Reading: what can be measured?

An IRA Research Fund Monograph from
the ERIC/CRIER Reading Review Series

The International Reading Association attempts, through its publications, to provide a forum for a wide spectrum of opinion on reading. This policy permits divergent viewpoints without assuming the endorsement of the Association.

Reading: what can be measured? was prepared pursuant to a contract with the Office of Education, U.S. Department of Health, Education, and Welfare. Contractors undertaking such projects under Government sponsorship are encouraged to express freely their judgment in professional and technical matters. Points of view or opinions do not, therefore, necessarily represent official Office of Education position or policy.

Reading: what can be measured?

Roger Farr
Indiana University

International Reading Association Research Fund
Newark, Delaware, 1969

ERIC/CRIER Reading Review Series

James L. Laffey
Series Editor

Gail Kelly
Publications Editor

Catherine F. Siffin
Director of Publications

Trends and practices in secondary school reading: a review of the research

A. Sterl Artley (1968)

Reading diagnosis and remediation

Ruth Strang (1968)

Reading: what can be measured?

Roger Farr (1969)

Reading in the content areas

James L. Laffey, *Series Editor* (1972)

These monographs are available from the

International Reading Association
Newark, Delaware 19711

Contents

Acknowledgments

This monograph could not have been prepared without the assistance and cooperation of a number of people. It should be emphasized that the opinions expressed and any interpretation of the research are the responsibility of the author. However, a number of people did make substantial contributions in ideas, organizational structure, and comprehensiveness of the review. The original idea for the manuscript was initiated in discussions with Edward G. Summers; Roy Kress provided the concept for the ERIC/CRIER index included in the test guide; James Laffey, Leo Fay, and Emery Bliesmer read the manuscript several times and provided many insights; Gail Kelly spent many, many hours in editing the manuscript and *Guide to Test and Measuring Instruments in Reading* and raising probing questions; Catherine Siffin coordinated the book design and layout and reviewed several chapters; Faye Branca coordinated the production of the final manuscript. Finally, I would like to thank William Eller who provided many stimulating discussions and broadened my concepts about the measurement of reading.

A number of research assistants and secretaries spent many hours in typing manuscript, editing references, and proofreading material. David Hunter IV and Diane Lapp patiently checked research and test references. Most of the final manuscript was typed by Jacqueline Clemenson; others who provided typing and proofreading help were Hazel Smith, Lynne Gelston, and Jayne Burnett. Special thanks are due to Mrs. Miriam Griffith for expediting the production of the manuscript.

Finally, I would like to thank my wife who put up with many, many evenings and weekends alone and provided the encouragement for me to complete this work.

Roger Farr

Introduction

The ERIC network of 19 decentralized information centers was created to serve the educational community. The creators of the system recognized that information is one of our nation's most valuable resources. Presently, knowledge is being created at a rate faster than it can be assimilated. There are more than three hundred education and education-related journals available today. For a teacher or researcher, numerous sources of information compound an already serious knowledge assimilation problem.

One of the major goals of the ERIC Clearinghouse on Reading is to prepare useful information products that organize, analyze, and synthesize information for the busy teacher, administrator, and researcher. One approach used in preparing such highly useful, interpretive papers for educators is to ask scholars in the field to prepare a manuscript on a specific research topic. *Reading: what can be measured?* is such an analytical paper.

This state-of-the-art monograph is an important contribution to the field of reading. The author not only explores measurement problems in reading but also raises some critical issues concerning the reading process and instructional practices in reading. Basic to further progress in the field of reading is an understanding of the reading process and the relationship between instructional practices and instructional objectives. While Roger Farr does not supply the answer or answers to understanding the reading process or resolving the dilemma of relating instructional practices to instructional objectives, he does clarify measurement issues related to both these problem areas. In addition, he delineates some new directions for research in measurement and evaluation in reading. One of the major virtues of the Farr monograph is that the author provides guidelines for the application of research to classroom practice. The Clearinghouse on Reading is proud to have sponsored this outstanding monograph and is pleased to publish it in cooperation with the International Reading Association.

James L. Laffey

Measurement in reading: general perspectives

This monograph organizes and describes the research literature on measurement and evaluation in reading. The review of the research is by no means exhaustive and while the major controversies in the field have been outlined, no attempt has been made to resolve them (although, in some instances, directions for possible solutions have been offered). The monograph is intended to serve as a guide to the researcher in pointing out both what is known and what is not known in measurement and evaluation in reading as well as to delineate those areas which need further research. The monograph also provides guidelines for the classroom application of research and explains how the teacher can and should use the wide array of measuring devices available. A guide to tests and measuring devices in reading has been included as a companion piece to the monograph. In it are listed reading tests currently in print. Information about the grade levels at which the test is appropriate, the kinds of sub-tests included within the test, the number of forms the test has, and the amount of time needed for administration are included. In addition, the Guide makes it possible for the teacher or researcher to obtain further information about any particular test either by writing to publishers (whose addresses appear in the Guide), by checking the reviews in Buros' (1968) *Reading Tests and Reviews,* or by consulting research which has used these tests, easily available through the published journal literature which is described in documents from the ERIC/CRIER system.

The major theme of the monograph is the use of tests in providing information about students' reading achievement. Such information is necessary to the teacher in setting instructional goals and in helping students to develop their reading skills. Thus, the first step in any discussion of testing and evaluation in reading is to define those skills which are essential to the reading act. Once this is done, then it is possible to consider whether reading tests accurately assess reading behavior. Can what they measure serve as a basis for organizing classroom instruction?

Before proceeding, something should be said about the limitations inherent in this monograph. Research on many aspects of measurement in reading is at best sparse. Even in those areas which have received a great deal of attention, more questions remain unanswered than answered. This monograph cannot be expected to definitively resolve all those questions posed by research, nor can it pretend to provide pat solutions to those problems with which the teacher is faced in the classroom. What it can do is summarize present research to enable the practitioner to gain some insights into the problem of measuring reading behavior. Hopefully the monograph will provide a foundation for further research which will begin to provide more conclusive evidence on the nature of the skills underlying reading ability, the validity of present devices for measuring these skills, and the most effective means for using those devices which are currently available.

Skills underlying reading ability

In order to measure any behavior it is necessary to know what the basic components of that behavior are. Research has been far from conclusive in defining reading. Much of it has taken the form of factor-analysis studies in which various kinds of tests (e.g., tests of reading ability as well as tests of language usage and general intelligence) are administered to a group of students and the test results are then analyzed to determine basic components of the reading act. In a review of twelve such research studies (Traxler, 1941; Gans, 1940; Davis, 1941; Thurstone, 1946; Langsam, 1941; Conant, 1942 Artley, 1944; Hall & Robinson, 1945; Harris, 1948; Maney, 1952; Sochor, 1952; Hunt, 1952; Stoker & Kropp, 1960), Lennon (1962) purported to find agreement on four factors basic to reading which could be measured. The four factors were: 1] a general verbal factor, 2] comprehension of explicitly stated material, 3] comprehension of implicit or latent meaning, and 4] appreciation. From a brief glance at Table 1 in which all twelve studies, including the test instruments used in each, and the factors each isolated are presented, it becomes obvious that Lennon's interpretation of the studies was perhaps an over-simplification. The studies showed only limited agreement as to the number of factors: some named only one factor (Conant, 1942, for instance) while others (such as Davis, 1941) found six. That there should be such disparity is not surprising: factor-analysis studies are dependent on both the data collected and the manner in which it is collected. The same tests were not used in each study and those which were used measured a wide array of elements ranging from personality factors, social studies and science achievement, and intelligence to reading, as defined by as many publishers and researchers as tests that were used. Given this situation, it is hardly surprising that the factors thought to comprise reading lack consistency from study to study.

One of the more extensive attempts to define reading through factor analysis was carried out in a series of studies by Holmes (1962) and Holmes and Singer (1964, 1966) in which, after administering a battery of reading tests, the matrix of all possible correlations were analyzed. A variety of sub-factors were isolated which Holmes and Singer believed accounted for the variance in students' speed of reading and power of reading and were, therefore, central to reading ability in general. The kinds of factors which they found are listed in Table 2. These particular factors appeared with fifth-grade students.

Table 1 Summary of the twelve studies reviewed by Lennon (1962)

Investigator(s)	Subjects		Factors isolated	Tests used
	Sample size	Grade		
Traxler (1941)	116	10	General reading level	Van Wagenen-Dvorak Diagnostic Examination of Silent Reading Abilities
Gans (1940)	417	3-5	Reading ability Selection-rejection (critical analysis) Delayed recall	Critical analysis of reading Thorndike-McCall Gates Silent Reading Test California Test of Mental Maturity (6 parts)
Davis (1941)			Word knowledge Reasoning ability Literal meanings Inference Ability to follow organization of a selection Knowledge of literacy devices and techniques	Davis Reading Test (designed to measure 9 factors)
Thurstone (1946)			General reading level	Reanalysis of Davis (1941) data

Langsam (1941)			Verbal (word meaning) Perceptual Word (fluency) Seeing relationships Numerical	6 reading tests (14 sub-tests) 1 intelligence test (7 sub-tests)
Conant (1942)			General comprehension	Nelson-Denny Reading Test American Council Psychology Examination 1 reading test (specially designed)
Artley (1944)	200	11	General comprehension	English Test C1: Reading Comprehension Application of Principles in Social Studies Test of Social Studies Abilities Test of General Proficiency in the Field of Social Studies Survey Test in the Social Studies Chicago Non-Verbal Examination
Hall & Robinson (1945)	100	College freshmen	Study attitude Inductive factor Verbal or word meaning Rate for unrelated facts Chart reading Unnamed	25 specially designed sub-scales (including tests of reading and non-prose material)

Table 1 Summary of the twelve studies reviewed by Lennon (1962) (cont'd.)

Investigator(s)	Subjects Sample size	Grade	Factors isolated	Tests used
Harris (1948)		Adults	General reading level	Battery specially designed to measure 7 sub-skills
Maney & Sochor (1952)	500	5	Non uni-factor	Gates Survey Test Pintner General Ability Test (verbal type) Tests specially designed to measure comprehension of science social studies material
Hunt (1952)			Reasoning ability Word knowledge	Tests specially designed to measure Davis' (1941) 6 factors
Stoker & Kropp (1960)		9	General	Iowa Test of Educational Development Ability to interpret reading materials

Holmes and Singer's research, subsequently labelled the substrata-factor theory of reading, has been criticized on both theoretical and technical levels (Sparks & Mitzel, 1966). The most serious question raised about the theory was put forth by Raygor (1966) and it applies to all such factor-analysis studies: How valid and reliable are the tests used to gather the data? Obviously, the validity and reliability of a given test determines the validity and reliability of any conclusions derived from its use. Another criticism leveled at the substrata-factor theory is that no comprehensive explanation of the skills needed for reading can be based solely on the results of reading tests. Factors such as personality variables, socio-economic background, and psycholinguistic experience have to be included. In fact, Goodman (1969) has gone as far as to suggest that Holmes and Singer have not developed a theory at all; instead, Goodman claimed, they have merely manipulated statistics generated by a set of reading tests.

That attempts have been made to define reading by examining performance on reading tests is not surprising since, on the surface, it appears a logical procedure. However, such attempts are severely limited. Performance on any one reading test is only a sample of an individual's behavior in one given situation under a single set of conditions. Significant differences in performance can occur when the time of day of test administration, the content of the reading material on the test, or the examiner administering the test are varied.

Several researchers have attempted recently to define reading in psycholinguistic terms. Goodman (1969) has developed a theory of reading which accounts for the nature of language and the reader's psycholinguistic background. According to Goodman, reading is a form of information processing: it occurs when an individual selects and chooses from the information available to him in an attempt to decode graphic messages. Thus, Goodman suggested that perhaps the reading process cannot be fragmented. Ryan and Semmel's (1969) review of

Table 2 Factors contributing to speed and power of reading (Holmes & Singer, 1964, 1966)

Factors contributing to speed of reading in order of per cent contribution to total variance	Per cent of total variance	Factors contributing to power of reading in order of per cent contribution to total variance	Per cent of total variance
Visual verbal meaning	20	Meaning of affixes	20
Spelling recognition	16	Visual verbal meaning	18
Speed of word perception	14	Word recognition in context	14
Meaning of affixes	11	Blending word elements	9
Visual verbal abstraction	6	Auding	8
Auditory verbal abstraction	6		

recent psycholinguistic theories of reading substantiated Goodman's point of view. They concluded:

> Research has demonstrated that the reader does not process print sequentially, but rather in a manner which reflects his use of language at every opportunity. Expectancies about syntax and semantics within contexts lead to hypotheses which can be confirmed (or disconfirmed) with only a small portion of the cues available in the text. Thus, not all the information needed by the reader is on the printed page—nor are all the printed details needed by him. (1969, p. 82)

If one were to extrapolate components of reading behavior from these psycholinguistic theories, they would probably include the ability to use knowledge of written syntax, knowledge of words used in context, and knowledge of how to use phonological cues.

Perhaps the psycholinguistic approach will provide a more viable definition of reading and lead to a more solid basis for test construction. It may well be that research will find, as the proponents of psycholinguistic theory have suggested, that attempts to define reading sub-skills on a group basis are fruitless. In that case, measurement in reading would have to be based on whether a reader has a strategy for decoding written messages and whether he understands reading as a communication process rather than whether he can simply decode written symbols, supply the meanings of words in isolation, or answer multiple-choice questions based on a literal understanding of a selection. Until research is carried out to develop tests which take into account the elements psycholinguistic theorists are finding central to reading ability, the teacher will still need to use present sub-tests of reading to evaluate reading ability, but this use of sub-tests must be done cautiously. Present reading tests can be helpful if the sub-tests are recognized merely as measuring the readers' different ways of interacting with printed messages and together are taken to represent a measure of the students' ability to utilize text material effectively.

It should be obvious by now that research has provided no clear-cut theoretical definition of reading and it is likely that this will be the case for some time to come. Yet, the classroom teacher needs some kind of operational definition or at least some idea of what is involved in reading in order to proceed with instruction. While research is far from unanimous that any one skill or combination of skills are, in fact, central to reading, there is general agreement that some skills are related to reading, even if that relation is questionable. The kind of skills which a teacher should be able to assess would center around the learner's ability to decode written symbols, the extent of his sight vocabulary, his knowledge of word attack skills, and his fluency in oral reading. Beyond this level of decoding, the teacher should have some idea of the learner's comprehension abilities, his ability to determine the pronunciation and meaning of words, his ability to read for the main idea, and his understanding of the author's intent. One skill area which is indicative of a mature reader and which is often overlooked by the teacher is the learner's ability to set his own goals and purposes for reading. Sub-skills here would involve the extent to which independent reading habits have been established, whether what is read can be applied to the solution of practical problems, and whether newly acquired information can be integrated with that obtained through previously read materials. Most of the skills which have just been mentioned can be measured by either formal or informal tests. Doubtless, there are other skills which were not included here, which are capable of measurement. For the purposes of this discussion, however, it suffices to point out that while there is no consensus as to what reading is, the teacher can still use tests which are based on seemingly inadequate theoretical foundations. Later chapters of this monograph deal in detail with the kinds of testing instruments that can provide the information described above and how these instruments might be used by the classroom teacher.

Variables affecting reading performance: the student's background

Measurement and evaluation in reading programs usually are concerned with determining how well a student reads. How well the student reads is influenced, to some extent or another, by his experiential background which he brings to the classroom and over which the classroom teacher has only partial control. Factors such as sex, socio-economic background, and personality do exert some influence. The problems that these present to the test user, however, are a matter of the degree of influence they exert on test performance. Do they so distort the performance that an accurate assessment of students' skills becomes impossible? A review of all the studies of the effect of student background on test performance is beyond the scope of this monograph. The studies included here emphasize that test performance cannot be the only means of assessing student capacity since it represents only a single sample of an individual's behavior which is affected by many immediate and long-term factors.

Sex differences

Of all the factors influencing test performance, sex differences have received the greatest amount of research attention. Their importance has been shown to vary at different age levels and to depend on a number of influences. Traxler and Spaulding (1954) compared the performance of 200 boys and 200 girls in private New York City area schools. Girls in grades three, five, and seven performed consistently higher than the boys in spelling and language, but the two groups were about equal in word meaning and paragraph meaning as measured by the Stanford Achievement Test. Traxler and Spaulding (1954, p. 80) suggested that separate sex norms should not be provided in the Stanford test because of the extensive overlap in achievement at various grade levels and because of the "similarity of the educational goals of boys and girls in independent elementary schools." However, caution should be exercised in interpreting these results because of the absence of statistical analysis in the study. In a more carefully controlled study, Hughes (1953) found that girls read significantly better than boys in grades three and four, but that these differences were not sustained beyond the fourth grade. American culture may well be *the* element in promoting differences by sex in reading performance. In Preston's (1962) study of American and German students, the superiority of girls over boys in the case of American children was reversed with German children. This was attributed to German cultural influences such as the predominantly masculine teaching body in Germany.

Studies of sex differences in reading test performance are generally quite consistent regarding American children: girls do perform better than boys, especially during the first years of school. However, few reading tests have taken this into account. Only a handful like the Gray Oral Reading Test provide separate norms for each sex. Traxler and Spaulding (1954) examined one hundred reading tests randomly selected from the files of the Educational Records Bureau. Only six tests provided separate sex norms; in addition, in the manuals of the one hundred tests surveyed only seven made any reference to the existence of sex differences.

While sex is a statistically significant variable affecting test performance, is it important in instruction? If understanding the existence of sex differences leads to a careful examination of the cause and subsequent adjustments in reading instruction, it is an important finding. However, because it is perhaps impractical to provide separate reading programs for boys and girls, any suggestion that separate test norms should be provided for boys and girls is probably not a valid one. In addition, most standardized tests are designed for comparing groups of children without regard to sex differences and the norms provided by the better test publishers carefully control variables such as sex, usually by random sampling procedures.

Socio-economic status

The influence of socio-economic status on test performance has become an extremely controversial issue. In the famous Hobson vs. Hansen case in the District of Columbia, a group of parents charged the school district with unconstitutionally depriving disadvantaged Negro pupils of equal access to educational opportunities. Included among the charges of discriminatory practices was the selection of biased tests for the placement and evaluation of pupils within the school (Lennon, 1968).

Reading test performance and socio-economic status have been shown to be highly related at all levels from the first grade through college. In a study of the relationship between socio-economic status and a number of variables including reading comprehension and vocabulary achievement, Hill and Giammatteo (1963) found that in a population of third-grade children, the high socio-economic group was eight months ahead of the low socio-economic group in vocabulary achievement. In reading comprehension, the range between the groups was equivalent to a full school term or nine months. Carson and Rabin (1960) investigated the verbal comprehension and verbal expression in Negro and white children. While this study did not use a reading achievement test as one of the variables, the importance of socio-economic class on test performance is worth noting. Three groups were studied: southern Negroes, northern Negroes, and northern whites. Subjects were matched for age, grade placement, sex, and level of comprehension; all the subjects were in the fourth, fifth, or sixth grades. Carson and Rabin found that white children scored higher than Negro children and that northern Negro children scored higher than southern Negro children on tests of verbal comprehension and communication.

The importance of the high correlation between socio-economic status and reading test performance is not in understanding that these differences exist, but rather in understanding what can be done to correct them. A first step in this direction was undertaken by Boykin (1955). Boykin studied the reading performance of Negro college students to assess in greater detail their reading problems, needs, and capabilities. Boykin's subjects scored only two-thirds that of the norming population on the Cooperative English Test: Reading Comprehension. The group also achieved lowest on vocabulary and highest on level of comprehension, while the norming population for the Cooperative test had scored highest on speed of comprehension. Further examination of Boykin's data indicates that the differences between the norming population and Boykin's subjects was about three-fourths of a standard deviation on level of comprehension; on speed of comprehension and vocabulary, the difference was about one and a half standard deviations. On all three sub-tests, the norming population scored significantly higher. Boykin's conclusion was not that the Cooperative test was inappropriate for Negro students, but that further research should be carried out to determine why the Negro students scored so poorly on it. Such studies, Boykin argued, should be focused on planning programs for improving the reading skills of Negro college students.

Socio-economic status and reading disability have also been shown to be highly related in studies with other disadvantaged groups (Chandler, 1966; Anastasi & D'Angelo, 1952; Klineberg, 1947). These studies are valuable not only because of the effect they have on the testing process such as the search for culture-free or culture-fair tests, but rather because of the contribution they can make to increasing educational opportunities through better teaching and school programs. After all, the fault does not lie with the tests or with the student; it lies with society and the educational system which produced the test performance.

Personality variables

Personality variables also seemingly affect student performance. A student's attitude toward a test, his concept of his own ability to perform on it, his physical well-being, and the attitude of his parents and siblings may well influence his performance. Sheldon and Carrillo's (1952) study of this problem compared students' reading performance on the Progressive Reading Test (now the California Achievement Tests) to home background information gathered through a questionnaire sent to the students' parents. A summary of their results indicated that student attitudes toward education strongly influenced their reading test performance and that these attitudes appeared to be shaped by parental attitudes.

In another study Edwards (1962) tried to assess students' attitudes toward reading by administering a concept test in which the students were asked to choose phrases characteristic of good readers. In a pilot study of six students reading six months above mental grade placement and six students reading six months below mental grade placement, a positive relationship was found between acquired concept of reading and the score on a reading achievement test. Further experimentation with a larger sample size did not reveal any significant correlation. Studies like Edwards' should always be interpreted cautiously because of the reliance on the correlation coefficient. In such studies, it is not always possible to determine which factor is the cause, which is the result, or whether some third factor is affecting both variables.

Other variables influencing test results

The choice of a particular test has also been shown to exert a great influence on students' reading grade scores (Ware, 1956). The demographic characteristics of the population used in norming a test, the reading difficulty level of the test used, and the relationship of a test to the specific objectives of the instructional program can all influence grade scores on that test. The effect of using an inappropriate test with a particular student is perhaps the most serious of these problems. If a test does not include enough lower limit for a poor reader or enough upper limit for a good reader, an inaccurate estimate of reading ability results.

Variables affecting reading performance: the reading program

While evaluation and measurement in reading have focused primarily on students' performance, there are variables within the reading program itself which influence that performance and which can be measured. Such variables include teaching procedures, the training and personality of the teacher, instructional materials, the physical setting for the reading program, and curriculum organization. All the studies dealing with these variables are not reviewed here. Only two of them—the difficulty level of materials and teaching procedures and teacher knowledge of those procedures—are discussed in any detail. It is hoped that this brief overview will emphasize the need for research on this aspect of the reading program.

Difficulty level of materials

The difficulty level of reading materials has probably received the most research of any instructional element within the reading program. The vast majority of studies on readability have tried to define the relationships between number of words and syllables to the difficulty of the selection. Chall's (1958) monograph, *Readability: An Appraisal of Research and Application,* is a comprehensive review of readability research. In it, Chall organized the research under three main categories: quantitative associational studies, surveys of expert and reader opinion, and experimental studies of one factor. The most commonly-reported type of study was the quantitative associational one, in which the outcome was "the readability formula based on the counting and weighing of several significant factors in the printed material to predict the reading skill necessary to understand it" (Chall, 1958, p. 155).

Early studies of readability emphasized vocabulary difficulty and average sentence length, both usually determined by counting words or syllables. More recent studies have attempted to assess more complex grammatical aspects of written prose. Bormuth (1965a, 1965b, 1966) has used the cloze procedure in several studies to investigate some of the underlying grammatical factors which are related to the reading difficulty of text material. Bormuth (1967) computed the correlation between comprehension of independent clauses and the frequency of independent clauses, mean word depth, and length (measured in letters). He concluded that all three factors had a significant correlation with comprehension, but that the frequency variable was too small to be of value in predicting readability.

A number of researchers have attempted to validate readability formulas by comparing readability scores with reading comprehension. A study of the comprehension of newspaper articles which were written at both easy and difficult levels according to the Flesch and Dale-Chall formulas was conducted with a group of adult employees of a midwestern company (Swanson & Fox, 1953). Differences in comprehension between the two versions were significant; however, the easier version did not attract more readers than the difficult version. Swanson and Fox pointed out that factors such as motivation and interest are at least as important as sentence length and vocabulary difficulty in attracting readers and in determining retention of information.

Several researchers who have validated and correlated readability formulas have suggested that while the formulas can provide an indication of relative difficulty of material, more extensive studies are needed to determine the effect of a broader range of factors. Russell and Fea (1951) in such an investigation of the Dale-Chall, Flesch, Lewerenz, Lorge, Washburne-Morphett, and Yoakam readability formulas stressed that the formulas do *not*:

1] give any measure of conceptual difficulty in the textual material,

2] take into consideration the way the material is organized or arranged,

3] allow for variations in the meaning of multiple meaning words,

4] accept the fact that a fresh or unusual word may make a sentence or idea clearer than a commonplace word,

5] vary their ratings in terms of different interests which persons may have at different developmental levels or in individual activities,

6] provide measures of difficulty below the fourth-grade level, and

7] take account of physical factors such as format and illustrations.

Because of the above factors, publishers do not generally seem to pay much attention to readability formulas. Mills and Richardson (1963) sent out questionnaires to twelve well-known publishers of children's books, asking if they used readability formulas in text preparation. Despite a great deal of follow-up effort, only seven questionnaires were returned. In half of these, the publishers responded negatively. Two of the publishers were quite disturbed at the suggestion that such formulas should be used: one stated that the wide range of reading abilities at a single grade in various parts of the country rendered readability formulas very unreliable; the other indicated that actual readability is probably not a function of mechanical factors, but rather is derived from motivational factors. A number of studies have been designed to demonstrate the effect of the readability of a test on student performance. Levy (1958) administered a revised form of the Study of Values to three groups with varying reading abilities. For the poorer readers, the two forms of the test were found not to be equivalent. Thus, Levy emphasized the importance of reading ability in all pencil-and-paper personality tests. Johnson and Bond (1950) after studying the reading difficulty of ten standardized group tests of personality and intelligence concluded that many of the tests would be too difficult for the less able readers to comprehend and would, therefore, not be valid measures of the trait being studied.

Research on the reading difficulty of materials has focused on a very narrow range of factors. While the most recent studies have employed a broader spectrum of grammatical elements, they have still neglected personality, motivation, and interest variables. It is clear from an overview of classroom practice that the results of the many studies on the readability of standardized tests have not had widespread application: test consumers more often than not have failed to take into account the reading difficulty of individual test items in assessing various personality traits and student abilities.

The concentration of research on the difficulty level of materials has overshadowed the importance of research into the effectiveness of those materials. Probably the reason for this has been the lack of consensus as to what the criteria should be for evaluating effectiveness. Recently, Goodman, Olsen, Calvin, and Vanderlinde (1967) have developed criteria for such evaluation. Their criteria include psychological, socio-cultural, educational, linguistic, and literary principles. What is badly needed now are studies which will employ these criteria and focus on making materials both more readable as well as more effective.

Teacher effectiveness Research on teacher effectiveness has been based almost exclusively on student performance on standardized tests. While this is certainly an acceptable criterion for evaluating the effectiveness of instruction and does reflect the effect of the teacher on student performance, there are many other ways to evaluate teaching that do not rely solely on students' test performance. In fact, there is a vital need to analyze teacher behavior in and of itself; it might well lead to a better and clearer conception of those factors which contribute to improved student performance.

The inconclusiveness of the U.S. Office of Education first-grade studies (Bond & Dykstra, 1967) cogently demonstrated the importance of having a clear delineation of experimental procedures being compared and how much work has to be put into doing this. In the first-grade studies, it was virtually impossible to know what was actually being compared within each of the 27 projects since many of the techniques purported to be different were, in fact, quite similar.

Prior to any evaluation of teacher behavior, a specific description of what constitutes good teaching is necessary. Hughes and his colleagues (1959) have identified a number of behaviors which could serve as standards for assessing effective instruction. Hughes indicated that if a child is to develop adequate communication skills, he must have opportunity to talk and listen to others. Therefore, the teachers' responses to a student should include the following:

1] seeking the student's opinion and experience;
2] giving the student an opportunity to use a variety of media of communication;
3] giving him a model of standard language usage;
4] providing him with a variety of books and other reading materials;
5] seeking to further his purposes in reading;
6] giving him opportunity to compare his reading with his new experience and to draw inferences and generalizations from his reading;
7] seeking the child's own idiomatic response in writing and other media of expression.

Other researchers, such as Sears (1963), Wallen and Wodtke (1963), and Spaulding (1963), have attempted to define "good" teaching through an inductive approach. They have investigated those teacher behaviors which appear to have the most positive influence on student behaviors. They also have developed elaborate lists of the behaviors characteristic of good teaching which include the teacher's willingness and ability to alter his behaviors to meet varying situations, to understand the students' point of view, to try new procedures, to ask effective questions, to use positive reinforcement of student behaviors, and to continue learning in a wide variety of subject areas.

Teachers' knowledge of specific skill areas involved in reading instruction has been explored by several researchers (Sheldon, 1960; Ramsey, 1962; Schubert, 1959). While their work as a whole has provided valuable information about the extent and limitations of teachers' knowledge, the information has not been applied to outcomes in the teaching of reading. In other words, research has failed to relate how a lack of knowledge of phonics, for instance, would influence teacher behavior and effectiveness. In one study of this type, Spache and Baggett (1965) administered a phonics knowledge test to a group of 99 graduate students enrolled in a graduate reading course. Ninety-three class members were in-service teachers pursuing graduate credit in reading. A very serious deficiency in teacher knowledge of phonic and syllabication rules was found. However, the investigators failed to provide evidence which would indicate the importance of this kind of knowledge to instruction. The implied assumption seemed to be that the ability to perform at a high level on a phonics principles and syllabication test is a very important element in the successful teaching of reading. Despite the fact that this is a logical assumption, failure to provide hard evidence does seriously limit any inferences that can be drawn from the study.

A variety of evaluation techniques need to be developed to enable the teacher to make an adequate assessment of his own instruction. Goodson (1965) developed such a multiple approach by analyzing the literature in reading and identifying areas which were essential to the competent reader: sight vocabulary, word attack, word meaning, mechanics of oral and/or silent reading, taste and enjoyment in reading, study skills, critical comprehension, and literal and interpretive comprehension. Goodson used these areas to develop a classroom observation guide, a questionnaire of instructional problems, and an inventory of teacher beliefs concerning the teaching of reading. He then tested these instruments out on nine educators and conducted studies of reading programs in 14 teachers' classes. While the conclusions of this study were not based on statistical analyses, Goodson found that the teachers and supervisory personnel who used the instruments found them to be helpful in aiding them to improve their reading instruction.

To determine the proficiency of elementary teachers in using a wide variety of information to improve reading instruction, Burnett (1961) constructed a problem-solving test. Significant differences in performance on the problem-solving test were found between reading specialists, undergraduate elementary education students, and experienced teachers. The reading specialist scored highest, the experienced teachers scored next highest, and the undergraduate elementary education majors scored lowest. The results of this study were limited because Burnett did not relate the relevance of this problem-solving ability to actual classroom teaching.

Some researchers, however, have discussed teacher knowledge in the context of student performance in the classroom. To measure teacher skill, Wade (1960) constructed a test consisting of ten problems. Those who scored highest were considered skillful in selecting books of the proper difficulty level, in placing children into homogeneous reading groups, in judging the amount of reading gains that pupils achieved after classroom instruction, in observing specific reading skill deficiencies, in diagnosing and correcting phonic and syllabication errors, in organizing a child's own word perception errors into meaningful instructional categories, and in recognizing the goals of various kinds of reading workbook exercises. The statistical analysis revealed that teacher performance on Wade's test was significantly related to student performance on a standardized reading test.

As more research begins to specify and define specific teacher behaviors and to relate these behaviors to accepted criteria for what constitutes a good reading program, adequate evaluation of teaching and teaching procedures will become possible. Another method of attack in evaluating teaching method and teacher effectiveness might be to ask teachers themselves to identify those areas in which they believe themselves to need additional training. If the sheer number of investigations carried out along these lines is any indication, this is a very popular technique for evaluating teacher skills. Typical of these questionnaire studies is one conducted by Hester (1953) in which teachers were asked to list the most serious problems they faced in reading instruction and indicate those problems with which they needed the most help. One interesting finding was that teachers wanted this help within their regular classroom situation. A second major result was that teachers seem to be relatively unconcerned with the teaching of reading in the content areas. Questionnaire studies were deemed valuable by Hester for determining those areas of teacher weakness which stand in need of remediation. Other research using questionnaires to determine teacher skills and needs were carried out by Aaron (1960) and Purcell (1958).

While questionnaire studies may point out some teacher-perceived weaknesses, many teachers are unable to identify those areas crucial to the teaching of reading in which they lack knowledge. In short, it appears that many teachers do not know what they do not know. One study which underlined this was initiated by Wilt (1950). Teacher awareness of listening as a factor in elementary education was compared with the actual amount of time spent on listening in a classroom. Wilt administered a questionnaire to teachers to determine the percentage of the school day that they expected children to listen and the relative importance they placed upon listening as compared to other facets of language art instruction. To verify the teacher answers, classroom observations were conducted. The most significant finding on the questionnaire was that teachers expected children to spend more time learning through reading than through any other language skill. Observations of teacher practices did not bear out the results of the questionnaire survey. In actual classroom activity, 57.5 per cent of the time was spent by the children in listening. When speaking and writing time were further subtracted from the remaining 42.5 per cent, it was obvious that the teachers were quite inaccurate in the amount of time that they expected the children to be learning through reading. Wilt's findings should certainly cause those who are evaluating teacher behaviors through questionnaire techniques to be cautious in interpreting results.

Austin and Morrison (1963) undertook a comprehensive nationwide study of the reading instruction in elementary schools. Questionnaires were used as well as classroom observations. One facet of the investigation was to compare problems in the teaching of reading reported by supervisory personnel and those reported by classroom teachers. Problems identified by supervisory personnel included:

1] providing for individual differences
2] teaching reading skills appropriate for the intermediate grades
3] teaching reading skills in the content areas
4] appropriate utilization of available materials
5] pacing
6] organizing children into flexible groups
7] creative teaching
8] understanding broad aspects of the reading program
9] understanding phonic principles
10] teaching children how to identify unfamiliar words

Teacher perceptions differed somewhat from those of the supervisory personnel. They believed the most frequent weaknesses of their reading programs to be:

1] the paucity and kind of materials available
2] the lack of motivation provided by the content of reading books
3] the lack of phonic practices in workbooks
4] the lack of aid in providing for homogeneous groups with large classes of children
5] a lack of sufficient time to teach basic reading skills
6] lack of necessary guidance from administrators

Studies such as the one by Austin and Morrison can provide reliable insights into the evaluation of the teaching of reading when they are both based on questionnaires and careful classroom observation. The problems in evaluating teaching are perhaps best exemplified by an analysis of the research conducted by Anderson and Hunka (1963). They concluded that research in teacher evaluation has been unproductive and has reached a dead end because of problems encountered in developing suitable criteria variables. They were alarmed not only because of the lack of these criteria variables, but also by the absence of reliable measurement for those variables which have been identified.

Another general problem in assessing teaching is the inability of research to isolate and define behaviors. The problems of conducting methods studies in teaching reading are always compounded by the lack of control over and description of teacher behaviors. It seems that research in this area must begin to focus on a broader spectrum of variables than merely teacher knowledge. Methods need to be developed for analyzing other aspects of teacher behavior including such facets as teacher motivation and personality. Most of all, future research should reveal how these variables promote effective teaching.

In conclusion

The preceding discussion is by no means definitive in terms of the kinds of variables which can affect measurement, but hopefully the reader will bear these in mind as he goes through the remainder of the monograph. The major concern of the present monograph is not on what variables influence student performance, rather it focuses on the kinds of measurement devices research has made available, what these devices measure, how they can be used, and their validity and reliability. The specific areas covered are organized around the measurement of specific skills related to reading, the types of testing procedures that exist for measuring these abilities, the evaluation of reading growth, and, last, but not least, measures of reading-related functions.

It is important, throughout the following pages, to bear in mind the fact that the art and science of measurement and evaluation is inexorably intertwined with all phases of reading education. It is virtually impossible to review research in this area without touching on all phases of the psychology and teaching of reading. At the same time, most reviews of measurement procedures in general cannot avoid discussing reading abilities. The broad study of measurement and evaluation presents a paradox in education. Research knowledge far outstrips classroom practice. Part of the problem is caused by the development of a technical vocabulary by the researcher which is seldom understood by most teachers. Added to this has been the deification of tests and test scores on the part of the classroom teacher.

Finally, the focus of this monograph is on presenting information and analyses useful to both the practitioner and researcher who want to keep abreast of the present state of knowledge in reading measurement. While academic and scholarly measurement problems are not avoided, they are deemphasized unless they form an integral part of the research under consideration.

References

Aaron, I. E. What teachers and prospective teachers know about phonic generalizations. *Journal of Educational Research*, 1960, *53*, 323-30.

Anastasi, Ann, & D'Angelo Rita Y. A comparison of Negro and white preschool children in language development and Goodenough Draw-a-Man I.Q. *Journal of Genetic Psychology*, 1952, *31*, 147-65.

Anderson, C. C., & Hunka, S. M. Teacher evaluation: some problems and a proposal. *Harvard Educational Review*, 1963, *33*, 74-96.

Artley, A. S. A study of certain relationships existing between general comprehension and reading comprehension in a specific subject matter area. *Journal of Educational Research*, 1944, *37*, 464-73.

Austin, Mary C., & Morrison, C. *The first R.* New York: Macmillan Company, 1963.

Bond, G. L., & Dykstra, R. The cooperative research program in first-grade reading instruction. *Reading Research Quarterly*, 1967, *2* (4), 5-142.

Bormuth, J. R. Validities of grammatical and semantic classifications of cloze test scores. In J. A. Figurel (Ed.), Reading and inquiry. *Proceedings of the International Reading Association*, 1965, *10*, 283-86. (a)

Bormuth, J. R. Optimum sample size and cloze test length in readability measurement. *Journal of Educational Measurement*, 1965, *2*, 111-16. (b)

Bormuth, J. R. Readability: a new approach. *Reading Research Quarterly*, 1966, *1* (3), 79-132.

Bormuth, J. R. Comparable cloze and multiple-choice comprehension test scores. *Journal of Reading*, 1967, *10*, 291-99.

Boykin, Leander L. The reading performance of some Negro college students. *Journal of Negro Education*, 1955, *24*, 435-41.

Burnett, R. W. The diagnostic problem solving proficiency of elementary teachers in teaching reading. Unpublished doctoral dissertation, Indiana University, 1961.

Buros, O. K. *Reading tests and reviews.* Highland Park, N. J.: Gryphon Press, 1968.

Carson, A. S., & Rabin, A. I. Verbal comprehension and communication in Negro and white children. *Journal of Educational Psychology*, 1960, *51*, 47-51.

Chall, Jeanne S. Readability: an appraisal of research and application. *Ohio State University, Bureau of Educational Research Monographs*, 1958, *34*.

Chandler, T. A. Reading disability and socio-economic status. *Journal of Reading*, 1966, *10*, 5-21.

Conant, Margaret M. *The construction of a diagnostic reading test.* N. Y.: Teachers Collge Press, Columbia University, 1942.

Davis, F. B. Fundamental factors of comprehension in reading. Unpublished doctoral dissertation, Harvard University, 1941.

Edwards, D. L. The relation of concept of reading to intelligence and reading achievement of fifth grade children. Unpublished doctoral dissertation, University of Buffalo, 1962.

Gans, Roma A. *A study of critical reading comprehension in the intermediate grades.* New York: Teachers College Press, Columbia University, 1940.

Goodman, K. S. Analysis of oral reading miscues: applied psycholinguistics. *Reading Research Quarterly,* 1969, *5,* 9-30.

Goodman, K. S., Olsen, H. C., Calvin, Cynthia M., & Vanderlinde, L. *Choosing materials to teach reading.* Detroit: Wayne State University Press, 1967.

Goodson, R. A. The development of three instruments to aid in the analysis of teacher practices, problems and theoretical beliefs concerning the teaching of reading in the later elementary grades. Unpublished doctoral dissertation, Columbia University, 1965.

Hall, W. E., & Robinson, F. P. An analytic approach to the study of reading skills. *Journal of Educational Psychology,* 1945, *36,* 429-42.

Harris, C. W. Measurement of comprehension of literature: II. studies of measures of comprehension. *School Review,* 1948, *56,* 332-42.

Hester, Kathleen B. Classroom problems in the teaching of reading. *Elementary School Journal,* 1953, *54,* 84-87.

Hill, E. H., & Giammatteo, M. C. Socio-economic status and its relationship to school achievement in the elementary school. *Elementary English,* 1963, *40,* 265-70.

Holmes, J. A. Speed, comprehension, and power in reading. In E. P. Bliesmer & R. C. Staiger (Eds.), Problems, programs and projects in college-adult reading. *Yearbook of the National Reading Conference,* 1962, *11,* 6-14.

Holmes, J. A., & Singer, H. Theoretical models and trends toward more basic research in reading. *Review of Educational Research,* 1964, *34,* 127-55.

Holmes, J. A., & Singer, H. *The substrata-factor theory: substrata factor differences underlying reading ability in known groups at the high school level.* (Final report covering contracts No. 538, SAE-8176 and 538A, SAE-8660) Washington, D. C.: U. S. Government Printing Office, 1966.

Hughes, Mildred C. Sex differences in reading achievement in the elementary grades. In Helen M. Robinson (Ed.), Clinical studies in reading. *Supplementary Educational Monographs,* 1953, *77,* 102-06.

Hughes, M. M., *et al. Development of the means for the assessment of the quality of teaching in elementary schools.* (Final report of Cooperative Research Project No. 353) Washington, D. C.: U. S. Department of Health, Education, and Welfare, 1959.

Hunt, L. C. A further study of certain factors associated with reading comprehension. Unpublished doctoral dissertation, Syracuse University, 1952.

Johnson, R. H., & Bond, G. L. Reading ease of commonly used tests. *Journal of Applied Psychology,* 1950, *34,* 319-24.

Klineberg, D. Negro intelligence and urban residence. In T. M. Newcomb & E. L. Hanlley (Eds.), *Readings in social psychology.* New York: Holt, 1947. Pp. 24-32.

Langsam, Rosalind. A factorial analysis of reading ability. *Journal of Experimental Education,* 1941, *10,* 57-63.

Lennon, R. T. What can be measured? *The Reading Teacher,* 1962, *15,* 326-37.

Lennon, R. T. *Testimony of Dr. Roger T. Lennon as expert witness on psychological testing.* New York: Harcourt, Brace, & World, 1968.

Levy, J. Readability level and differential test performance, a language revision of the study of values. *Journal of Educational Psychology,* 1958, *49,* 6-12.

Maney, Ethel Swain. Literal and critical reading in science. Unpublished doctoral dissertation, Temple University, 1952.

Mills, R. E., & Richardson, Jean R. What do publishers mean by "grade level"? *The Reading Teacher,* 1963, *16,* 359-62.

Preston, R. C. Reading achievement of German and American children. *School and Society,* 1962, *2,* 350-54.

Purcell, Barbara A. Methods of teaching reading: a report of a tri-state survey. *Elementary School Journal,* 1958, *58,* 449-53.

Ramsey, W. C. Will tomorrow's teachers know and teach phonics? *The Reading Teacher*, 1962, *15*, 241-45.

Raygor, A. L. Problems in the substrata-factor theory. *Reading Research Quarterly*, 1966, *1* (3), 147-50.

Russell, D. H., & Fea, H. R. Validity of six readability formulas as measures of juvenile fiction. *Elementary School Journal*, 1951, *52*, 136-44.

Ryan, Ellen Bouchard, & Semmel, M. I. Reading as a constructive language process. *Reading Research Quarterly*, 1969, *5*, 59-83.

Schubert, D. G. Teachers and word analysis skills. *Journal of Developmental Reading*, 1959, *2*, 62-64.

Sears, Pauline S. *The effect of classroom conditions on the strength of achievement motive and work output on elementary school children.* (Report of Cooperative Research Project No. 873) Washington, D. C.: U. S. Office of Education, 1963.

Sheldon, W. D. Specific principles essential to classroom diagnosis. *The Reading Teacher*, 1960, *14*, 2-8.

Sheldon, W. D., & Carrillo, L. Relation of parents, home and certain developmental characteristics to children's reading ability. *Elementary School Journal*, 1952, *52*, 262-70.

Sochor, E. Elona. Literal and critical reading in social studies. Unpublished doctoral dissertation, Temple University, 1952.

Spache, G. D., & Baggett, Mary E. What do teachers know about phonics and syllabication? *The Reading Teacher*, 1965, *19*, 96-99.

Sparks, J. N., & Mitzel, H. E. A reaction to Holmes' basic assumptions underlying the substrata-factor theory. *Reading Research Quarterly*, 1966, *1* (3), 137-45.

Spaulding, R. L. *Achievement, creativity, and self-concept correlates of teacher-pupil transactions in elementary school classrooms.* (Report of Cooperative Research Project No. 1352) Washington, D. C.: U. S. Office of Education, 1963.

Stoker, H. W., & Kropp, R. P. The predictive validities and factorial context of the Florida state wide ninth-grade testing program battery. *Florida Journal of Educational Research*, 1960, *1*, 105-14.

Swanson, C. E., & Fox, H. G. Validity of readability formulas. *Journal of Applied Psychology*, 1953, *37*, 114-18.

Thurstone, L. L. Note on a reanalysis of Davis' reading tests. *Psychometrika*, 1946, *11*, 185-88.

Traxler, A. E. A study of the Van Wagenen-Dvorak Diagnostic Examination of Silent Reading Abilities. *Educational Records Bulletin,* 1941, *31,* 33-41.

Traxler, A. E., & Spaulding, Geraldine. Sex differences in achievement. *Educational Records Bureau,* 1954, *63,* 69-80.

Wade, E. W. The construction and validation of a test of ten teacher skills used in reading instruction, grades two to five. Unpublished doctoral dissertation, Indiana University, 1960.

Wallen, N. E., & Wodtke, K. H. *Relationships between teacher characteristics and student behavior—part I.* (Report of Project No. 1217) Washington, D. C.: U. S. Office of Education, 1963.

Ware, Florence E. Effect on reading achievement of undertesting pupils in low third grade. *California Journal of Educational Research,* 1956, *7,* 22-24.

Wilt, Miriam E. A study of teacher awareness of listening as a factor in elementary education. *Journal of Educational Research,* 1950, *43,* 626-36.

Test references

An asterisk after a test listing indicates the test is included in the *Guide to Tests and Measuring Instruments in Reading* which appears after Chapter 6.

California Achievement Tests E. W. Tiegs & W. W. Clark. Monterey, Calif.: California Test Bureau, 1933, rev. 1963.

Cooperative English Test: Reading Comprehension Test C. Derrick, D. P. Harris, & B. Walker. Princeton, N. J.: Educational Testing Service, Cooperative Test Division, 1940, rev. 1960*.

Gates Reading Survey A. I. Gates. N. Y.: Bureau of Publications, Teachers College, Columbia University, 1939, rev. 1960.

Gray Oral Reading Test W. S. Gray. Indianapolis: Bobbs-Merrill Co., 1963, rev. 1967*.

Stanford Achievement Test: Reading Tests T. L. Kelley, R. Madden, E. F. Gardner, & H. C. Rudman. N. Y.: Harcourt, Brace, & World, 1922, rev. 1964*.

2

Problems in measuring reading sub-skills

Standardized tests, the most common device for measuring reading ability, divide reading into a number of sub-skill areas. In every instance, this division is arbitrary since there is almost no research evidence supporting it. However, since most standardized reading tests are organized around separate sub-skill areas and since the teacher has to work with existing tests, the problems of measurement are discussed in this chapter as they apply to the most commonly found sub-skill divisions. These sub-skill areas include reading vocabulary, rate, comprehension, and rate of comprehension. The discussion of these sub-skill areas is organized so that the reader is presented with a review of methods used for measuring each skill and the problems involved in such measurement. This is followed by an examination of validity and reliability studies relevant to measuring each skill and by projections for further research.

Reading vocabulary

Over ninety per cent of group survey tests of silent reading ability include a separate measure of reading vocabulary. The inclusion of such a measure is, on the surface, highly reasonable. In fact, it has been suggested by several reading authorities (Karlin, 1964; Wilson, 1967) that vocabulary scores provide teachers with diagnostic insight into the reading ability of students. However, the wide array of procedures used to measure reading vocabulary cast doubt as to whether reading vocabulary is a *specific* sub-area of reading.

Kelley and Krey (1934) studied standardized vocabulary and reading tests and delineated 26 different approaches for measuring knowledge of word meanings. In a list adapted from Dolch (1927), they categorized the approaches as follows:

1] Unaided recall
   A. Checking for familiarity
   B. Using words in a sentence
   C. Explaining the meaning
   D. Giving a synonym
   E. Giving an opposite
2] Aided recall
   A. Recall aided by recognition
     1. Matching tests
     2. Classification tests
     3. Multiple-choice tests
       a. Choosing the opposite
       b. Choosing the best synonym
       c. Choosing the best definition
       d. Choosing the best use in sentences
     4. Same-opposite tests
     5. Same-opposite-neither tests
     6. Same-different tests
   B. Recall aided by association
     1. Completion test
     2. Analogy test
   C. Recall aided by recognition and association
     1. Multiple-choice completion test
     2. Multiple-choice substitution test
         (Kelley & Krey, 1934, p. 103)

In conclusion, Kelley and Krey stated that there did not seem to be any one best technique for measuring word meaning knowledge. They added that with present instruments there was little hope of accurately determining the extent or the quality of the reading vocabulary of an individual.

An attempt to analyze the behavior involved in a child's knowledge of the meaning of a word was undertaken by Cronbach (1942). Cronbach's categorization of such behavior can be presented as follows:

1] Generalization—Can the child define the word?
2] Application—Can the child recognize an illustration of the word if properly named by the word?
3] Breadth of meaning—Can the pupil recall different meanings of the word?
4] Precision—Can the pupil apply the term correctly in all possible situations?
5] Availability—Does the child actually use the word?

The methods of measuring vocabulary listed by Kelley and Krey and the categories of behaviors involved in vocabulary skills devised by Cronbach suggest that the measurement of reading vocabulary is indeed a complex task. If one just looks at standardized reading tests, it is obvious that many sub-tests are labelled vocabulary. However, on closer examination it becomes hard to believe that all these sub-tests of vocabulary are measuring the same thing since the procedures used and the types of behaviors sampled vary from sub-test to sub-test. For example, the Gates-MacGinitie Reading Test includes a reading vocabulary sub-test of fifty items to be completed within fifteen minutes; for each item, a word is given in isolation and the examinee is asked to select the best synonym from five alternatives. But, the Diagnostic Reading Tests: Upper Level differs from the Gates-MacGinitie: it has a vocabulary sub-test consisting of sixty items to be completed within ten minutes; for each item, a definition is given and the examinee is to select from five alternatives the word defined. The vocabulary sub-test of the Nelson-Denny Reading Test: Vocabulary-Comprehension-Rate contains one hundred items to be completed within ten minutes;

for each item, an incomplete definition statement is given and the examinee is to select from five alternatives the best word to complete the definition. In each of these three *vocabulary* tests the task is quite different. Time is a stringent factor on one test but not on the other two; the words to be defined are in isolation in one test but not on two others; and, on one test, the match is between a word and a synonym and in the other between a word and a definition.

The confusion caused by the diversity of methods for measuring reading vocabulary poses a serious problem for the test consumer: which reading vocabulary sub-test should be selected from the many available? Assuming that reading vocabulary is a distinct and measurable sub-skill of reading, the problem of test selection can be mitigated somewhat if when choosing a test, the goals of the test are matched with the instructional goals. For example, if a variety of procedures have been used to foster vocabulary growth, then the vocabulary test used to assess this growth should include a wide range of tasks. What is important is that the test sample the same behaviors as those developed through the instructional program. This is not teaching for a test, rather it is selecting a test which measures growth toward the specified objectives of the reading program.

While the use of tests which do not measure reading vocabulary as it has been developed in the classroom constitutes a prevalent problem in measuring vocabulary, there are important problems which should be considered. A number of vocabulary tests at every grade level impose such severe time limits that many students are unable to complete the test. This happens most in upper level reading tests. Time limits do tend to increase the reliability of any given test, but, at the same time, they reduce the test's validity as a vocabulary measure. When speed and vocabulary are tested together, what is being measured is some unknown combination of the two, rather than just reading vocabulary or just reading speed. A test which confounds the two cannot validly assess the reading vocabulary of a slow but methodical reader.

The inclusion of a speed factor in measuring reading vocabulary may partially account for the significant improvement of an experimental group over a control group reported in many research studies. A speed factor in measurement also allows the well-known Hawthorne effect to have more effect than usual. Such an effect would be easy to demonstrate. For example, a Hawthorne effect could be built into two parallel studies of reading vocabulary improvement: in the first study, the vocabulary tests would be untimed; in the second study, the tests would be timed so that only the top quarter of the class would have enough time to finish. The test results might well show more significant reading gains in the study in which the tests were timed.

Another source of confusion in vocabulary measurement arises from the vast number of tests which attempt to assess vocabulary skills by presenting words in isolation and directing students to select the "best" synonym from a number of alternatives. This method does not reflect reading vocabulary skills as an individual actually applies such an ability in a practical reading situation. Goodman (1968) has pointed out that reading is a psycholinguistic guessing game and that a student relies quite heavily on the semantic and syntactic context clues of a reading passage in determining the meaning and pronunciation of a word. H. L. Smith (1956), another well-known linguist, has seriously questioned the validity of defining any word out of context.

Still another problem in measuring vocabulary improvement relates to the use of so-called equivalent forms of tests. The equivalency of most reading vocabulary tests is based on a statistical rather than a logical basis. An analogy may be drawn from the high jumping and long jumping ability of students. It is possible to determine the distance (long jumping) and height (high jumping) ability for a group of students and compute the equivalency between the two; the raw scores from each could then be changed to grade equivalents and presented in a table. If the long jump measure is used as an indication of improved performance following a semester of high jumping classes, this would constitute a *statistically* equivalent test but not a *logically* equivalent test because the content of the two measures would not be the same. This same situation is true of vocabulary tests despite test developers' attempts to control the content validity of equivalent forms. If two forms of a test were equivalent, a raw score of fifty on one test would mean exactly the same thing as a raw score of fifty on another form. A number of factors about the nature of the words used on each test, however, make any two forms of a vocabulary test far from equivalent: relative word length, subject matter, part of speech, difficulty of discrimination among alternatives, word lists used for the selection of items, poor items, etc. Very few studies have investigated these types of problems related to test equivalency. However, a start has been made by Hinton (1959) who found that the sub-tests of two forms of the Diagnostic Reading Tests were quite unequal in difficulty.

Validity of reading vocabulary measures

Are standardized tests of reading vocabulary valid measures of the quality or depth of a student's vocabulary power? Several researchers have dealt with this question. Dolch and Leeds (1953) examined five tests of reading vocabulary: the Thorndike, the Gates, the Durrell-Sullivan, the Stanford, and the Metropolitan. They concluded that the tests do not measure depth of word meaning because they: 1] ignore all but the most common meaning of words; and 2] when synonyms are used, a very indefinite amount of knowledge is tested. Dolch and Leeds suggested that the most serious weakness of the five tests is that they fail to recognize that words have different meanings for different people and that there is no one "meaning" for any particular word. Instead, they claimed, each word has a variety of meanings. While these points are well taken, they are severely limited by the lack of statistical evidence and specific validity criteria.

The fact that most reading vocabulary tests are quite similar to one another regardless of their intended grade level use has led researchers to question the validity of using the same type of vocabulary test at all grade levels. Feifel and Lorge (1950) examined the types of *oral* vocabulary responses of 900 children between the ages of 6 and 14 and found: 1] older children (ages 10 to 14) more often use a synonym-type definition than younger children (ages 6 to 9), and 2] younger children supply and use description-type definitions more than older children. If *spoken vocabulary* can be used as an indication of reading vocabulary development, Feifel and Lorge's study could be used as a basis for the development of differentiated procedures for measuring reading vocabulary at different age levels.

Kruglov (1953), in investigating the quality of reading vocabulary responses of students at various age levels, administered a ten-item five-option multiple-choice test to pupils in grades three, five, seven, and eight and to a group of college graduates. For each test item, three or four options were correct but were of different qualitative levels. Therefore, Kruglov concluded that: 1] there is an increase in the choice of a synonym as the correct response for older students; 2] there is a significant decrease in the per cent of repetition, illustration, and inferior explanation-type responses between students in grades three through eight and college graduates; and 3] there are no differences in the use of description-type responses and explanation-type responses between any of the groups tested.

The preceding studies present rather conclusive evidence that there are qualitative differences in students' responses to vocabulary items: younger students tended to choose more concrete definitions (description and use) while older students chose more abstract definitions (synonyms and classifications). The ability of present vocabulary tests to measure these differences in student responses has been studied by several of the preceding authors who consistently pointed out that the tests are inadequate for measuring all but the very lowest level of vocabulary ability.

Russell (1954) made various suggestions for improving the validity of reading vocabulary measures. The most serious problem in testing vocabulary, according to Russell, is that of determining verbalization—whether or not students supply correct answers without a real understanding of the concept to which they are responding. As have many others in the field of reading such as Kruglov (1953) and Dolch and Leeds (1957), Russell recommended that words to be used as test items be placed in as meaningful a situation as possible and that vocabulary tests be developed which evaluate the quality of students' reading vocabulary. Such measuring devices would include items designed to assess students': 1] precision in knowledge of words, e.g., the ability to discriminate between words such as *valley* and *canyon;* 2] breadth of vocabulary indicated by the number of words recognized and knowledge of multiple meanings of words such as *run* and *strike*; and 3] ability to use vocabulary in speaking, writing, and reading.

Another point of controversy has been the usefulness of standardized reading tests in determining the size of a student's vocabulary. Mary K. Smith (1941) conducted a number of studies which have shown that the usually accepted estimates of the size of students' listening vocabulary may be vastly underestimated because the test constructors used abridged dictionaries in selecting the words included in that test. Estimates of vocabulary size based on a sampling from unabridged dictionaries by Smith indicated that the average first grader knows 24,000 different words, the average sixth grader knows 49,500 words, the average high school student knows 80,000 words, and the average university student knows 157,000 different words. Most other estimates (Buckingham & Dolch, 1936; Rinsland, 1945; Thorndike, 1931; Seashore & Eckerson, 1940) of vocabulary size, upon which instructional materials and tests have been based, are much lower than this. Bryan (1953) claimed that the estimates by Smith may also be too low. To determine vocabulary size, Bryan used three vocabulary tests: a free association test, a stimulus-response test, and a multiple-choice recognition test. The estimates of the number of words that children knew were larger when the following methods were used: 1] testing the children in a greater number of socio-economic areas of the country; 2] testing children more often during the year so that various holidays, seasons, and recreational activities would serve to recall additional words; 3] reconstructing for children a greater number of their common areas of experience.

The studies cited thus far cast considerable doubt on the ability of present standardized tests to measure the qualitative or quantitative aspects of vocabulary. Perhaps a more important question is whether standardized tests can validly measure reading vocabulary as distinct from other reading skills. Most validity studies of reading skills have used correlation techniques to point out that there is so much overlap between subskills that almost all of the variance on the standardized reading tests is taken up by some kind of general factor.

V. H. Hughes (1953) correlated scores of 332 fifth graders on tests of word meaning and reading comprehension with scores made on tests of other aspects of language ability such as spelling, punctuation, capitalization, language usage, paragraph organization, and sentence sense. Despite the fact that the study was not designed specifically to isolate sub-test variance, Hughes found that there is a very high degree of overlap between all the tests of language skills.

Another study which emphasized the lack of discriminant validity for vocabulary tests was conducted by Garlock, Dollarhide, and Hopkins (1965). The Wide Range Achievement Test (a reading recognition vocabulary test) and the Gilmore Oral Reading Test were found to provide almost identical interchangeable information. However, the findings of Garlock and his colleagues are somewhat limited because of the atypical population of mentally retarded pupils they studied.

Farr (1968) in a convergent-discriminant validity study of three upper level reading tests reported that none of the three subtests of reading vocabulary evidenced any discriminant validity (the validity of tests as measures of distinct skills or abilities).

For example, the vocabulary test of the Nelson Reading Test correlated .76 with the vocabulary sub-test of the California Reading Test; however, the vocabulary sub-test of the Nelson correlated with the comprehension sub-test of the California test also at .76; and the vocabulary sub-test of the California test correlated at .73 with the comprehension sub-test of the Nelson test. Certainly the specific (discriminant) validity of the sub-tests of vocabulary as measured by these two tests should be seriously questioned.

Reliability of measures of reading vocabulary

Research on the reliability of reading vocabulary tests is a rarity. The reliability coefficients provided by most test publishers have been based on an internal consistency procedure. In reporting them, the test publishers often fail to describe in detail the population used in determining the coefficients. This kind of omission seriously limits their usefulness.

Two factors which have been shown to influence the reliability of vocabulary test scores are related to directions on guessing and the timing of tests. Swineford and Miller (1953) investigated the effects of three sets of directions on the amount of guessing on reading vocabulary tests. Students either were told 1] they should avoid guessing, 2] they should guess even when they did not know the answer, or 3] they were given no directions regarding guessing. The group which was told not to guess responded to substantially fewer items than either of the other two groups. Swineford and Miller found that too many difficult items on a test or too much guessing seriously reduces the test's reliability.

Slakter (1967) has shown that if examinees are discouraged from guessing because a penalty has been imposed for it, the test scores of the examinees reflect the risk-taking of the examinees as well as their achievement. If the test maker is more concerned with validity than reliability, Slakter urged that he construct tests in which examinees are encouraged to answer all questions. If such directions are used, it is crucial that the test be of appropriate difficulty. A test which is extremely difficult for a particular group and in which students are encouraged to guess would have an exceedingly low reliability.

Boag and Neild (1962) explored the effects of timing on the reliability of the vocabulary section of the Diagnostic Reading Test. They found that the relative standings of some high school students changed when they were given additional time on the vocabulary test. Thus, it was concluded that speed and power of reading scores should be not used interchangeably. One additional finding was that changes in relative standings under timed and untimed conditions occur with considerably greater frequency through the middle range of scores than they do at either extreme of the distribution.

The measurement of reading vocabulary is far from an exact science. The studies reviewed here indicate that there is confusion about how to measure reading vocabulary or whether there is a unitary trait which can be labelled reading vocabulary. Perhaps the most important conclusion that can be derived from this review is that there is a lack of evidence to support the contention that vocabulary can be measured as a distinct sub-area of reading.

Reading vocabulary: needed approaches

The most important research need in measuring reading vocabulary is the development of tests based on sound theoretical and empirical evidence concerning the components of reading ability (Kingston, 1965). While it has been logically argued that a person can know the meanings of many words he reads and, at the same time, lack the ability to weave these meanings together in reading sentences and paragraphs, this contention has no empirical basis. Until such evidence is forthcoming, any attempts to "diagnose" reading vocabulary as distinct from reading comprehension or other areas should proceed on very cautious grounds. It seems possible that research may reveal that the logical analyses of sub-skills constituting reading behavior have been quite inaccurate and that such skills need to be re-examined from a radically different point of view. This conclusion would not only have serious implications for test design and content, but also for the development of reading programs and instructional materials.

If past test developers' and researchers' attempts to measure vocabulary as a distinct sub-area prove to be successful, the study of the qualitative differences in reading vocabulary responses at different age levels should then become the focal point of future research. Studies already carried out have indicated that the usual methods do not supply adequate information concerning many aspects of reading vocabulary. An initial undertaking along these lines might well take the form of verifying Kelley and Krey's (1934) 26 methods for measuring reading vocabulary.

Estimates of the size of students' vocabularies need updating. The availability of computer techniques as well as newly developed sampling procedures certainly would facilitate the task of developing grade and age level vocabulary lists. Such studies should be able to profit from the early work of Thorndike (1931) and Seashore and Eckerson (1940) and more recently from that of Dale (1949) and Bryan (1953).

Speed of reading

For the purposes of the review which follows, reading speed is defined as the number of words read within any given time period. Comprehension as it relates to reading speed is discussed separately later in this chapter.

The development of faster reading speed is an important, if not central, goal of many high school and college reading programs. This is certainly justifiable on both logical and empirical grounds—the large volume of reading required in most academic and vocational endeavors is reason enough for the development of speed reading programs. The realization that many

high school and college students read at a rate below their potential and that reading speeds can easily be increased has led to
the rapid expansion of these programs over the past decade.

Because of the recent emphasis on reading speed, a number
of standardized tests—Burnett Reading Series: Survey Test,
Diagnostic Reading Tests, and the Gates-MacGinitie Reading
Tests—have been developed. Most of these include some type
of comprehension check for two reasons: 1] the belief that
faster reading results in better comprehension; 2] the belief
that reading speed is unimportant unless some minimal level of
comprehension is maintained. That faster reading results in
better comprehension is not at all substantiated by research evidence. In fact, the validity of correlations between reading speed
and comprehension has been a point of controversy for many
years. In the 1930's, Eurich (1930), Anderson and Tinker
(1932), and many others began reporting moderately high correlations between rate and comprehension. In 1942, however,
Stroud pointed out that most of the early studies relating speed
to comprehension were invalid because they were based on
comprehension scores derived from timed tests and, therefore,
the comprehension score was contaminated by a speed factor.

A study by Flanagan (1937) emphasized this point.
Flanagan collected two scores for subjects on a literary comprehension test: a level of comprehension score and a rate of comprehension score. The level of comprehension score was based
on the average number of comprehension items answered correctly on four twenty-item scales. The rate of comprehension
score was the total number of items answered correctly on all
eighty items minus a correction for guessing. Flanagan computed a positive correlation of .77 between these two scores,
thus indicating a great deal of trait similarity. However, when
he correlated a rate of reading score (determined by the total
number of items completed within a time limit) with the level of
comprehension score, the correlation was only .17.

The belief that reading speed is unimportant unless some
minimal level of comprehension is maintained seems quite

logical. Certainly a reader should not increase his reading speed if by so doing, he is unable to comprehend what he is reading. However, if reading speed and comprehension are unrelated, there appears to be justification for measuring speed separately from comprehension. Many students who are slow readers are good comprehenders, but there are also many slow readers who are poor comprehenders. On the other hand, both good and poor reading comprehension occurs among relatively fast readers. Stroud (1969) has emphasized that there is as much point in one's reading rapidly what he does not understand as there is in his reading it slowly.

Applying comprehension checks to measure reading speed has resulted in another problem. Comprehension scores have been used on many reading rate tests as if they formed a perfect ratio scale, that is, as if there were an absolute zero point on the test. On one such test, an individual's score is determined by multiplying his reading rate with his per cent of comprehension. The reason for this, according to the test developer, is that the reading speed score should be reduced by the reader's level of comprehension. The invalidity of this procedure is easily illustrated through the following hypothetical situation. Suppose an examinee reads 300 words per minute and scores 85 per cent on comprehension. Multiplying the two would result in a reading speed score of 255 words per minute. If the examinee merely reads the title of the selection and then reports that he had read the material, his speed would be taken as being approximately 20,000 words per minute. A subsequent comprehension score of 55 per cent would result in a rate of reading score of 11,000 words per minute. Such a comprehension score without reading would not be unusual since examinees can always answer several questions correctly on the basis of their prior knowledge and several other items can be guessed correctly. ⌊The main point here is that combining comprehension with measures of reading rate detracts from the validity of measuring speed of reading.⌋

The failure of test developers to provide specific purposes for reading a given selection also poses a measurement problem. Several studies (McDonald, 1966; Sheldon, 1955) have shown that purpose can have a strong influence on rate of reading. Most tests of reading speed merely require that the examinee read the material and answer the questions that follow. McDonald (1958) attempted to deal with this problem by developing a reading versatility inventory. McDonald's inventory tries to measure the reader's ability to change his reading speed and approach to suit his purpose for reading. The inventory is composed of three reading selections each containing different directions. The first set of directions asks the student to read the material carefully; the second asks him to read rapidly; and the third asks him to skim. McDonald reported that flexible readers complete each succeeding part of the inventory 1.8 to 2 times faster than the preceding one. Two important points about McDonald's inventory should be made: 1] while both speed and comprehension scores are determined for each reading selection, there is no attempt to combine the scores; 2] the subjects in McDonald's study were not allowed to look back when answering the questions. Whether or not examinees should be permitted to look back at the reading selection when answering test items is a controversy in measuring reading comprehension which is discussed later.

Despite McDonald's attempts to build a measure of reading flexibility, there is little evidence that most students have any ability to adjust their reading rate to suit specific purposes. McDonald (1966), in an overview of research studies, concluded that the vast majority of readers are untrained in reading flexibility and, therefore, do not change their reading rate to any great extent even when instructed to read for different purposes. In a more recent study of fourth graders, Gifford and Marson (1966) supported McDonald's conclusion. The subjects in their study did not vary their reading speed to suit the specific purposes of reading for main ideas and details. The fact that readers do not adjust their speed in different situations should not be taken as an indictment of reading tests; if anything, it points out the shortcomings of reading programs which develop such inflexible readers. If reading tests were to include more specific directions about purposes for reading and would vary these purposes, more reading programs might begin to teach flexibility.

Several studies which test developers as well as consumers should particularly heed have focused on the effects of typography on reading speed. In Hvistendahl's (1965) study, subjects were presented the same magazine page in four different formats: one with paragraph heads, another with boldface lead-ins, another with boldface paragraphs, and a final one containing no typographical aids. Each was also presented in two- and three-column format. Rate of reading was determined by asking the subjects which page they thought they could read fastest. The results were statistically significant in favor of all the pages containing typographical aids, but there were no significant differences in the use of two- versus three-column format. These findings are limited, however, because of the criteria used to determine rate of reading.

The effect of print size on the reading speed of first, second, and third graders was examined by McNamara, Patterson, and Tinker (1953). The print used ranged in size from 8 to 24 point. Little difference in the rate of words read for any of the type sizes were found at the first two grade levels. In grade three, there was a definite trend indicating students read material set in 10, 12, and 14 point type faster. Therefore, McNamara, Patterson, and Tinker advised that the type size of reading material should not be a consideration in selecting materials in the first two grades only because of rate which is not an important factor in reading instruction in these grades. There are other factors which do make size of print important at this age. As reading skills develop to the level found at the third grade where rate is more important, size of type does have an effect on speed and should be considered in selecting materials. While size of print may exert the greatest single influence on rate of reading, other factors such as type style, line width, page format, color of print and background, illumination, and the reading situation also should be considered (Tinker, 1963).

A number of studies have pointed out that there is a maximum limit in the number of letters that can be effectively perceived by a reader at any one time (Newman, 1966, p. 272). According to a review of the research made by Stroud (1942), this limit is generally thought to be five to eight letters or about six to eight fixations per line by the average mature reader (Anderson, 1937; Buswell, 1922). Newman's (1966) study was concerned with determining the reader's lower limits in effectively perceiving letters. Using rather unique equipment, Newman contended that when the number of letters presented to a reader at a single exposure falls below a minimal level, the subject does not receive enough contextual help from surrounding letters and reading is disrupted.

Validity and reliability of tests of reading speed

The validity of reading speed tests has been questioned in a number of instances. The most significant factor affecting validity is the attempt to combine reading speed with comprehension. This factor has resulted in the construction of tests of rate or speed or comprehension, not speed of reading.

The effect on reading rate scores of the difficulty level and interest appeal of the reading selections included in a particular test is in itself a basis for raising the validity question in any facet of reading measurement. However, because of the susceptability of reading speed tests to the Hawthorne effect, it is more of a problem in measuring reading rate than in measuring other reading skills. One attempt to investigate the relationship between reading rate and the interest appeal of reading selections was undertaken by Bryant and Barry (1961). They concluded that interest did not significantly influence reading rate in the case of relatively simple, narrative articles. The procedure used by Bryant and Barry involved asking subjects which of two articles they found more interesting. From a sample of one hundred cases, two groups of 17 were selected: one group had favored the first selection while the other had favored the second. This procedure does not seem valid for selecting materials with much positive or negative attraction; the small number of students choosing selections as "most interesting" would seem to support this contention. Thus, the mildly positive or negative attitudes which Bryant and Barry found is not surprising, neither is the lack of significant differences in reading speed.

Significant differences were found in reading speed for varying difficulty levels of reading material by Carlson (1951). The primary statistical procedure used in the study was a Pearson Product-Moment correlation. As would be expected, all of the correlations between reading rate and level of difficulty were significant at the .01 level, but they were not large enough for any predictive use. Carlson's study also pointed out the limitation of measuring reading speed when the difficulty level of the reading material is not controlled. The effects of the reading level of materials on the measurement of reading rate is a problem which is often overlooked. If a student is unable to read seventh-grade material, despite the fact that he may find himself in a seventh-grade class, a test of reading speed utilizing material of seventh-grade difficulty is probably not a valid measure of reading speed for this student. Should a subject's reading speed be determined on material of relatively easy reading? Or, should he be reported as having several reading speeds depending on the difficulty and interest appeal of the material? These questions have not been answered in research studies and are generally ignored by most constructors of reading rate tests.

Another problem affecting the validity of reading speed scores is the apparent "slack" that most readers seem to have in normal reading speeds. Laycock (1955) investigated the effect of giving students a mental set to read faster without decreasing their comprehension. Under these conditions, subjects increased reading speed by as much as forty per cent. These results suggest the possibility that supposed gains in reading speed, following a session of reading improvement classes, may be due to the new "mental set" students have established.

Few studies focus on the reliability of tests of reading rate. Traxler (1938), for one, studied the relationship between the length and the reliability of one of these tests. Seventy-eight high school juniors were given two forms of a 177-line reading rate test in alternate order. The students were asked to mark the line they were reading at the end of each hundred seconds. Traxler then correlated the number of lines read at each hundred seconds between forms A and B. The correlations were significantly higher (.86) for four hundred seconds than for one hundred seconds (.62). Traxler concluded that the time allowed for most tests of reading rate (one minute to five minutes) is too short for high reliability. He called for the development of tests two or three times the length of those extant. This same plea is valid today.

The most important research need in the measurement of reading rate is a thorough analysis of how students develop faster reading speeds that can serve as a basis for test construction. In particular, the phenomenal reading rates achieved by students in some rate improvement programs should be studied more closely, especially since some of the rates reported have exceeded the physiological limits of the normal progression of eye movements across and down the page. Another area demanding further study concerns the difficulty and interest-appeal of selections used to measure reading rate. Probably the best approach for such research would be through a series of studies combining purposes for reading, difficulty of selections, and interest level of selections in a three-way analysis of variance. Such an investigation could help to determine the effects of each of these factors individually as well as the unique interaction effects among all three factors. Replication could then be conducted with a number of different age groups. Finally, the reliability of reading rate measures should also prove a fertile area for future study. Traxler in 1938 provided valuable insight into this problem, but since then very little effort has been expended in this area. The interchangeability of test forms, the effects of test length at various age levels, and the effects of typography all need to be examined if the reliability of reading rate measures is to be improved.

Reading comprehension

A review of the factors that should be considered in measuring reading comprehension reveal that this measurement task is extremely complex. These factors include the length, interest-appeal, subject matter, reading difficulty, and organization of the material to be read; the reader's purpose, mental set, environmental conditions for reading, and command of basic decoding skills; the type of question to be used; and whether examinees are allowed to look back at the selection when answering questions. Kerfoot (1968, p. 42) stated that the measurement of reading comprehension is a "problem of inconsistency in both theoretical base and descriptive terminology." He suggested that, to overcome this problem, both researchers and practitioners should seek to operationally define reading comprehension in terms of specific reading tasks. Barrett (1968) has provided a partial response to Kerfoot's plea for an operational definition of comprehension by developing a taxonomy of the cognitive and affective domains of reading comprehension. The major sections of this taxonomy include literal comprehension, reorganization, inferential comprehension, and evaluation and appreciation.

As part of a review of research on reading comprehension, Davis (1968) cited an analysis of reading comprehension by Richards (1929), which Davis considered perceptive. Among the abilities which Richards included in his analysis of reading comprehension were literal comprehension, recognizing the writer's mood, comprehending the writer's tone, and recognizing the writer's purpose.

There are presently many sub-tests of standardized reading tests purporting to measure sub-skills of reading comprehension.

Testing

However, the division of comprehension into distinct sub-skill areas has not been based on any validity studies. Stroud (1969), realizing this deficiency, suggested that reading comprehension tests include measures of the reader's ability to recall specific facts, generalize, draw inferences, and determine the author's purpose. However, Stroud did issue a caution: he suggested that such sub-tests not be used for diagnostic purposes. Instead, he urged that the sub-tests be combined.

Ward (1956) in analyzing the results of four tests which he developed specifically to measure reading comprehension, also urged that a variety of approaches be used to measure comprehension. The tests Ward designed, however, contained much broader elements than those usually thought of as sub-skills of reading comprehension; they included speed, flexibility, understanding of ideas, and knowledge of words.

Early attempts to isolate specific reading comprehension skills employed factor-analysis techniques. Davis (1944) developed tests of nine skills which he believed to be components of reading comprehension. The list of nine reading skills that were appraised by Davis' tests included:

1] knowledge of word meanings
2] ability to select the appropriate meaning for a word or phrase in the light of its particular contextual setting
3] ability to follow the organization of a passage and to identify antecedents and references in it
4] ability to select the main thought of a passage
5] ability to answer questions that are specifically answered in a passage
6] ability to answer questions that are answered in a passage but not in words in which the question is asked
7] ability to draw inferences from a passage about its contents
8] ability to recognize the literary devices used in a passage and to determine its mood and intent

9] ability to determine a writer's purpose, intent, and point of view, i.e., to draw inferences about a writer.

A factor-analysis of the results of these tests administered to a group of college freshmen produced only five statistically significant skills; two of them—word knowledge and reasoning—accounted for 89 per cent of the total variance. The five statistically significant reading comprehension skills were: 1] word knowledge, 2] ability to reason in reading, 3] ability to follow the organization of a passage and to identify antecedents and references in it, 4] ability to recognize the literary devices used in a passage and to determine its tone and mood, and 5] tendency to focus attention on a writer's explicit statements to the exclusion of their implications.

Thurstone (1946) questioned the validity of Davis' findings on two bases: 1] Davis' data showed that the nine tests were measures of the same reading function, and 2] the tests revealed no evidence about the components of reading comprehension. Davis (1946) refuted Thurstone's re-analysis and suggested that the factors he had revealed

> ought to provide individuals actually engaged in teaching children to read and in constructing tests of comprehension in reading with improved insight into the nature of reading comprehension and with clues for improving the teaching of reading and the measurement of reading. (1946, p. 188)

In a more recent study, Hunt (1957) examined the correlations of a number of sub-tests of reading comprehension to determine if each of the measures of reading comprehension which he developed were distinct and measurable skills. Hunt concluded that each sub-test was measuring essentially the same thing and that, therefore, diagnostic measures of reading comprehension needed further study. Davis (1968) interpreted Hunt's study in a summary of research on measuring reading comprehension and concluded that the results of Hunt's study were in harmony with Davis' (1944) findings:

> Hunt, therefore, concluded that only the vocabulary items were measuring a skill in comprehension (knowledge of word meanings) that was significantly different from the others. This implies that comprehension in reading involves two skills: word knowledge and paragraph comprehension. These results are in harmony with Davis' findings that word knowledge and reasoning in reading account for virtually all of the variance of comprehension. (1968, p. 508)

Whether, in fact, they were in agreement is open to question. In a more recent study, Davis (1968) reinvestigated the unique variances of sub-tests of reading comprehension with a set of carefully constructed tests designed to measure specific aspects of reading comprehension. The five skills which Davis isolated, listed in order of unique variance contributing to total comprehension scores, included: 1] memory for word meanings; 2] drawing inferences from the content; 3] following the structure of a passage; 4] recognizing a writer's purpose, attitude, tone, and mood; and 5] finding answers to questions asked explicitly or in paraphrase. These factors are quite similar to those listed by Davis in 1944; however, this is not surprising since the tests used by Davis in 1968 closely paralleled those used in the 1944 study.

In all of the factor-analysis studies reported above, multiple-choice tests were used. Vernon (1962) questioned whether the overlap between measures of reading comprehension might be caused by not only the methods of testing but also by students' ability to take certain kinds of tests. The tests used by Vernon in this study included multiple-choice vocabulary questions, filling in the blanks in sentences, vocabulary definitions supplied by the examinee, reading comprehension questions for which the examinees were allowed to look back at the passages after reading, and reading comprehension questions for which the examinees could not look back at the passages. Vernon's tests of various aspects of comprehension did result in higher correlations within than between the types of comprehension. Vernon pointed out that this uniqueness could have been the result of the technical bias of the passages rather than the measurement of unique aspects of comprehension.

McCullough (1957) studied whether different aspects of comprehension were measured by different types of questions. Data consisted of the responses of elementary school children to common types of reading comprehension questions. Included were questions designed to measure comprehension of main ideas, facts, or details; sequence or organization; and creative reading. McCullough found a statistically significant correlation between all four types of reading comprehension questions. However, because the correlations were not substantial, McCullough cautioned that the measurement of any one of the skills could not be substituted for any of the other four.

While McCullough's suggestion is perhaps valid, there is still a lack of understanding about basic aspects of reading comprehension. The results of the preceding studies do demonstrate that most attempts thus far to validly measure specific sub-skills of reading comprehension have not been consistent. Because of this failure to delineate the basic measurable components of reading comprehension satisfactorily, the best procedure involves using a variety of measures. Included could be tests of the reader's ability to recall specific facts, make generalizations, draw conclusions, draw inferences, and reorganize and organize ideas. Sub-scores from any of these tests should not be used independently in any attempt to diagnose reading comprehension, but rather should be combined to measure reading comprehension or, as Stroud put it, the effective use of reading text. In selecting a test of reading comprehension, the potential test consumer should select one which appears to measure reading comprehension as he has taught it. Despite the lack of evidence regarding the individual aspects of reading comprehension, it still is more valid to select a test which appears to measure the skill which has been taught. If, for example, the instructional program has focused on teaching students to draw inferences from reading selections, then the reading comprehension test used to measure growth toward this objective should not consist of a series of questions which measure immediate retention of specifically stated facts.

What are the problems affecting the measurement of reading comprehension? Certainly the effects of timing, of allowing examinees to look back at the reading selection, of prior knowledge of the content or the topic of the reading selection, of the language structure, and length of the selection, personality traits of the examinees, and purposes for reading all contribute to the complexity of measuring reading comprehension.

The effects of time on reading comprehension are quite considerable. Indeed, if the measurement of reading comprehension is timed, then speed of reading comprehension rather than power of reading comprehension is being evaluated. Because of the fairly common practice of timing reading comprehension tests and the contemporary stress on speed, speed of reading comprehension is discussed as a separate skill later. The present discussion involves only *untimed* tests of reading comprehension or, as it may be labelled, power of reading comprehension.

One variable which has received little attention is the effect of allowing examinees to look back at the selection while answering questions about it after they have completed reading it. The decision as to whether to allow this should be made by the examiner, based on the objectives of the instructional program. If subjects are allowed to look back, is reading comprehension actually being measured? If they are not allowed to look back, does the test become a measure of immediate memory span? Perhaps some of the findings of studies such as Anderson and Tinker's (1932), Eurich's (1930), Gray's (1917), and Tinker's (1932), all of which showed a strong relation between rate of reading and comprehension resulted from not permitting subjects to look back. Flanagan (1938) found an inverse relationship between rate of reading and extent of comprehension when subjects were allowed to look back at the selections. In a study reported previously, Vernon (1962) compared comprehension scores based on subjects' responses when they were not allowed to refer back to the text in answering questions with when they were allowed to. Vernon concluded that the two procedures did indeed appear to measure different skills and that the latter procedure of allowing students to refer back to the text was more predictive of academic achievement.

The influence of prior knowledge is another factor which must be considered when attempting to measure reading comprehension. Preston (1962) administered the first thirty comprehension questions of the Cooperative English Test: Reading Comprehension to 128 college freshmen. The reading selections did not accompany the multiple-choice items. Greater than chance scores were achieved by 77 per cent of the students. Preston, therefore, concluded that there are many reading comprehension items that are probably invalid because students are able to recognize correct answers without reading the passages.

Marks and Noll (1967) have proposed a technique for dealing not only with this problem but also with the broader question of what reading comprehension tests measure. They suggested administering the comprehension items without reading selections and then re-administering them several weeks later with the reading selections. If the number of students answering a particular item correctly under both testing conditions is greater than chance, it is highly probable that the item is testing something other than reading comprehension.

Another area which might influence reading comprehension is language structure and length of the reading selection. Ruddell (1965) examined the relationship between reading comprehension scores and the similarity of the structure of oral language used by children. The analysis of the language structures was based on work done by Strickland (1962). The primary factor of language structure manipulated was word order. Ruddell (1965, p. 273) concluded: "Reading comprehension scores on materials that utilize high frequency patterns of oral language structure are significantly greater than reading comprehension scores on materials that utilize low frequency of oral language structure." It is certainly clear from this particular study that children's language patterns should be considered when parallel test forms are being constructed.

Length of reading selections has been shown not to have any differential effect on the reading comprehension of examinees (Traxler, 1938; Humphrey, 1957). Students who score high on comprehension tests covering short selections also tend to score high on comprehension tests covering relatively longer selections. However, while there does not seem to be any discriminant validity involved, it does seem worthwhile to suggest that both longer and shorter selections should be included on any general test of reading comprehension. But the scores derived from each should not be considered separately; for the most part, short selections are used on standardized reading tests. The use of these tests in research studies may have led to the conclusion that length of the selection does not affect reading comprehension.

There has been a noticeable absence of significant findings in studies relating personality variables to reading comprehension test scores. Most of the studies [for example, the Gann (1945), Garrett (1949), and Spache (1954) studies] have failed to reveal any personality patterns for poor readers. Kleck and Wheaton (1967) did find that dogmatism was highly related to reading comprehension scores on opinion-consistent and opinion-inconsistent information.

Establishing purposes for reading has been shown to significantly influence the reading comprehension of good readers but not of poor readers (Helen K. Smith, 1961). Henderson (1965) found that fifth graders differed in their ability to formulate a purpose for reading and that this ability was positively related to reading comprehension scores. It should be noted, however, that all of the students in Henderson's study were average readers.

The cloze procedure is a relatively new technique for measuring reading comprehension. The procedure involves deleting certain words from a reading selection and then requiring the examinee to supply the missing word; usually every fifth word is deleted. Bormuth (1967) tried to establish a frame of reference for the interpretation of cloze scores. He administered a fifty-item cloze test and a 31-item multiple-choice test for each of nine passages to 73 pupils in grades four and five. The results indicated that a score of 38 per cent correct completions on the cloze test was equal to a comprehension score of 67 per cent and that a cloze score of 50 per cent was equal to a comprehension score of 87 per cent.

Hafner (1964), using college students as subjects, investigated the relationship of various measures to cloze scores. In this study, not only did cloze scores correlate positively and significantly with measures of intelligence, vocabulary, and information, they also compared favorably with standard prediction of course grades.

The confusion concerning the components of reading comprehension have led to several serious problems for the test consumer. Of prime importance are the problems concerning what reading comprehension test to select, whether that test should include a variety of sub-tests, whether it should be timed, and what format the content and language structure of the reading selections should follow. On the basis of the review of present research on measuring reading comprehension, it is probably best to select an untimed test which includes a variety of kinds of questions, but these should not be combined in any attempt to develop diagnostic sub-tests. The reading comprehension measures selected are likely to be valid if the language structure and content of the selection follow patterns familiar to the examinees. In addition, the selections used in the tests should be of various lengths and cover a variety of topics. Also, for some of the selections, the examinees should be allowed to look back at the selection; for others, they should not. Finally, the test should provide specific purposes for reading. A test along the lines described here might well provide a useful measure of general reading comprehension power.

Validity and reliability of reading comprehension measures

Relatively few predictive validity studies of reading comprehension have appeared in the literature. In one study, Webb and McCall (1953) used reading comprehension scores to predict academic performance for college freshmen. In another, Murphy and Davis (1949) found a negative relationship between ability to reason in reading and academic achievement for college freshmen. According to Murphy and Davis, this might be due to the heavy emphasis placed on acquisition of factual material in freshmen courses. However, the procedure used in determining reasoning in reading was somewhat questionable: the vocabulary score was subtracted from the level of comprehension score on a reading test and the difference was labelled reasoning in reading.

Construct validity studies of reading comprehension tests have been more common. If reading comprehension test scores are valid measures of reading comprehension, then increased scores on these tests should be related to increased comprehension of common reading materials. One approach to testing this supposition would be to compare reading comprehension test scores with students' ability to comprehend a series of increasingly difficult selections. Peterson (1956) followed this procedure in developing a set of ten 100-word passages ranging in difficulty according to the Flesch formula from 5 to 95; six multiple-choice questions followed each selection. The high school seniors in the study were also administered the General Reading and Comprehension sub-tests of the Diagnostic Reading Test: Upper Level. A statistically significant relationship was found between the standardized reading test scores and the comprehension scores for the 100-word passages; comprehension of the passages decreased as the Flesch reading difficulty scores increased. The small number of questions used by Peterson resulted in a very small variance on the reading comprehension test and this limited the applicability and interpretation of his findings.

Studies comparing reading grade scores derived from a standardized reading test with actual reading performance on reading material for that grade level represent a validity index for the reading grade scores. Most of this kind of research has compared informal reading test performance to standardized reading test performance (McCracken, 1962; Sipay, 1964; Glaser, 1964). In general, the research points to the conclusion that the reading grade scores from standardized reading tests are approximately two grades higher than performance on individually administered informal tests. Michaelis and Tyler (1951) supported this finding when they compared scores on the Iowa Silent Reading Tests to comprehension of social studies material. The mean standard score on the Iowa test was 174, which corresponded to a grade equivalent of 13.0. The social studies materials, which were designed for use in high school classes, averaged about grade-thirteen difficulty according to the Lorge, Flesch, and Dale-Chall readability formulas. A total of 69 questions followed the selections; the mean percentage correct was only 62 per cent. The difficulty of the comprehension items was a significant factor in Michaelis and Tyler's study. Despite this finding, there is considerable doubt about the usefulness of the grade scores of standardized reading tests for determining students' functional reading levels.

Another attempt to understand the composition of reading comprehension test scores was undertaken by O'Donnell (1963). O'Donnell hypothesized that reading comprehension scores would be more highly related to awareness of structural relationships of words in sentences than it would be to the ability to verbalize grammatical rules and terminology. The two tests used by O'Donnell to measure these abilities included a specially designed test of recognition of structural relationships in English and the Iowa Grammar Information Test. The findings support the hypothesis that the two variables (awareness of structural relationships and ability to verbalize rules and terminology) correlated about equally with reading comprehension scores (.44 and .46, respectively). These correlations, however, indicate that only about 19 per cent of the variance in the reading comprehension scores can be accounted for by the two grammar tests. Thus, it would appear that knowledge and awareness of grammatical structures are not major factors contributing to reading comprehension. On the other hand, Jenkinson (1957), by employing the cloze procedure, found that good comprehenders (those with high cloze scores) had a better understanding of language structure. The differences between the Jenkinson and O'Donnell findings can probably be accounted for by the two different methods of measuring reading comprehension used. It is possible that while the ability to respond to multiple-choice factual recall questions is not related to awareness of language structure, they become related when comprehension is based on ability to supply missing words in text. This ability is probaby based on a combination of skills involving the use of semantic and syntactic clues.

The validity of reading comprehension scores as indicators of the amount of knowledge retained has also been subjected to study. Most reading comprehension tests are given immediately following the reading of a selection and it is entirely possible that this comprehension does not result in retention. Sharpe (1952) found that comprehension tests given immediately after reading a selection and also at 1, 7, 14, 21, 28, and 56 day intervals showed a similar forgetting curve to classroom learned material: there was a gradual process of forgetting and not an abrupt falling away as might be expected. Sharpe's study seemed to indicate that reading comprehension tests are usually measures of the amount of material learned and do not represent a unique behavior syndrome.

Most standardized reading comprehension tests report split-half correlation studies as reliability evidence. While this evidence has some value, it should be noted that the effects of test format (i.e., both halves of the test contain the same type of items) probably increases this reliability index (Kerlinger, 1965). The manuals of many standardized reading tests also fail to report sub-test reliabilities. Perhaps this is because many of the sub-tests are too short to have adequate reliability. It has also been hypothesized by Sharpe (1952) that it is possible to raise reliability indexes by allowing examinees to look back at the material rather than forcing them to rely more on memory without looking back.

Needed research in measuring reading comprehension

The most pressing research need in measuring comprehension is for a clear understanding of the nature of reading comprehension. At this time, there is no conclusive evidence regarding the components of this skill. Is it a unitary skill or is it a composite of sub-skills? If it is a composite of sub-skills, can each of the sub-skills be measured independently? As research progresses, it is likely that reading comprehension will be found to be composed of a variety of skills; at the same time, it also probably will be discovered that the skills are dependent on a particular set of conditions. These conditions might well include the topic of a particular selection, the purpose for reading, the reading difficulty of the selection in comparison to the reading skill of the examinee, the measure of comprehension utilized, and the length and language structure of the selection.

It seems reasonable to suggest that reading comprehension as a global skill is non-existent and that measurement attempts should be narrowed down to specific conditions. For example, a reading comprehension test for a student reading at about the seventh-grade level could be developed from a 200-word science selection of fifth-grade readability level. The student could be asked to read to understand and recall specific directions on how to conduct a scientific experiment. The reading comprehension test could consist of a set of multiple-choice questions in which the student is not allowed to look back at the material. *By varying any of these conditions, the skill being measured would probably be altered.*

Another research need is the development of criterion tests for measuring reading comprehension. What is the reading comprehension level needed for effective citizenship? What level of skill is needed to comprehend articles in daily newspapers? The goal of diagnostic teaching is to provide instruction based on individual needs and to determine progress toward specific goals. This implies that some goal has been defined. Usually standardized reading tests have been developed to compare one student's reading performance with that of another rather than with some specific goal. This constitutes one of the major shortcomings of all such tests.

With the exception of the cloze procedure, which was used in intelligence testing many years ago, there have been few new procedures for measuring reading comprehension in over forty years. If these "old" methods have been shown not to be valid, new ones should be tried. Perhaps, more importantly, the widespread notion that comprehension is a separate measurable sub-skill of reading should be thoroughly investigated.

Rate of comprehension

A review of the literature on the measurement of reading rate and reading comprehension reveals that most researchers are concerned with the degree of relation between these two variables. The general conclusion regarding this relationship which seems tenable, given the research available (Letson, 1958; Shores & Husbands, 1950), has been summarized by Rankin (1962, pp. 4-5):

> In conclusion, it appears that the confounding of rate and comprehension in measurement is, at least in part, responsible for some of the earlier findings that "fast readers are good readers." Other studies of the relationship between rate and "power of comprehension," find only a slight relationship. When the material is more difficult, when more critical thought processes are involved, and when the reader's purpose is more exacting, the relationship between reading rate and comprehension is minimal.

Rather than a continued assault on the relationship between rate and comprehension, it seems worthwhile to pursue the measurement of rate of reading comprehension as a unique skill. Certainly, the independent measurement of rate and comprehension may have diagnostic value, but the measurement of the speed at which a reader comprehends a reading selection also has value. Several tests, Cooperative English Test: Reading Comprehension and the Gates-MacGinitie Reading Tests: Survey, include measures which are combinations of reading rate and comprehension.

In previous discussions of the various reading skills, a review of validity and reliability studies followed the presentation of the problems involved in measuring that particular skill. Because of the lack of such studies on the rate of comprehension, this section includes only those studies related to defining rate of comprehension and apparent problems in its measurement.

Rate of comprehension is a useful variable in measuring reading achievement. Teachers should be legitimately concerned with how fast a student can accomplish a particular reading comprehension task. What is the construct of this skill? Buswell (1951) investigated whether rate of silent reading (speed) varied directly with rate of thinking (comprehension); if it did, schools might provide special reading instruction for slow readers who are fast thinkers. Buswell did find a positive relationship between rate of thinking and rate of reading. However, his population—77 college seniors at the University of California—seriously limits generalizations from the study.

The concept of rate of comprehension is very closely related to that of reading flexibility. In measuring rate of comprehension, what the teacher needs to know is how fast a reader achieves his purpose, i.e., how quickly he understands the selection (McDonald, 1965; Sheldon & Carrillo, 1952). The teacher does not have to know that a reader can pass over words at 300, 800, or 1200 words per minute; what he needs to know is how long it takes the reader to *comprehend* the material for a given purpose. The purpose is, of course, very important. If a student is asked to determine the general content of a selection, he would be expected to read at a rate different from that which he would use if asked to read to determine the specific causes leading up to a certain event. Whenever a test utilizes specific purposes for reading, the examiner should be aware that the test's purpose is always modified by the reader's purpose.

According to McDonald (1958), most research has failed to reveal that readers tend to change their reading rate to satisfy particular purposes unless special instruction is provided to this effect. The most meaningful measures of reading flexibility should include comprehension and speed when reading for a *particular purpose*. Sheldon (1955) found that college students who had been identified as good readers varied their reading speed considerably depending on the type of material read. Their comprehension scores were also uniformly high. The poor readers, on the other hand, had a very uniform (about 300 words per minute) reading rate regardless of the type of material read or purposes given for reading, while their comprehension varied greatly.

The difficulty level of the material to be read is a limiting factor in measuring rate of comprehension. [Hill (1964) found that purpose for reading had little influence on reading rate and comprehension when college students were asked to read for one of three different purposes: 1] to read a particular selection as a course assignment over which the reader was to be tested the following day; 2] to read the selection to identify its main ideas; and 3] to read the selection to analyze critically the motives and attitudes of the author.] The reading selections, which Hill stated dealt with relatively complex concepts, were used as experimental tests. They were written for the well-educated adult and presented organizational patterns and author attitude in a definite but subtle manner. It is quite possible that the complexity of the reading material prevented any reader flexibility.

[A somewhat contradictory finding was reported by Letson (1958) who studied the relationship of reading speed and comprehension on easy and difficult reading material for college freshmen. Letson's results indicated: 1] the relationship between speed scores on difficult and easy materials was high; 2] the relationship between comprehension scores on difficult and easy materials was moderate; and 3] the relationship between speed and comprehension scores was high for easy material, but decreased as the difficulty of the material increased. However, the readers in the study tended to maintain a reading rate independent of the difficulty of the material or the purpose for reading.

A major problem in the measurement of rate of comprehension resides in the fact that such measures are bound to be confounded by artifacts resulting from the measurement procedures. Letson noted that when speed and comprehension are measured simultaneously, the resulting score includes the time taken to read the selection, to read the question, and to look back and re-read the text—perhaps several times. Letson suggested that such a measure would be a speed of working, rather than a speed of reading score.

Another measurement problem is the effect of interrupting students during their reading when the examiner is attempting to determine rate of comprehension. The Nelson-Denny Reading Test, for example, asks students to note how far they have read after reading a selection for one minute; students then go on to complete reading the selection and answer the comprehension questions which follow. The Gates-MacGinitie Reading Tests: Survey measure rate by a modified cloze procedure. This interrupts the student's reading to the extent that he must consider the correct alternative to fill a blank in the reading text. There is some evidence that this interruption could affect any attempts to measure rate of reading comprehension.

McDonald (1960) studied the reading rate and comprehension of 117 college students under four timing procedures involving various amounts of interruption. Reading performance was significantly hampered by periodic interruptions; reading rate was not affected, but significant reduction in reading comprehension was noted. McDonald concluded: "Timing procedures which produce periodic interruptions during the reading process should be avoided. Methods of timing reading which minimally interrupt the students should be selected" (1960, p. 33).

Differential effects on reading comprehension scores, as the result of an interruption, have been found for slow and fast readers. Cook (1957) attempted to discover if time announcements during the administration of reading tests given to all entering students at the University of Iowa affected comprehension scores. Significantly poorer comprehension was noted for the slower readers than for the fast readers.

The content of the reading selections has also been shown to be a significant factor in the relationship between reading rate and comprehension. Thurstone (1944) obtained correlations between rate and comprehension of .11 on physical science material, .42 on literary material, and .44 on social science material.

A further measurement problem is caused by the finding that students can increase their reading speed, without any loss in comprehension, under a set of instructions to read faster. Maxwell (1965, p. 186) supported this hypothesis in a study involving 104 college students, concluding that the " . . . study has shown that instructing students to read faster on a standardized test results in a significantly faster reading rate, and further suggests that reading test speed increases as a function of a warm-up period."

Fricke (1957) studied the results of the Cooperative English Test: Reading Comprehension to determine if speed of reading scores and level of reading scores could be replaced by two new scores: rate and accuracy. Both the speed and accuracy scores were rate of comprehension scores; however, the speed score suggested by the manual for the Cooperative test was the number of correct answers less one quarter of the wrong answers. Fricke stated that this score does not validly measure the rate of comprehension of the fast but careless reader. He suggested that the rate score (speed of comprehension) should be simply the number of correct responses.

Research on the measurement of rate of reading comprehension must first focus on the utility of such a measure. There is no research evidence that has been found which relates this score to the objectives of the reading instructional program. How can such a score be utilized? Is the knowledge of student performance on this measure of educational value to the classroom teacher? Is the improvement of speed of comprehension when it is related to specific purposes an important objective of reading programs? Future research should certainly focus on these questions.

Specific research in measuring rate of comprehension should investigate more carefully the effects of the difficulty of material, the interest level of the selections, readers' purposes, and the effects of certain timing and scoring procedures. Almost all of the studies which have begun to examine these variables have used college students. Much work needs to be done at younger age levels. If flexible reading patterns are important for college readers, then they would also seem to be important for elementary and high school students. Perhaps future research will conclude that there is no general rate of reading comprehension; instead, it might well prove that for each reader there are a number of reading rates dependent upon some of the previously mentioned variables such as purpose and difficulty of materials. If this should be the case and if there is general agreement that improvement in rate of comprehension is an important objective of the reading program, a variety of tests for use in differing class situations need to be developed and/or teachers need to be trained to assess this skill informally in each learning situation.

What can be measured?

From a review of the previous studies, it is quite clear that the measurement of reading behavior is based on logical rather than empirical evidence. Research studies regarding the measurement of sub-skills of reading are very limited. Where there have been studies, there is more negative than positive evidence to support existing measures of the sub-skills of reading. In addition, for the common sub-test of reading behavior, there is great confusion concerning the most appropriate method of measurement. There are far more procedures utilized for measuring any single sub-skill of reading than there are hypothesized sub-skills of the total reading act. Many studies also conclude that the tests of reading skills fail to measure the more important aspects of the skill but focus instead on the superficial.

Researchers in this area have also voiced a fairly consistent plea that teachers employ more specific measures of reading ability. This means that teachers need to more carefully define their teaching objectives and then select or construct a test which matches those program objectives. This procedure would automatically increase the validity of the test.

Now that it has been established that many tests fail to measure validly what they purport to measure, that no one seems to know whether sub-skills of reading can be measured, and that there is a lack of measures for assessing more complex reading behaviors, it seems appropriate to focus on research on procedures for assessing students' reading abilities.

References

Anderson, I. H. Studies in the eye movements of good and poor readers. *Psychological Monographs*, 1937, No. 215.

Anderson, Verna L., & Tinker, M. A. The speed factor in reading performance. *Journal of Educational Psychology*, 1932, *27*, 621-24.

Barrett, T. C.—cited by T. Clymer, What is reading? some concepts. In Helen M. Robinson (Ed.), Innovation and change in reading instruction. *Yearbook of the National Society for the Study of Education*, 1968, *67*, 7-29.

Boag, Audrey K., & Neild, Margaret. The influence of the time factor on the scores of the Triggs Diagnostic Reading Test as reflected in the performance of secondary school pupils grouped according to ability. *Journal of Educational Research*, 1962, *55*, 181-83.

Bormuth, J. R. Comparable cloze and multiple-choice comprehension test scores. *Journal of Reading*, 1967, *10*, 291-99.

Bryan, F. E. How large are children's vocabularies? *Elementary School Journal*, 1953, *54*, 210-16.

Bryant, N. D., & Barry, N. E. The relationships between interest and reading rate and between interest and reading comprehension. In E. P. Bliesmer & A. J. Kingston (Eds.), Phases of college and other adult reading programs. *Yearbook of the National Reading Conference*, 1961, *10*, 127-30.

Buckingham, B. R., & Dolch, E. W. *A combined word list.* Boston: Ginn & Co., 1936.

Buswell, G. T. Fundamental reading habits: a study of their development. *Elementary Education Monographs*, 1922, No. 21.

Buswell, G. T. The relationship between rate of thinking and rate of reading. *School Review*, 1951, *59*, 339-46.

Carlson, T. R. Effect of certain test factors in measurement of speed of reading. *Journal of Educational Research*, 1951, *44*, 543-49.

Cook, D. L. A comparison of reading comprehension scores obtained before and after a time announcement. *Journal of Educational Psychology*, 1957, *48*, 440-46.

Cronbach, L. J. Analysis of techniques for diagnostic vocabulary testing. *Journal of Educational Research*, 1942, *36*, 206-17.

Dale, E. *Bibliography of vocabulary studies.* (Rev. ed.) Columbus, Ohio: Ohio State University Press, 1949.

Davis, F. B. Fundamental factors of comprehension in reading. *Psychometrika*, 1944, *9*, 185-97.

Davis, F. B. A brief comment on Thurstone's note on a re-analysis of Davis' reading tests. *Psychometrika*, 1946, *11*, 249-55.

Davis, F. B. Research in comprehension in reading. *Reading Research Quarterly*, 1968, *3*, 499-545.

Dolch, E. W. *Reading and word meaning.* Boston: Ginn & Co., 1927.

Dolch, E. W., & Leeds, D. Vocabulary tests and depth of meaning. *Journal of Educational Research*, 1953, *47*, 181-89.

Eurich, A. C. The relation of speed of reading to comprehension. *School and Society*, 1930, *32*, 404-06.

Farr, R. C. The convergent and discriminant validity of several upper level reading tests. In G. B. Schick & M. M. May (Eds.), Multidisciplinary aspects of college-adult reading. *Yearbook of the National Reading Conference*, 1968, *17*, 181-91.

Feifel, H., & Lorge, I. Qualitative differences in the vocabulary responses of children. *Journal of Educational Psychology*, 1950, *41*, 1-18.

Flanagan, J. C. A proposed procedure for increasing the efficiency of objective tests. *Journal of Educational Psychology*, 1937, *28*, 17-21.

Flanagan, J. C. A new type of reading test for secondary school and college students which provides separate scores for speed of comprehension and level of comprehension. (Official report of the American Educational Research Assn.) Washington, D. C.: National Education Assn., 1938. Pp. 195-99.

Fricke, B. G. Speed and level versus rate and accuracy of reading. In E. M. Huddleston (Ed.), Measurements used in education. *Yearbook of the National Council of Measurement in Education*, 1957, *14*, 73-77.

Gann, E. *Reading difficulty and personality organization.* New York: King's Crown Press, 1945.

Garlock, J., Dollarhide, R. S., & Hopkins, K. D. Comparability of scores on the Wide Range and the Gilmore Oral Reading tests. *California Journal of Educational Research*, 1965, *16*, 54-57.

Garrett, H. F. A review and interpretation of investigations of factors related to scholastic success in colleges of arts and science and teachers colleges. *Journal of Experimental Education*, 1949, *18*, 102-03.

Gifford, Edith M., & Marson, A. R. Test anxiety, reading rate, and task experience. *Journal of Educational Research*, 1966, *59*, 303-06.

Glaser, N. A. A comparison of specific reading skills of advanced and retarded readers of fifth grade reading achievement. Unpublished doctoral dissertation, University of Oregon, 1964.

Goodman, K. S. The psycholinguistic nature of the reading process. In K. S. Goodman (Ed.), *The psycholinguistic nature of the reading process.* Detroit: Wayne State University Press, 1968. Pp. 13-26.

Gray, W. S. Studies of elementary school reading through standardized tests. *Supplementary Educational Monographs*, 1917, No. 1.

Hafner, L. E. Relationships of various measures to the "cloze." In E. L. Thurston & L. E. Hafner (Eds.), New concepts in college-adult reading. *Yearbook of the National Reading Conference*, 1964, *13*, 135-45.

Henderson, E. H. A study of individually formulated purposes for reading. *Journal of Educational Research*, 1965, *58*, 438-41.

Hill, W. R. Influences of directions upon the reading flexibility of advanced college readers. In E. L. Thurston & L. E. Hafner (Eds.), New concepts in college-adult reading. *Yearbook of the National Reading Conference*, 1964, *13*, 119-25.

Hinton, E. A. Doubts about equivalent forms. *Journal of Developmental Reading*, 1959, *2*, 59-62.

Hughes, V. H. A study of the relationships among selected language abilities. *Journal of Educational Research*, 1953, *47*, 97-106.

Humphrey, K. H. An investigation of amount-limit and time-limit methods of measuring rate of reading. *Journal of Developmental Reading*, 1957, *1*, 41-54.

Hunt, L. C. Can we measure specific factors associated with reading comprehension? *Journal of Educational Research*, 1957, *51*, 161-72.

Hvistendahl, J. K. The effect of typographic variants on reader estimates of attractiveness and reading speed of magazine pages. *Communications Research Report*, 1965, *20* (3).

Jenkinson, M. D. Selected processes and difficulties of reading comprehension. Unpublished doctoral dissertation, University of Chicago, 1957.

Karlin, R. *Teaching reading in high school.* New York: Bobbs-Merrill, 1964.

Kelley, T. L., & Krey, A. C. *Tests and measurements in the social sciences.* New York: Scribner, 1934.

Kerfoot, J. F. Problems and research considerations in reading comprehension. In Mildred A. Dawson (Ed.), *Developing comprehension including critical reading.* Newark, Delaware: International Reading Association, 1968. Pp. 38-44.

Kerlinger, F. N. *Foundations of behavioral research.* New York: Holt, Rinehart, & Winston, 1965.

Kingston, A. Is reading what the reading tests test? In E. L. Thurston & L. E. Hafner (Eds.), The philosophical and sociological bases of reading. *Yearbook of the National Reading Conference,* 1965, *14,* 106-09.

Kleck, R. E., & Wheaton, J. Dogmatism and responses to opinion-consistent and opinion-inconsistent information. *Journal of Personality and Social Psychology,* 1967, *5,* 249-52.

Kruglov, Lorraine P. Qualitative differences in the vocabulary choices of children as revealed in a multiple-choice test. *Journal of Educational Psychology,* 1953, *44,* 229-43.

Laycock, F. Significant characteristics of college students with varying flexibility in reading rate. *Journal of Experimental Education,* 1955, *23,* 311-30.

Letson, C. T. Speed and comprehension in reading. *Journal of Educational Research,* 1958, *52,* 49-53.

McCracken, R. A. Standardized reading tests and informal reading inventories. *Education,* 1962, *82,* 366-69.

McCullough, Constance M. Responses of elementary school children to common types of reading comprehension questions. *Journal of Educational Research,* 1957, *51,* 67-70.

McDonald, A. S. A reading versatility inventory. In O. S. Causey (Ed.), Significant elements in college and adult reading improvement. *Yearbook of the National Reading Conference,* 1958, *7,* 48-53.

McDonald, A. S. Factors affecting reading test performance. In O. S. Causey & E. P. Bliesmer (Eds.), Research and evaluation in college reading. *Yearbook of the National Reading Conference,* 1960, *9,* 28-35.

McDonald, A. S. Research for the classroom: rate and reading flexibility. *Journal of Reading,* 1965, *8,* 187-191.

McDonald, A. S. Flexibility in reading approaches: measurement and development. In J. A. Figurel (Ed.), Combining research results and good practices. *Proceedings of the International Reading Association,* 1966, *11,* 67-71.

McNamara, W. J., Patterson, D. G., & Tinker, M. A. The influence of size of type on speed of reading in the primary grades. *Sight Saving Review*, 1953, *23*, 28-33.

Marks, E., & Noll, G. A. Procedures and criteria for evaluating reading and listening comprehension tests. *Educational and Psychological Measurement*, 1967, *27*, 335-48.

Maxwell, Martha J. An experimental investigation of the effect of instructional set and information on reading rate. In E. L. Thurston & L. E. Hafner (Eds.), The philosophical and sociological bases of reading. *Yearbook of the National Reading Conference*, 1965, *14*, 181-87.

Michaelis, J. U., & Tyler, F. T. A comparison of reading ability and readability. *Journal of Educational Psychology*, 1951, *42*, 491-98.

Murphy, H. D., & Davis, F. B. College grades and ability to reason in reading. *Peabody Journal of Education*, 1949, *27*, 34-37.

Newman, E. B. Speed of reading when the span of letters is restricted. *American Journal of Psychology*, 1966, *79*, 272-78.

O'Donnell, R. C. A study of the correlation between awareness of structural relationships in English and ability in reading comprehension. *Journal of Experimental Education*, 1963, *31*, 313-16.

Peterson, Margaret J. Comparison of Flesch readability scores with a test of reading comprehension. *Journal of Applied Psychology*, 1956, *40*, 35-36.

Preston, R. C. A new approach to judging the validity of reading comprehension tests. In J. A. Figurel (Ed.), Challenge and experiment in reading. *Proceedings of the International Reading Association*, 1962, *7*, 166-67.

Rankin, E. F. The relation between reading rate and comprehension. In E. P. Bliesmer & R. C. Staiger (Eds.), Problems, programs and projects in college-adult reading. *Yearbook of the National Reading Conference*, 1962, *11*, 1-5.

Richards, I. A. *Practical criticism*. New York: Harcourt, Brace, & World, 1929.

Rinsland, H. D. *A basic vocabulary of elementary school children*. New York: Macmillan Co., 1945.

Ruddell, R. B. The effect of oral and written patterns of language on reading comprehension. *The Reading Teacher*, 1965, *18*, 270-75.

Russell, D. H. The dimensions of children's meaning vocabulary in grades four through twelve. *University of California Publications in Education,* 1954, *11,* 315-414.

Seashore, R. H., & Eckerson, L. D. The measurement of individual differences in general English vocabularies. *Journal of Educational Psychology,* 1940, *31,* 14-38.

Sharpe, J. F. The retention of meaningful material. *Catholic University of America Educational Research Monograph,* 1952, *16,* 1-66.

Sheldon, W. D. Diagnostic techniques and tools: the flexibility of reading rate. In O. S. Causey (Ed.), Exploring the goals of college reading programs. *Yearbook of the Southwest Reading Conference for Colleges and Universities,* 1955, *5,* 116-17.

Sheldon, W. D., & Carrillo, L. W. The flexibility of reading rate. *Journal of Educational Psychology,* 1952, *43,* 37-45.

Shores, J. H., & Husbands, K. L. Are fast readers the best readers? *Elementary English,* 1950, *24,* 52-57.

Sipay, E. R. A comparison of standardized reading scores and functional reading levels. *The Reading Teacher,* 1964, *17,* 265-68.

Slakter, M. J. *The measurement and effect of risk taking on objective examinations.* (Final Report, Project No. 5-8428) Washington, D. C.: U. S. Office of Education, 1967.

Smith, Helen K. Research in reading for different purposes. In J. A. Figurel (Ed.), Changing concepts of reading instruction. *Proceedings of the International Reading Association,* 1961, *6,* 119-22.

Smith, H. L. *Linguistic science and the teaching of English.* Cambridge, Mass.: Harvard University Press, 1956.

Smith, Mary K. Measurement of the size of general English vocabulary through the elementary grades and high school. *Genetic Psychology Monographs,* 1941, *24,* 311-45.

Spache, G. D. Personality characteristics of retarded readers as measured by the picture-frustration study. *Educational and Psychological Measurement,* 1954, *14,* 186-92.

Strickland, Ruth G. The language of elementary school children: its relationships to the language of reading textbooks and the quality of reading of selected children. *Bulletin of the School of Education, Indiana University,* 1962, *38,* 1-131.

Stroud, J. B. A critical note on reading: rate and comprehension. *Psychological Bulletin,* 1942, *39,* 173-78.

Stroud, J. B. Background of measurement in reading improvement.

In W. Eller & D. A. Brown (Eds.), *College and adult reading*, 1969, in press.

Swineford, Frances, & Miller, P. M. Effects of directions regarding guessing on item statistics of a multiple-choice vocabulary test. *Journal of Educational Psychology*, 1953, *44*, 129-39.

Thorndike, E. L. *A teacher's word book of the twenty thousand words found most frequently and widely in general reading for children and young people.* New York: Bureau of Publications, Teachers College, Columbia University, 1931.

Thurstone, L. L. *A factorial study of perception.* Chicago: University of Chicago Press, 1944.

Thurstone, L. L. Note on a reanalysis of Davis' reading tests. *Psychometrika*, 1946, *11*, 185-88.

Traxler, A. E. The relationship between the length and the reliability of a test of rate of reading. *Journal of Educational Research*, 1938, *32*, 1-2.

Tinker, M. A. The relation of speed to comprehension in reading. *School and Society*, 1932, *36*, 158-60.

Tinker, M. A. Legibility of print. Ames, Iowa: Iowa State University Press, 1963.

Vernon, P. E. The determinants of reading comprehension. *Educational and Psychological Measurement*, 1962, *22*, 269-86.

Ward, L. R. Measuring comprehension in reading. *College English*, 1956, *17*, 481-83.

Webb, S. C., & McCall, J. N. Predictors of freshman grades in a southern university. *Educational and Psychological Measurement*, 1953, *13*, 660-63.

Wilson, R. M. *Diagnostic and remedial reading.* Columbus, Ohio: Charles E. Merrill Books, 1967.

Test references

An asterisk after a test listing indicates the test is included in the *Guide to Tests and Measuring Instruments in Reading* which appears at the end of Chapter 6.

Burnett Reading Series: Survey Test R. Burnett. Bensenville, Ill.: Scholastic Testing Service, 1966, rev. 1967*.

California Reading Test E. W. Tiegs & W. W. Clark. Monterey, Calif.: California Test Bureau, 1957, rev. 1963*.

Cooperative English Tests: Reading Comprehension Test ...C. Derrick, D. P. Harris, & B. Walker. Princeton, N. J.: Educational Testing Service, Cooperative Test Division, 1940, rev. 1960*.

Diagnostic Reading Tests. F. Triggs. Mountain Home, N. C.: Committee on Diagnostic Tests, 1947, rev. 1963*.

Gates-MacGinitie Reading Tests A. I. Gates & W. H. MacGinitie. N. Y.: Teachers College Press, Columbia University, 1926, rev. 1965*.

Gates-MacGinitie Reading Tests: Survey A. I. Gates & W. H. MacGinitie. N.Y.: Teachers College Press, Columbia University, 1926, rev. 1965*.

Gilmore Oral Reading Test J. Gilmore & V. Gilmore. N. Y.: Harcourt, Brace, & World, 1951, rev. 1968*.

Iowa Grammar Information Test F. D. Cram & H. A. Greene. Iowa City: Bureau of Educational Research and Service, 1935.

Iowa Silent Reading Tests H. A. Greene, A. N. Jorgensen, & V. H. Kelley. N.Y.: Harcourt, Brace, & World, 1927, rev. 1942*.

Nelson-Denny Reading Test: Vocabulary—Comprehension—Rate M. Nelson, E. Denny, & J. Brown. Boston: Houghton Mifflin, 1931, rev. 1960*.

Nelson Reading Test M. J. Nelson. Boston: Houghton Mifflin, 1931, rev. 1962*.

Wide Range Achievement Test (WRAT) J. F. Jastak & J. R. Jastak. Austin, Texas: Guidance Testing Associates, 1936, rev. 1965*.

3
Methods for assessing reading achievement

While there is no question that standardized, formal, and informal reading tests supply information, there is little agreement among reading specialists as to the nature of this information and the value it has for the classroom teacher. Standardized tests obviously indicate how a student performs in relation to other students at one point in time, but they rarely account for why the student performs as he does. As mentioned earlier, many factors can influence student performance. These factors range from the student's experiential background to the interest appeal of selections included on any given test. They can both limit the accuracy of testing devices and their usefulness as valid indicators of student performance. Because tests merely describe reading behavior rather than explain it, it may well be the case that tests can supply only limited information as a basis for classroom instruction. However, it is assumed for the purposes of the present chapter that knowing how a student performs is information enough to allow the teacher to proceed with instruction. Thus, it is legitimate to raise the question of whether testing instruments actually provide a true estimate of student achievement. Research has dealt with this problem in one form or another many times. A good example of this is Glaser's (1964) study in which the performance of a group of third graders was compared with that of seventh graders on the Gates Reading Survey. While the two groups scored the same on the Gates survey (between 5.0 and 5.9), their performance on an informal reading inventory differed considerably. This was due to the fact that on the Gates, assessment of skills takes place by comparing an individual's performance with other students' performance; on the informal inventory, how well a student reads is determined by his performance on a set of criteria tasks. If anything, the Glaser study underlines the dangers inherent in depending on any one measure as an indicator of student performance. Therefore, if one seeks to get an accurate assessment of student achievement, it is advisable to use a wide variety of reading measures including informal inventories, standardized tests, teacher observations, and teacher assessment of performance in content areas. The validity of using a variety of measures has been well substantiated in the research literature. For instance, Croft (1951) used intelligence tests, medical histories, arithmetic and reading achievement tests, social adjustment and interest inventories, sociograms, and social background data to assess the achievement of a group of students. He found that this particular combination of measures provided a more useful and accurate basis for planning instructional programs than any one of the measures did when used singly.

The previous paragraph should give the reader a general idea of some of the problems inherent in using testing devices. The following pages expand these ideas and provide some suggestions for test usage. The focal point of this chapter is not on the philosophical aspects of testing, rather it is on the viability of two kinds of devices commonly used in evaluating reading performance: standardized diagnostic tests and informal reading inventories.

Standardized tests

The teaching of reading, if it is to be effective, should be based on a thorough knowledge of the reading strengths and weaknesses of students. The central issues discussed in this section are whether standardized tests do provide such information accurately and reliably. The most serious deficiency in using standardized tests to diagnose reading achievement is the lack of discriminant validity (the validity of tests as measures of distinct skills or abilities) for the various sub-tests of reading. This problem was discussed in some length in the preceding chapter; without a doubt, it constitutes a major shortcoming of most standardized reading tests. If a teacher is planning an instructional program geared to improve those specific reading skills which a test has shown to be weak, the teacher has to be reasonably confident that the tests he has used validly measure those skills. Most research on measuring specific reading skills has been either too limited or too equivocal to support the logical contention that specific sub-skills of reading can be validly measured. For instance, Hunt (1957) and Farr (1968) both questioned the diagnostic validity of sub-tests of reading. The lack of such diagnostic validity was attributed by Goodman (1968) to a lack of understanding of the reading process.

The discussion which follows focuses primarily on reading and psychological tests which have been used for diagnostic purposes and on the reliability and validity of group and individual tests. A separate sub-section on the Wechsler Intelligence Scale for Children has been included because of numerous studies devoted to its use as a diagnostic tool.

Group tests

This monograph has already discussed the limited validity of group tests and sub-tests of reading skills. What has yet to be explored is the use of group tests as diagnostic tools and the possibility of improving these tests so that they accurately assess reading ability.

Davis (1961, p. 86) outlined four steps which should be adhered to if standardized group tests are used:

1] Carefully and explicitly define the variable being measured.

2] Administer a test of the variable, or as close an approximation as possible, under conditions that assure a high degree of cooperation on the part of the pupil.

3] Compare a pupil's obtained score with suitable norms, such as percentile ranks in his own age or grade group.

4] Consider the possibility that the pupil's obtained score represents a sizeable deviation from his true score.

These four steps emphasize the importance of matching instructional objectives to test objectives if the test is to validly measure specific reading skills. Hills (1964) has elaborated on this point and has offered ten questions that should be fully answered before any particular measure of skills is selected for use.

1] Is the test appropriate for the consumer's purposes?

2] What does the test purport to measure?

3] What do reviewers think it measures?

4] What are the item content and style?

5] Is the test a test of speed or of power?

6] Does the test contain a correction for guessing?

7] Does the structure of the items provide clues to the answers?

8] Are there alternate forms? How well are they matched?

9] What are the norm groups (kind, quality, characteristics)?

10] Is the range wide enough (is there enough top and bottom)?

Even if a test consumer carefully adheres to both Davis' and Hills' guidelines, the tests he selects still may not validly assess reading achievement. Several studies have cast doubt on the diagnostic validity of any group reading test. Murray and Karlsen (1960) conducted a concurrent validity study of the Gates Reading Diagnostic Tests, an individually administered test, and the Developmental Reading Tests: Silent Reading Diagnostic Test, a group test. They found no agreement between the sub-tests of these two tests. The ten sub-tests Murray and Karlsen compared were perception of words in isolation, orientation reversals, initial errors, middle errors, ending errors, word elements, letter sounds, beginning sounds, rhyming sounds, and word synthesis. It is very difficult to interpret this study because of the very small sample size (only twenty students). In addition, the use of grade level scores when examining differences between mean scores is of questionable validity. Such a procedure is valid only if the two tests are normed on the same populations and this is very unlikely in the Murray and Karlsen study.

Chall (1958) used two procedures in an attempt to validate the Roswell-Chall Diagnostic Reading Test of Word Analysis Skills. The first procedure involved comparing scores on the word analysis test with various criterion tests for three different populations: second graders, fifth graders, and a reading clinic group from various elementary grades. Second graders were administered the Gray Oral Reading Test, a silent reading test, and the spelling sub-test of the Metropolitan Achievement Tests. The clinic population took the same spelling and oral reading tests as did the second graders; however, the silent reading test they were administered was taken from the Metropolitan. The fifth-grade population in the study was administered only the oral reading test. All these measures seem to be questionable criteria for validating a word analysis test. The second graders' scores all correlated at a high level with the three criteria tests, but this may have been due to the fact that the second graders probably scored at the top of the scale of the word analysis test and there was, therefore, little variability in their scores. The clinic population, whose scores on the word analysis test would be more variable, had much lower correlations with the three tests: .73 with oral reading, .64 with silent reading, and .57 with spelling. These correlations indicate that in all three cases less than fifty per cent of the variance was shared in common by the two tests—this is not very conclusive validity evidence. Chall's second procedure involved investigating the number of errors on each of the subtests of the word analysis test according to eight reading grade levels. The sub-test scores gave a very impressive picture of a decrease in the number of errors from the first through the eighth grade, thereby indicating a mastery of these skills as students progress through school.

The evidence from these studies as well as from those studies cited in Chapter 2 are consistent in pointing out that group tests of reading achievement are quite limited as valid measures of sub-skills of reading. Indeed, there does not seem to be any degree of consistency between or among test publishers and researchers about what these group tests actually measure. Yet there are valid uses for group tests in the instructional reading program. First of all, the tests are reliable for comparing students in terms of general reading achievement. Secondly, the tests can be used as a screening device in determining the need for and possibly the type of further assessment necessary. For example, a student who performs very poorly on a group test designed for intermediate grade children would probably need a more detailed assessment of his word attack skills, while a student who performs quite well perhaps needs more detailed evaluation of his ability to use sources of information more effectively. Individual reading tests and informal testing procedures—both the subject of subsequent parts of this chapter—are valuable procedures for continuing the diagnosis which is barely started by group standardized tests.

Individual tests

For the purposes of this section, individual tests are defined as those tests which can be administered to only one examinee at a time. A variety of such individual tests have been used in

an attempt to diagnose the reading achievement of students and
there has been considerable amounts of research devoted to assessing their validity and reliability.   One such study, conducted
by Sheldon and Hatch (1950, 1951) at Syracuse University, focused on the Durrell Analysis of Reading Difficulty.   In the initial study (Sheldon & Hatch, 1950), third-grade students served
as subjects.   The criterion used for determining good and poor
readers were reading achievement tests and teacher ratings of
reading ability.   The lowest and the highest five per cent of the
readers who had intelligence scores above 90 were administered
the Durrell test.   Results indicated that the Durrell test was a
valid measure of reading achievement.   Because the mean
scores of the intelligence tests for the good and poor readers
were significantly different, it is possible that the Durrell test was
merely comparing intelligence levels and not reading levels.   In
a similar study with sixth-grade children, Sheldon and Hatch
(1951) obtained almost identical results.   While neither of the
two investigations were undertaken primarily as validity studies
of the Durrell test, they did provide substantial evidence that
the Durrell Analysis of Reading Difficulty is a valid measurement device for diagnosing reading difficulties when the criterion used is teacher ratings and specific standardized reading
test scores.   However, neither of these studies supplied any validity evidence for the Durrell test as a diagnostic measure of
specific reading sub-skills.

A concurrent validity study of three of the most popular individual reading tests—the Durrell Analysis of Reading Difficulty, the Diagnostic Reading Scales, and the Gates-McKillop
Reading Diagnostic Test—was undertaken by Eller and Attea
(1966).   They found that the word analysis and oral reading
sub-tests of the three tests were highly correlated.   It also would
have been quite interesting if correlations across sub-tests had
been supplied by the researchers so that it would be possible to
determine if the correlations had indicated any discriminant
validity. Despite the high correlations between these tests, there
were significant differences between the grade level scores for

the oral reading sub-tests. The Durrell test was, on the average, about half a grade level lower than the Diagnostic Reading Scales and about a third of a grade level lower than the Gates-McKillop test. Eller and Attea used multiple t tests to study all of these differences. Unfortunately, this left the significance of their findings open to question.

Some very interesting discrepancies in the scaling properties of a few of the sub-tests of the Durrell, the Diagnostic scales, and Gates-McKillop tests were found in the Eller and Attea study. Particularly striking are the weaknesses found in the listening comprehension sub-test of the Durrell and the silent reading sub-test of the Diagnostic scales. The Durrell listening comprehension test is composed of a series of paragraphs of increasing difficulty which are read orally to an examinee after which he is asked a set of questions. This would seem to be a useful procedure for estimating reading potential. However, in Eller and Attea's study, 99 per cent of the third-grade pupils passed the third-grade paragraph test, only 10 per cent passed the fourth-grade test, while 32 per cent of the same students passed the fifth-grade test. In determining silent reading level on the Diagnostic scales, the examinee is required to read orally a set of paragraphs of increasing difficulty until a certain number of errors are made. The examinee then continues reading on the next level silently. The assumption on which this procedure is based is that silent reading is always more highly developed than oral reading. Yet, Eller and Attea were not able to determine silent reading scores for 47 per cent of the third graders because their silent reading achievement was not, according to the test, as well developed as their oral reading achievement.

Oral reading tests have been used extensively to diagnose reading in general. This is especially evident when one realizes that most standardized individual reading tests include oral reading sub-tests. For example, the Durrell Analysis of Reading Difficulty, the Gates-McKillop Reading Diagnostic Test, and the Diagnostic Reading Scales all include sub-tests of oral reading. The use of oral reading tests to diagnose reading achievement is based on the assumption that there is a high correlation between silent and oral reading, as some researchers (Fairbanks, 1937; Gilmore, 1947) have found, and that the use of oral reading tests as measures of silent reading achievement is, therefore, justifiable. This assumption has been criticized by Buswell (1947) on the grounds that oral reading involves different skills than silent reading.

The use of oral reading tests as a measure of silent reading achievement above the elementary grades has also been questioned by Gray and Reese (1957). Gray and Reese cogently pointed out that silent reading achievement surpasses oral reading achievement, at least in terms of rate, after children reach a second-grade reading level. Wells (1950) studied oral reading tests on the college level. He sought to determine whether the analysis of oral reading errors would correlate with silent reading achievement for college freshmen of low academic ability. Non-significant correlations were found between oral reading mispronunciations and tests of silent reading comprehension and vocabulary. This alone would cast considerable doubt on the value of an oral reading test for diagnosing silent reading achievement with more mature readers. In referring to data presented by Gilmore (1947), Wells suggested that the progressively lower correlations found between oral and silent reading as the higher grade levels are reached indicates an increasing tendency on the part of each of the two reading skills to become independent.

A second problem in using oral reading performance as a basis for assessing silent reading involves the significance of categorizing certain word call errors. Weber (1968) studied the classification systems of a number of researchers in the area of oral reading and those of a number of oral reading tests and concluded that these systems were based, for the most part, on whole word errors. Weber emphasized that the two most serious weaknesses of these tests were their treatment of word errors as isolated sets of letters rather than as part of a sentence. In addition, Weber found that the standardization of the tests relied on the *total number* of errors made, rather than the *type* of errors made. This would lead to a situation where a student who made five minor mispronunciations which did not interfere with his understanding of a selection would be grouped with a student who made five gross mispronunciations and failed to understand most of the selection.

Contradictory evidence, however, has been reported by Spache (1950) in a study in which he attempted to compare the various norms given for the oral reading test of the Diagnostic Reading Scales, the Oral Reading—Unaided Oral Recall Test of the Durrell Analysis of Reading Difficulty, and Gray's Oral Check Test. Under certain specified test procedures, Spache found the tests to be quite comparable. This finding indicates that it is possible to use tests, or at least these three particular tests, in various combinations to determine reading improvement during the course of a remedial program. The major difference between Weber's conclusion and Spache's is that Weber was concerned with the diagnostic validity of recording oral word call errors while Spache was attempting to compare students' general performance on several oral reading tests.

The relation between psychological test scores and reading

A number of psychological tests have been used to diagnose reading achievement. Their validity for diagnosing reading disability has been questioned. Validity studies of this nature have focused on the Stanford-Binet Intelligence Scale, Marianne Frostig Developmental Test of Visual Perception, the Bender-Gestalt, the Wepman Test of Auditory Discrimination, and the Rorschach Test.

A study of the auditory memory span sub-test of the Stanford-Binet Intelligence Scale, Form-L was undertaken by Rose (1958) to determine its diagnostic potential for poor readers. Rose found a strong relation between poor reading in general and poor performance on this test. This, by the way, was consistent with the findings of the WISC studies cited later.

However, Rose cautioned against thinking that all poor readers are deficient in auditory memory span and, therefore, need instruction in improving it. Rose reached this conclusion because one-third of the remedial readers in the study did not have any more difficulty on the auditory memory span sub-test than did the students of average reading achievement.

Contrary to Rose's findings, Bond and Fay (1950) discovered that poor readers, when compared to good readers, tended to perform better on memory items on the Stanford-Binet. They also cautioned against using their finding for diagnostic purposes because there was a lack of consistently superior performance on these memory items by the poor readers.

The Marianne Frostig Developmental Test of Visual Perception was found to be of little value in predicting the reading achievement of second-grade students (Olson, 1966). The low correlation reported by Olson between the scores on the Frostig test and chronological and mental age should also raise some questions concerning the validity of the test for determining perceptual development.

A validity study carried out by Krippner (1966) of the Minnesota Percepto-Diagnostic Test resulted in quite different findings. In the Child Study Center at Kent State University, the diagnostic categorization of the Minnesota test was compared to the diagnostic findings of reading clinicians. The diagnostic categories were based on the major etiological factors behind reading disability according to Rabinovitch (1959). The three categories were: organic, primary, and secondary retardation. In 24 reading clinic cases, the Minnesota Percepto-Diagnostic Test and the reading clinicians' diagnoses agreed in all but two cases. This finding is amazing when it is realized that the reading clinicians were graduate students in training and the three diagnostic categories were not defined in specific behavioral terms. This report of highly positive concurrent validity would have been more useful if the tests or procedures used by the reading clinicians were described more fully.

Contradictory findings concerning the use of the Bender-Gestalt as a diagnostic instrument of reading achievement were reported in two recent studies. Keogh (1965), in a longitudinal study of 127 children, evaluated the use of the Bender-Gestalt at the kindergarten level as a predictive measure of reading achievement and at the third-grade level as a diagnostic test of reading performance. The third-grade criterion measures of reading were teacher ratings and the California Reading Test. Keogh concluded that the Bender-Gestalt was useful in identifying potentially good readers but was of limited value as a diagnostic test of reading difficulty.

The second recent study on the Bender-Gestalt was carried out by Parrish (1962). Parrish administered the Bender-Gestalt to a group of first-grade male readers and a group of first-grade male non-readers of average intelligence. The results indicated that the two groups did not differ significantly in copying or in discrimination on the perceptual phase of the test. Significant differences were found, however, in the reproduction of the Bender designs. This was attributed to interpretive factors. Parrish concluded that the clinical utility of the Bender-Gestalt with young children was confirmed and the test seemed capable of discriminating between reader and non-reader first-grade boys.

The use of the Rorschach Test as a diagnostic tool for analyzing reading behavior was conducted by Knoblock (1965) who administered it to 62 second-grade children. The children were divided into good (upper quartile) and poor (lower quartile) readers on the basis of their Gates Advanced Primary Reading Test scores. In general, Knoblock found that the Rorschach Test failed to discriminate between the good and poor readers. As a result, he rejected the hypothesis that good readers generally function at a more mature level on all psychological measures.

The relation between WISC scores and reading   Many recent studies have attempted to use the sub-test patterns of the Wechsler

Intelligence Scale for Children to identify and diagnose students with reading disability. Deal (1965) reviewed some of these studies (Altus, 1956; Burks & Bruce, 1955; Coleman & Rasof, 1963; Graham, 1953; Hirst, 1960; Kallos & Grabow, 1961; Muir, 1962; Neville, 1961; Paterra, 1963). In order to compare these studies, Table 3 has been devised. The table also contains additional studies on the WISC not included in Deal's review (Richardson & Surko, 1956; Sheldon & Garton, 1959; Dockrell, 1960; Robeck, 1960; McClean, 1968; McCleod, 1965; Reid & Schoer, 1966).

A number of problems should be borne in mind as the studies are compared:

1] Many of the studies used quite small and restricted populations.

2] The criteria used to determine reading retardation differed considerably from study to study.

3] Subjects' age ranges varied in some studies, while they were quite restrictive in others.

4] The intelligence scores of the subjects in some of the studies were controlled so that some of the comparisons were between high and low scores on intelligence tests rather than between good and poor readers of similar intelligence levels.

5] A number of the studies included only males.

6] The criteria for determining the significance of high and low scores on the sub-tests of the WISC were not similar in each study.

7] Several studies only compared verbal to performance scores for good and poor readers and were not concerned with WISC sub-test patterns.

Despite these limitations, it appears from Table 3 that fairly consistent patterns of WISC scores for retarded readers are discernible from the sixteen studies included. Inspection of the patterns of scores indicates that poor readers perform at a lower level than they score on the rest of the WISC on the following

Table 3 The sub-test patterns of WISC scores for retarded readers

Researcher	Subjects' age or grade	Sample size	Verbal tests						Performance tests				
			Information	Comprehension	Arithmetic	Similarities	Digit span	Vocabulary	Picture completion	Block design	Picture arrangement	Object assembly	Coding
Altus (1956)	Grade 3-8	25			low		high	high	high		high	high	low
Burks & Bruce (1955)	Grade 3-8	42	low	high	low					high	high		low
Coleman & Rasof (1963)	7.5-16 yrs.	146	low	high	low		low	low	high	high			low
Dockrell (1960)	8-14 yrs.	34	low	high	low	high		low			high		low
Graham (1953)	8-17 yrs.	96	low	high	low	high	low	low	high	high	high	high	low
Hirst (1960)	8-13 yrs.	30			low	low	low	low	high	high	high	high	low
Kallos & Grabow (1961)	9-14 yrs.	37	low		low					high			low
McClean (1968)			low		low		low		high				low
McCleod (1965)	10-14 yrs.	393	low		low	low	low	low	high				low

Table 3 The sub-test patterns of WISC scores for retarded readers (cont'd.)

Researcher	Subject's age or grade	Sample size	Verbal tests						Performance tests				
			Information	Comprehension	Arithmetic	Similarities	Digit span	Vocabulary	Picture completion	Block design	Picture arrangement	Object assembly	Coding
Muir (1962)		50	low	high	low			low	high	high		high	low
Neville (1961)		35	low		low		low			high	high		
Paterra (1963)	6-14 yrs.	33		high	low	high		low	high				
Reid & Schoer (1966)	Grade 4	87			low	low	low		high				
Richardson & Surko (1956)	8-18 yrs.	105	low		low		low		high	high	high	high	low
Robeck (1960)			low	high		high	low	high	high	high	high	high	low
Sheldon & Garton (1959)	7-14 yrs.	36								high		high	low

sub-tests: Information, Arithmetic, Digit Span, Coding, and sometimes Vocabulary. The poor readers usually perform better on the following sub-tests than on the rest of the WISC battery: Comprehension, Picture Completion, Block Design, Picture Arrangement, and Object Assembly.

Several of these researchers (Paterra, 1963; Burks & Bruce, 1955; Hirst, 1960) suggested that the WISC sub-test patterns could be employed to determine the type of remedial reading program needed by these students; but not one of the studies undertook to validate this suggestion. Future research could use at least two approaches to interpreting these sub-test patterns. The first would be to relate the good and poor performances on the WISC tests to the lack of opportunity to learn which was caused by the inability to read. For example, Information, Arithmetic, and Vocabulary sub-tests are probably most affected by the broadening of knowledge through reading; however, this analysis does not account for the poor performance on Digit Span and Coding. The sub-tests on which the poor readers scored relatively high would probably not be increased by further experience through reading. Such an analysis of the WISC patterns would hypothesize that poor readers are not deficient in particular abilities caused by the reading disability, but rather, that poor reading skill has prevented the student from developing in certain areas.

A second path for future research might involve relating the WISC performance patterns to perceptual-motor development. Performance on the Arithmetic, Digit Span, and Coding appear to rely on auditory and visual discrimination as well as immediate memory span. These same skills also seem to be highly related to learning to read. While some perceptual-motor skills are required on the Picture Completion, Block Design, and Object Assembly, these sub-tests tend to be more gross in nature and more closely related to concrete objects in contrast to the more abstract symbols and numbers of Arithmetic, Digit Span, and Coding.

One last problem should be mentioned in analyzing WISC sub-test patterns: researchers have limited their studies to pupils within the average range of mental ability. If it is accepted that poor readers are at a serious disadvantage on WISC sub-tests such as Vocabulary, Information, and Arithmetic, it logically follows that if such students are to attain average intelligence test scores, they must perform at a higher level on several of the remaining tests. It may be that some of these studies are, therefore, not comparing good and poor readers of average intelligence; rather, they are comparing bright students who are poor readers with average students who are average readers. The sub-test patterns of the WISC have been shown to be related to reading retardation. What is now needed are studies which attempt to relate this test performance to instructional programs in order to investigate the validity of these scores for planning effective remediation.

A note on the use of standardized tests

From the preceding review of research on tests diagnosing reading ability, several key problems are apparent. First, there is no consistent definition of the sub-skills constituting reading on present standardized tests, thereby leading to confusion concerning their discriminant validity. This confusion has filtered down to the classroom where teachers have been left in a quandary about how to proceed with instruction. Although available diagnostic tests seem to be quite limited, teachers can still plan effective reading programs which meet the needs of their students. This has been the case and will continue to be the case as long as the practitioner is aware of the limitations of the various diagnostic tests and realizes that the tests probably at best represent an obstacle course for the students. The best diagnosis takes place when the teacher brings "enough sophistication to the test sessions to evaluate pupils' reading abilities and weaknesses as they succeed or fail" on the various test items (Eller & Attea, 1966, p. 566).

Adequate criterion measures of reading achievement need to be delineated before diagnostic testing can be improved. Standardized tests usually compare a student's performance to some norm groups. What is needed are tests which compare a student's performance to some criterion of adequate reading. For example, at present, only vague notions exist about what "good" third-grade reading is. Until such criteria, or perhaps more importantly, some criteria for determining reading levels adequate for "effective" citizenship for adults can be devised, the value of diagnostic tests will continue to rely more on the sophistication of the reading teacher than the sophistication or the intrinsic value of the tests.

Finally, it appears that the attempts to use psychological tests such as the WISC, the Frostig, the Bender-Gestalt, and the Rorschach in diagnosing reading achievement have been largely futile. While correlations between poor reading and performance on these tests have been found, the reasons for them have never been determined. Unless researchers begin to validate these correlations against remedial programs or some other valid criterion, attempts to use psychological tests as diagnostic reading tests should be abandoned. Instead, efforts might best be channeled toward improving diagnostic testing through a more valid sampling of reading behavior rather than through an assessment of behaviors which are related to reading in some unknown manner. The test consumer can increase the validity of his diagnostic attempts in two ways. First, when selecting a standardized group or individual test, he can carefully match his teaching objectives to the test objectives. Secondly, he can develop informal procedures to assess students' reading behaviors in the classroom situation.

Informal measurement of reading

Informal approaches to assessing reading achievement include a wide range of methods such as measuring student use of the library, determining out-of-school reading habits, using teacher-made check lists of reading skills, and diagnostic evaluations made by both the student and his parents. There have been very few studies which have investigated the validity and usefulness of most of these approaches. Research on informal reading assessment has focused on either comparing informal reading inventories with standardized reading tests (Sipay, 1964; Patty, 1965; Williams, 1963), validating students' self-evaluations (Purcell, 1963; Spaights, 1965), or comparing teacher judgments of students' reading with their performance on standardized reading tests (Kermonian, 1962; Henig, 1949; Hitchcock & Alfred, 1955).

Because informal approaches use such a wide variety of procedures to assess reading performance over a number of different occasions, it is not surprising that they are more reliable and more valid measures than standardized reading tests. After all, the more behavior which is sampled, the more likely the assessment is to be accurate. However, a word of caution is needed on the use of informal approaches. Evaluations based on informal means are more reliable estimates of the student's true reading behavior than standardized reading tests precisely because they are not based on the comparison of any one student to any other student. If a teacher wishes to compare student performance with that of other students, informal inventories are inappropriate because they evaluate each student individually under different conditions. In this case, standardized tests should be used since they have consistent administrative procedures.

However, when they are used to plan instruction, informal measurement procedures have more validity than standardized reading tests. In using informal assessments of students' reading in daily classroom situations, the teacher can evaluate the students' ability to apply their reading skills to various learning tasks. In this way, not only can the teacher learn about the development of students' basic reading skills, but he can also learn about student attitudes toward reading tasks, their reading interests, and their ability to apply their reading skills.

Informal reading inventories

The use of informal reading inventories (IRI's) for determining students' functional reading levels and diagnosing reading skills is a fairly well established practice. For an excellent discussion of informal reading inventories, the reader is referred to Johnson and Kress' (1966) work, *Informal Reading Inventories*. The inventory or IRI, as it is known, is composed of a series of graded paragraphs which are usually read aloud by the examinee to the examiner; comprehension checks follow each paragraph reading. As the student reads, the examiner keeps track of such errors as mispronunciation of words, unknown words, reversals, repetitions, substitutions, word by word reading, and other word call errors. On the basis of these readings, the teacher determines the students' functional reading levels. Some informal reading inventories occasionally include additional paragraphs to be read silently, an assessment of the size of a student's sight vocabulary, a procedure for assessing oral language development, and other measures which have been developed to assess aspects of the student's reading developments which the teacher feels are vital to reading success. These inventories range from tests which teachers devise for use in their own classrooms to more standardized inventories developed for use in reading clinics. There are even more carefully standardized inventories which are published for sale like the Standard Reading Inventory.

These informal inventories are highly regarded for their usefulness in determining students' reading levels. Johnson (1960) pointed out the difference between standardized tests and informal tests on the basis of the information they convey.

Standardized tests rate an individual's performance as compared to the performance of others. By contrast, an informal

> inventory appraises the individual's level of competence on
> a particular job without reference to what others do. (1960,
> p. 9)

Johnson suggested that the classroom teacher determine appropriate levels for independent and instructional work solely through the use of informal reading inventories.

Despite the accepted worth of informal reading inventories, there are several problems that limit their use. First of all, the criteria for evaluating IRI performance is quite subjective; reading specialists have suggested various criteria for evaluating reading performance (Betts, 1940; Sipay, 1964). Secondly, the performance a student exhibits is quite dependent on the reading selection selected for a particular IRI. For example, a story may be selected from a third-grade reader for inclusion on an IRI because it is supposed to represent third-grade reading difficulty. However, the reading difficulty of any short selection taken from a basal reader may be quite different from the reading level it is supposed to represent. A third problem in using IRI's relates to the examiner's knowledge of the basic reading process and his ability to record errors and make judgments about reading performance.

Research concerned with informal reading inventories has focused primarily on the relation between IRI's and standardized reading tests as well as the usefulness of the IRI as a diagnostic tool. In particular, research has concentrated on assessing the accuracy of informal versus standardized testing procedures in determining an individual's reading level. Betts (1940) attempted to study the accuracy of standardized as compared to informal procedures for assessing reading grade placement. He administered five silent reading tests—the Gates Reading Survey, the Stanford Achievement Test: Reading, the Durrell-Sullivan Reading Achievement Test, the Sangren-Woody Reading Test, and the Iowa Silent Reading Tests: Advanced—to fifth graders and compared their performance on them with that on an author-constructed informal reading inventory. Betts offered the following conclusions:

1] The results from one test are not highly comparable with the results secured from another test.

2] None of the standardized reading tests used provide an accurate index to the levels at which reading instruction should be initiated for the low achievers. For example, 11 per cent of the fifth graders experienced difficulty in typical third-grade reading activities, but only one of the standardized tests used placed these pupils below the third-grade level. The tests did identify the low achievers whose reading difficulties needed further analysis.

Another early study comparing performance on a standardized reading test—the Gates Reading Survey—with that on an informal inventory was undertaken by Killgallon (1942) with a group of 211 fourth graders. The various functional reading levels determined by Killgallon's reading inventory are presented in Table 4. Among other things, Killgallon found that the IRI for his group of fourth-grade children yielded three functional reading levels:

the mean Independent Reading grade level was .86, the range was 0 to 5.0;
the mean Instructional Reading grade level was 3.16, the range was 0 to 9.0;
the mean Frustration Reading grade level was 6.3, the range was 4.0 to 9.0.

In addition, Killgallon found that the reading ability of the 211 students in the original sample on the Gates Reading Survey ranged from 2.0 to 10.4, while the mean was 4.6. Killgallon pointed out that, on the average, pupils tend to score about one year higher on the standardized reading test than their instructional level determined by the informal reading inventory. As an example of the difficulties encountered in using the Gates Reading Survey to identify reading levels for students at the lower end of the scale, Killgallon reported that a student who

Table 4 Functional reading levels determined by Killgallon's informal reading inventory

	Basal (or independent) reading level	Instructional reading level	Capacity level	Frustration level
Minimum comprehension	90%	50%	75% when a selection is read to subject by examiner	20% or lower
Word perception error	No errors	Maximum ratio of 7%		1 error per each 10 running words
Silent reading	Characterized by: a] Adequate rate of comprehension b] Freedom from poor silent reading habits such as pointing and all forms of vocalization.	Excessive lateral head movements and finger pointing. Various forms of vocalization during silent reading were interpreted as indicating undue difficulty when appearing in conjunction with low comprehension or high error ratio.		
Oral reading		Oral reading performance if characterized by lack of emphasis upon meaning,		

Behavior

Clearly observable tension-type behavior

inadequate phrasing, or word-by-word reading was considered sufficient justification for assigning a lower instructional level unless comprehension was 75% or above.

scored 2.8 on the Gates survey was found to be utterly incapable of reading a pre-primer when tested with the IRI.

Table 5 Criteria used to estimate functional reading levels by Sipay (1964)

Level	Accurate word pronunciation	Minimum comprehension
Instructional		
Cooper—Criteria 96	96%-99%	60%
Betts—Criteria 90	90%-95%	60%
Frustration	less than 90%	less than 50%

Sipay (1964) attempted to obtain objective evidence on the extent to which the level of reading achievement as measured by standardized reading achievement test scores differed from the functional reading levels as estimated by an author-constructed informal reading inventory. He administered the Metropolitan Achievement Test: Reading, the Gates Reading Survey, and the California Reading Test to 202 subjects from eight fourth-grade classes. The students were given an individually administered informal inventory which was based upon selections from the Scott, Foresman reading series. The criteria for determining the functional reading levels are presented in Table 5. The statistical analysis of the test scores indicated the following results:

1] When the more stringent criteria were used to estimate the instructional level, all three standardized tests tended to overestimate the instructional level by approximately one or more grade levels.

2] When Criteria 90 was used, the mean score on the Metropolitan test was 0.11 grade levels higher, while the Gates survey overestimated the Criteria 90 instructional level by 0.29 of a grade level, and the mean of the California test was 1.02 higher than that of the Criteria 90 instructional level.

3] The standardized tests, when compared with the frustrational level criteria, were significantly lower in the case of Metropolitan and Gates test.

4] A comparison of the means of the frustration level and the California test revealed that the California Reading Survey underestimated the frustration level by 0.24 of a grade level. This difference was significant at the .05 level.

In conclusion, Sipay (1964, p. 268) stated:

> These findings suggest that it is impossible to generalize as to whether standardized reading achievement test scores tend to indicate the instructional or frustration level. Rather, it appears that in making such judgments, one must consider the standardized reading test used and the criteria employed to estimate the functional reading levels.

In still another study of the relation between results on informal reading inventories and standardized tests, Glaser (1964) compared the functional reading levels of retarded seventh-grade and advanced third-grade students to their score on the Gates Reading Survey. All of the students in both groups had scored between 5.0 and 5.9 on the Gates survey. The findings of Glaser's study indicated:

1] The instructional levels of the advanced and retarded readers were consistently lower than the levels of their standardized reading test scores with a slightly larger spread evident for retarded readers.

2] Sixteen (52 per cent) of the retarded seventh-grade readers reached frustration level in passages of fifth-grade difficulty; 17 (57 per cent) of the third-grade pupils met the criteria for frustration at this level.

3] The instructional levels were consistently below the standardized reading test scores for the two groups.

4] Providing reading instruction and materials for students on the basis of standardized reading test scores could hinder their progress and possibly affect their attitude toward reading.

McCracken (1962) compared the performance of 56 sixth-grade pupils on the Iowa Every-Pupil Tests of Basic Skills, Test A: Silent Reading Comprehension to the reading comprehension and vocabulary scores on an informal reading inventory which included both oral and silent reading. The three levels of performance on the informal reading inventory were the immediate instructional reading level, the maximum instructional reading level, and the word recognition level. McCracken concluded that the use of standardized test scores to determine the level of instruction would place 63 per cent of the students at a frustration reading level and suggested that the standardized test scores should be lowered by two grades. He urged that this score be used to determine instructional level. If McCracken's recommendations were followed through with the students in his study, only four per cent would have been reading books which would be too difficult and seven per cent would have been reading books which would be too easy. McCracken's suggestion, however, only has validity for the Iowa Every-Pupil Tests of Basic Skills (which he used in the study) and the reading materials which formed the basis for his informal inventory.

A validity and reliability study of a standardized informal reading inventory—the Standard Reading Inventory—was carried out by McCracken (1964). McCracken attempted to develop the content validity of the inventory by controlling the vocabulary, sentence length, content, and style of the reading selections. Construct validity was studied by administering the oral reading paragraphs contained in the inventory to 664 children in grades one through six. The significant differences found in student performance as paragraphs of increasing difficulty were read were quite substantial. Reliability evidence for the alternate forms of the inventory was obtained by having two examiners administer alternate forms of the Standard inventory to sixty elementary school children. Correlations of reading levels between the two forms for the independent, instructional, and frustration reading levels ranged from .86 to .91. The correlations between the two forms for the eight reading sub-skills measured by the inventory ranged from .68 for word recognition errors to .99 for vocabulary in isolation. From the results of this study, it certainly appears that the Standard Reading Inventory should validly determine students' functional reading levels. In addition, the reliabilities between alternate forms of the inventory suggest that they could be used interchangeably in determining growth during a reading program.

Seven doctoral dissertations reported since 1961 have compared performance on informal reading inventories to that on standardized reading tests. McCracken's (1963), Sipay's (1961), and Glaser's (1964) have already been discussed in some detail. In a dissertation, Williams (1963) compared the performance of fourth, fifth, and sixth graders on an informal reading inventory, based on their classroom basal readers, with their scores on the California Reading Test, the Gates Reading Survey, and the Metropolitan Achievement Tests: Reading. When an informal reading inventory was used which contained selections from basal readers with which the students were familiar, the standardized tests were found to place students relatively near their instructional level. This finding is somewhat different from those of other researchers. Another result of Williams' study is that the disabled readers showed more standardized test versus inventory variance at the instructional reading level than did normal readers in any one grade.

Leibert (1965) compared informal reading inventory performance and scores on the Gates Advanced Primary Reading Test for second-grade students. Leibert reported differences in grade placement for the two measures, but suggested that these differences may be due to the wider range of skills included in a group standardized test, while reading as measured by an informal reading inventory is more narrowly defined.

Patty (1965) contrasted the Gilmore Oral Reading Test and the Gray Oral Reading Test with IRI performance. Patty found that it was impossible to generalize as to whether standardized oral reading tests indicate the functional reading levels of children as accurately as informal reading inventories do. Because of the economy of administration and the usefulness of the information they provided, the Gray Oral Reading Test and an informal reading inventory were deemed the most desirable instruments for determining functional reading levels. Brown (1963) came to a similar conclusion in a study using the following silent reading tests: the California Reading Test, the Metropolitan Achievement Test: Reading, the Stanford Achievement Test: Reading, the Iowa Every-Pupil Tests of Basic Skills, and the Gates Reading Survey. Brown found no consistent relationship between performance on these tests and on informal inventories. However, the Brown and Patty studies are not directly comparable: Brown used standardized *silent* reading tests while Patty used standardized *oral* reading tests.

In reviewing the findings of the studies cited above, several generalizations appear appropriate. First, it is important to remember that the purposes of standardized tests and informal inventories differ. Most publishers of standardized tests do not suggest that the grade score norms be used as indicators of the levels at which reading instruction should be provided. Rather, the standardized tests are designed merely to compare students to each other in terms of their reading skills. Secondly, performance on one informal reading inventory based on only one set of materials or set of basal readers in all likelihood will differ from performance on another reading inventory based on another set of materials. If an informal reading inventory is based on the materials used in classroom instruction, students perform better on that inventory than they would when presented with an inventory based on an unfamiliar set of materials. At the same time, estimates of student performance on classroom instructional materials is probably of greatest value to teachers. Third, any comparisons between IRI performance and standardized test scores are entirely dependent on: 1] the standardized test used, 2] the materials used to construct the IRI,

3] the criteria used to evaluate performance, and 4] the ability and skill of the examiner in recording errors and judging performance on the inventory. Finally, it seems that informal reading inventories are not as useful at the upper grade levels as they are at lower grade levels. Evidence (Wells, 1950) has already been cited which indicates that at the upper grade levels oral and silent reading abilities may be quite different skills. As it has been pointed out:

> above the sixth-grade level, certain limitations inherent in available reading textbooks render the estimates of grade placement based upon them probably less reliable and less refined than those of the standardized tests at corresponding levels. Prominent among the limitations referred to is the lack of a carefully graded vocabulary and the absence of any satisfactory control of comprehension difficulties arising from sources other than vocabulary difficulty such as, sentence length, sentence structure, extent of reference to subjects foreign to the experiential background of the pupil, and unrestricted use of fiction, or words for which concrete referents are unavailable. (Killgallon, 1942, p. 180)

Diagnosis through self-appraisal

In addition to the informal reading inventory, another procedure which has been proposed for diagnosing reading achievement is the use of the reader's self-evaluations. The major research concerns in this area have focused on the validity of self-evaluations—whether reader self-evaluations are useful in providing the teacher with added insight into a pupil's reading difficulties. While it has been well established that self-evaluations are a sound procedure in psychology, it has yet to be shown that it is sound practice in evaluating student reading abilities. There is also sparse research evidence supporting the validity of student self-evaluations in terms of assessing performance. Purcell (1963) polled college and adult students in reading improvement classes to determine the relative importance the students assigned to the factors which could have been causing them to read slowly. The factors were taken from a reading workbook and were explained by the instructor. Purcell's procedure appeared to limit the number of factors available for evaluation despite the fact that students were allowed to include additional factors. The factor which was rated as most important and was checked by 645 of the 827 students was back tracking; following in order of importance were daydreaming, word-by-word reading, vocalizing, and monotonous plodding. The validity of these as separate skills of reading is certainly open to serious question. It would be quite surprising if students would be able to identify these skills in other students; it is also probable that teachers would, likewise, be unable to do so. Certainly, the value of Purcell's study would have been considerably enhanced if these student ratings had been related either to test performance or teacher ratings. Spaights (1965) actually did this in his study comparing the self-estimates of eighty junior high students with their performance on the California Achievement Tests. Comparisons were made for each track of the school's four track system: able class learner (mean I.Q. 116), regular class learners (mean I.Q. 95), modified class learners (mean I.Q. 83), and slow learners (mean I.Q. 64). Students' self-ratings in slow learner classes correlated at the highest level with California Achievement Test reading grades .79; the regular class learners, .70; the modified class, .55; and the able class students' self-ratings correlated lowest at .36. Several elements weakened Spaights' study: foremost was Spaights' assumption that the California test was reliable for all four groups. Perhaps many of the more able learners scored at the upper end of the test scale and, therefore, many of them were not being accurately measured by the test because the test was not difficult enough for them. The use of teacher ratings would have added useful insights into this problem. Another factor detracting from the study was the questionable practice of employing student ratings based on grade score ratings. Spaights did not describe the rating sheet, but if product moment correlations were used, it is probable that the students were asked to rate themselves 7.1, 7.2, and so forth on the reading scale. It is highly unlikely that students know the difference between a seventh- or sixth-grade reading level much less the difference between 7.1 and 7.2.

A study which examined the usefulness of self-ratings as compared to formal evaluations was undertaken by Darby (1966). In this investigation, self-referred students and formally referred students were found not to differ in amount of reading growth during a reading improvement program nor were they found to differ in the length of time they remained in the program. However, at the conclusion of the program the self-referred students did score higher on the Brown-Holtzman Survey of Study Habits and Attitudes.

Most of the studies of self-evaluation have failed to relate the self-analyses to growth in the areas of identified weakness. If a student is able to identify his own reading deficiencies, he should then make greater improvements in those areas which he has specified as being weak. The comparison of student self-ratings to standardized test scores would not seem to be a useful approach to studying the value of self-diagnosis. Even if perfect correlations are established between these two measures, it would not indicate whether the self-diagnoses are more useful than the standardized tests; rather, it would show that one measurement procedure could be substituted for another.

Teacher ratings

Comparisons of teachers' ratings of student achievement with standardized test scores has also received some research attention. Studies of teacher ratings have been concerned primarily with comparing the predictive validity of reading readiness tests and teacher forecasts (Kermonian, 1962; Henig, 1949), the ability of teachers to diagnose and classify readers (Burnett, 1963; Hitchcock & Alfred, 1955; Preston, 1953; Emans, 1964), and teachers' skill in the selection of reading tests (Fisher, 1961; Bauernfeind, 1967).

Kermonian (1962) compared teacher ratings of reading readiness with scores on the Metropolitan Readiness Test. This study was undertaken to update Kottemeyer's (1947) findings which indicated that:

1] the subjective judgment of teachers as to first-grade reading success of children is as valid as results obtained by standardized tests;

2] teachers with more than ten years of experience predict reading success with greater accuracy than those with less experience;

3] Errors in appraisal occur mainly when teachers credit potential first-grade reading success to children who do not later attain this end.

Kermonian in his study found that teacher ratings and the Metropolitan Readiness test scores correlated .73 and that the majority of errors which were made by teachers were in the direction of overrating students. The major weakness of Kermonian's study was that no comparison of the teacher ratings or Metropolitan test scores were made with later reading achievement. Because of this, the conclusion that the use of reading readiness tests should be optional and teachers should be allowed to exercise their own judgment in appraisal is quite untenable.

Henig (1949) conducted a study similar to Kermonian's except that both the readiness test and the teachers' forecasts were compared to later reading achievement. The Lee-Clark Reading Readiness Test was used in this study. Henig used a five-level categorization of readiness ratings for both the readiness tests and the teachers' ratings (excellent, good, fair, poor, very poor) and compared these to a five level categorization (assigned grades from A to E) for first-grade reading achievement. The results indicated that the teacher ratings were as valid as the readiness tests in predicting later reading achievement.

From these two studies, there seems to be substantial evidence that teacher forecasts and at least two standardized tests of reading readiness are highly correlated. There is also some evidence that these two procedures are equally valid in predicting later reading achievement.

Teachers' ability to make diagnostic evaluations of students' reading performance has been shown to be related to amount of training the teachers have had in reading courses, amount of teaching experience, and type of college attended (Burnett, 1963). The studies in which teacher judgments were compared to standardized reading tests seem to be most dependent on the type of test which teachers ratings were being compared to and the amount of teacher knowledge of reading education.

When the comparison tests are general reading proficiency tests, teachers' judgments show a high degree of relationship with the tests. Hitchcock and Alfred (1955) found the correlations presented in Table 6 between English teacher ratings and the Stanford Achievement Test: Reading for 101 eighth-grade students. The correlations indicate that there is much

Table 6 Correlations between English teacher ratings and Stanford Achievement test scores (Hitchcock & Alfred, 1955, p. 423)

Test rating	Paragraph meaning	Word meaning	Average reading
Paragraph meaning	.74	.75	
Word meaning	.73	.79	
Average reading	.78	.83	.83

agreement between the results of the test scores and the teacher ratings. However, there also is a great deal of trait overlap between the paragraph meaning and word meaning categories, indicating, therefore, that the diagnostic proficiency of the tests and the teachers' rating were somewhat limited.

Several studies (Preston, 1953; Emans, 1964) have found that the more experience teachers have with making diagnostic evaluations, the less agreement their ratings have with diagnostic tests. Preston (1953) found that elementary teachers tended to classify students as retarded readers when they were actually reading up to or near capacity. In comparing teacher classifications to test scores, Preston divided the reading grade of each child by his mental age. He concluded that any student whose index or ratio fell below .80 was a retarded reader. In two schools in which this procedure was followed, 43 and 60 per cent of the normal readers were, according to Preston's index, incorrectly classified as retarded by the teachers. The most serious deficiency of Preston's index is that the mental ages of each child were taken from group standardized intelligence tests. The tests he used were the Kuhlmann-Anderson Intelligence Tests and the California Test of Mental Maturity. Both of these tests are highly correlated with reading achievement. Therefore, a student who was a poor reader probably scored poorly on the intelligence test (which would certainly be expected) and, therefore, would not be classified by the index as a retarded reader. In discussing his findings, Preston indicated that this may have occurred in a number of instances.

Emans' (1964) study compared remedial reading teachers' rankings of the reading skills with which students needed help with the skills indicated by the individually administered Gates Reading Diagnostic Tests. The twenty teachers involved in Emans' study each had worked individually for at least 25 hours with the two students they rated. Emans found that teachers do not perceive children's individual reading needs according to the test results. He concluded that individualized reading programs would be doomed from the start unless a standardized diagnostic reading test were used to identify the reading skills needs of the students. A shortcoming of the study was Emans' failure to describe the procedures used by the teachers in making their diagnostic evaluations—the directions to teachers, the definitions of the skills, and the format of the rating procedures all would influence the results of the teachers' ratings. Emans also did not discuss the possibility that the lack of agreement might not be due to the lack of validity of the teacher evaluations, but rather might be attributed to the lack of diagnostic validity of the Gates test.

Perhaps the best criterion for determining the usefulness of diagnostic evaluations would be to compare the amount of improvement made by students selected for a remedial program on the basis of teacher ratings versus those selected on the basis of standardized test scores. A study of this type was conducted in Scotland by Lytton (1961). Lytton found that it made no difference whether children were selected for remedial reading instruction by teachers' judgments or by standardized tests when the criterion was standardized test score improvement in reading.

What kinds of tests do teachers prefer as diagnostic tools? How skillful are teachers in selecting tests? There are very few studies which provide any answers to these questions. It is highly probable that teacher selection of reading tests is related to their educational backgrounds and to their teaching responsibilities. There is some evidence that teachers at the elementary and secondary level would like to have reading comprehension and vocabulary tests administered to the students they teach (Bauernfeind, 1967). Fisher (1961) conducted a study with 1,041 elementary school children which indicated that "out of grade" reading tests were better measures of the reading ability of advanced and retarded readers. By "out of grade" tests, Fisher meant tests that were used at a higher or lower grade level than the level where the publisher suggested they be used. He believed that such tests are consistently better suited to the actual performance of advanced and retarded readers. In this study they provided better discrimination between the abilities of advanced and retarded students and contained materials with better content validity. Fisher further concluded that "out of grade" tests merit more extensive use in cases where pupils' abilities are markedly different from the norm of his particular grade. Fisher's results indicated that the selection of tests should involve more than merely examining the technical and logical properties of the test; it should also entail some under-standing of the abilities of the individual students being adminis-tered the tests.

The informal procedures discussed in the previous section all seem to provide useful information for assessing students' reading behaviors. However, the use of any of these tech-niques should be limited by an understanding of the strengths and weaknesses of each. Informal assessment of students' reading performance should also include an examination of the students' ability to apply their reading skills in content subjects. The diagnosis of this ability is extremely important if the teacher is concerned about the ultimate objective of reading de-velopment—the utilization of text material to further learning.

Assessing reading in content areas

The appraisal of students' reading in social studies, math, science, literature, and other subject areas can provide the read-ing teacher with relevant diagnostic information about how well the student can apply the reading skills he is taught. Such ap-praisal can also provide the content teacher with information about how a student can be helped to learn more efficiently in a given subject area. In an early study of reading skills in the content areas, Artley (1944) found that while some relation-ship exists between tests of general comprehension and compre-hension in the social studies, there is also a high degree of spe-cificity in the factors relating to reading comprehension in the social studies. A command of the specialized vocabulary of so-cial studies was found to be at least as important as knowledge of social studies facts on tests measuring knowledge of facts in social studies. Several studies since Artley's early investigation have also concluded that comprehension of reading material is different in each subject area (Shores, 1960; Maney, 1958; Halfter & Douglass, 1960). If this finding is accurate, it means that the diagnosis of a student's reading performance in a con-tent area must be concerned with more than his general reading comprehension.   Students may be performing poorly in academic subjects not because they lack reading comprehension abilities in general, but because they lack the specific ability to apply this skill to various subject areas.   The diagnosis of reading ability, therefore, needs to go beyond an evaluation of general reading power and should examine the reader's ability to apply his reading skills.

Shores (1960) found that comprehension of science materials for sixth-grade students was related to their purposes for reading.   The purposes Shores established for the reading were: 1] reading for the main idea and/or 2] reading to keep a series of ideas in sequence.   Shores found that reading for the main idea is more like what is measured by tests of general reading achievement than is reading for a series of ideas in sequence.

In an earlier study with fourth, fifth, and sixth graders, Shores and Saupe (1953) investigated whether the type of reading comprehension demanded of a student in each content area differs qualitatively beyond the primary grades.   It was discovered that the kind of reading used in grades four, five, and six for problem-solving in science has "a large factor in common with mental ability and general achievement as these are commonly measured and yet is somewhat unique in a manner which cannot be accounted for by these generalized factors" (Shores & Saupe, 1953, p. 157).   They added that better testing instruments were needed to define the nature of this unique variance and its relation to general reading comprehension.

Further support for the hypothesis that reading comprehension is a specific ability related to specific purposes for reading and various subjects was reported in a study with 513 fifth-grade students (Maney, 1958). Maney administered an author-constructed test of science reading comprehension, the Gates Reading Survey—Level of Comprehension and the Pintner General Ability Tests. Intercorrelations between the test items were then examined. Of great importance is that literal reading comprehension correlated with each critical science reading

test item from − .15 to + .47. This finding lends considerable credence to Maney's conclusion that critical reading of
science materials cannot be predicted from general reading tests
or from a test of literal reading comprehension.

Each of the studies cited thus far have emphasized the need
for tests of reading comprehension in each subject area.
Maney (1958) developed such a test for use in science classes
with fifth graders. Researchers in other content areas have also
attempted the development of reading comprehension tests for
specific subjects. Halfter and Douglass (1960) developed a
test designed to measure a student's general competence in
reading skills peculiar to the field of commerce. Their test correlated highly with successful performance in a business school.
Comparative validations of the test were provided by correlating
high school grades and the Ohio State University Psychological
Test. The Ohio State test correlated with later grades .64 as
did the Commerce Reading Comprehension Test. The two
tests and high school grades provided a multiple correlation of
.77 with first semester grades in business school. However,
Halfter and Douglass failed to indicate the amount of variance
contributed by high school grades which limits their conclusion
that the Commerce Reading Comprehension Test is a useful
predictor of later grades in business courses.

Comprehension of vocabulary in a particular academic area
has also been suggested as an important predictor of success in
that content field. The reading vocabulary sub-test of the California Reading Test—Upper Level is divided into specific subject matter areas. While there have been few studies which
have examined the validity of tests of vocabulary in specific subjects, several researchers (Johnson, 1952; Wyatt & Ridgeway,
1958; Dunlap, 1951) have concluded that subject-oriented vocabulary tests reveal students' weaknesses in understanding the
vocabulary of textbooks in that field.

Mary E. Johnson (1952) constructed a vocabulary test consisting of 150 multiple-choice items designed to test fifth graders'
understanding of vocabulary in six content fields: arithmetic,

geography, history, science, health, and literature. The words used in the test were taken from the fifth-grade books which the students used for daily study. Because the pupils tested did not seem to be equipped to deal with the vocabularies of the texts used in content fields, it was concluded that a program of word enrichment was needed. Similar findings have been reported with high school students (Wyatt & Ridgeway, 1958; Dunlap, 1951).

Belden and Lee (1961) compared Dale-Chall readability scores of five general biology textbooks adopted for use in Oklahoma high schools. Three hundred fifty-seven tenth graders in six Oklahoma high schools were then administered the Nelson-Denny Reading Test and students' reading ability and the readability level of the textbooks were compared. Only one of the five biology texts was found to have a readability level suitable for at least fifty per cent of the students who were using it. This conclusion is limited, however, by the lack of reliability evidence for the Dale-Chall formula and the Nelson-Denny test. The lack of agreement between readability level and students' reading ability could have been due to either the invalidity or unreliability of these two measures, but the findings do suggest that a complete diagnosis of a student's reading ability must include an assessment of his ability to read textbook material.

The number of investigations related to the measurement of reading ability in content areas indicates that many researchers and teachers feel there is a need for tests of specific reading skills. Most of these studies (Maney, 1958; Halfter & Douglass, 1960; Shores & Saupe, 1953) are related to attempts to measure reading comprehension as it relates to a specific subject. Others (Johnson, 1952; Wyatt & Ridgeway, 1958; Dunlap, 1951) have pointed out the need for measuring students' vocabulary ability in each subject area so that the needed vocabulary instruction can be provided and students can learn more effectively from textbooks in each subject.

How successful have these attempts been? First of all, there is a serious lack of research related to the basic components of reading comprehension and their relation to various subjects. The majority of investigations have relied on the correlation coefficient for their analyses. While such a procedure does indicate that two variables are related, it does not provide the reasons underlying such a relation. A given reading comprehension test in science may be related to later success in science not because the test is a test of specific science reading ability, but because the student who has had past experience with science not only achieves at a high level on such a test but he has a high probability of performing well in a science class.

More basic research has been conducted on the elements composing general reading comprehension than on those composing reading comprehension in specific subject areas. This research, reported previously in the present monograph, has been quite equivocal in the validation of attempts to measure specific reading skills. Hunt (1957) cautioned against the use of measures of specific reading comprehension skills:

> However, it seems to this writer that the whole question of the construction of diagnostic measures of reading comprehension needs further examination. There have been several efforts to use the procedure of naming the important skills of reading comprehension, constructing items designed primarily to measure each of the skills as labelled, and then studying the responses to the items by a sample or group of examinees. This conventional procedure has usually been least exhaustive in the two most important steps: namely, item construction and the analysis of student responses to the different sets of items. (1957, p. 169)

Hunt obviously was pleading for more careful definitions of the skills which are to be measured. If a test constructor suggests that reading comprehension is different in science than it is in social studies, he must describe exactly how they differ. It is not enough for him to build two reading comprehension tests, one based on science material and one on social studies material. Furthermore, attempts to validate such tests must be related to students' responses. Correlating a test of science reading ability with grades in science is not a valid procedure for examining the unique qualities of reading comprehension in science. By studying students' responses, it may be possible to determine if the student goes through a different mental procedure in comprehending science material than he does in comprehending social studies material.

Finally, there is a lack of tests on the market which measure reading achievement in specific subjects. If content area teachers desire information regarding students' reading performance in that content area, it would be most useful for them to develop informal reading inventories designed to measure students' skill in learning from text material. To determine reading levels and specific skill weaknesses, Eller (1965, p. 188) has suggested on the college level a procedure of using informal "tests which include samples from the texts used in the basic freshman courses in science, social science, and English." Eller further recommended that this informal approach be used by the reading teacher or the subject matter teacher to diagnose other skills: ". . . he can easily begin to 'specialize' in the development of special collections of exercises for the appraisal of note-taking skills, evaluation skills, abilities concerned with the organization of information and locational and reference skills" (1965, p. 188).

A note to the practitioner

This chapter has attempted to review some of the more important studies dealing with the problems of using formal and informal tests to assess students' reading achievement. It has also tried to point out explicitly the implications this research has for the test consumer, what devices might be most helpful for diagnosing skills and at what levels they are most appropriate. The major conclusion, if any, from the preceding review must, of course, be that much research is needed before definitive suggestions for classroom practice can be made. However, such a conclusion is scarcely helpful to the practitioner who is faced with immediate problems of how to assess an individual student's achievement. If anything, though, the research should have said to him that no one method can solve his problems. Knowledge about the diagnosis of reading achievement is not so scant that the teacher need be paralyzed. Given a variety of procedures, teachers can make a reasonably accurate assessment of students' skills, capabilities, and needs. Both standardized and informal tests can help in grouping students for instruction, determining reading levels, and diagnosing reading achievement.

The most efficient procedure for determining instructional groupings or for comparing students in general reading development is to use a group standardized reading test. The selection of the appropriate test should be done by comparing instructional objectives to the test objectives and by selecting a test which has the broadest coverage. In using the test results for comparing students, the teacher should not depend upon grade norms, instead he should rely on standard scores. In addition, no attempt should be made to use sub-test scores for diagnostic purposes. Care should also be taken to make sure that the test is not too easy or too difficult for more able or less able students. A standardized test is valid for comparing students only when the standardized administration procedures are carefully followed for all the students who are to be compared. After the teacher has obtained some idea from the standardized tests about who the good, the average, and the poor readers are, the next step is to determine their functional reading levels. This can be done by using standardized reading tests in a procedure outlined by Farr and Anastasiow (1969). This procedure is based on determining the relationship between a particular standardized reading test and an informal reading inventory.

An informal reading inventory, developed by the classroom teacher and based on the classroom instructional materials, provides a very useful measure of each student's ability to read at increasingly difficult levels. Most often overlooked in the use of informal reading inventories is their use as a daily, continuous part of reading instruction. By constantly being alert to each student's reading performance and applying the criteria for assessing informal reading inventory performance, the teacher can adjust the instructional materials to insure continued student success. After determining appropriate reading levels for students, the teacher's next concern relates to the diagnosis of reading skills development.

The validity of the teacher's diagnosis of students' reading skills can be increased if he selects or develops measurement devices which assess those skills which he has concluded are most important for the students' reading skill development. This would mean the teacher would accumulate a collection of procedures and tests for the continuous diagnosis of students' reading achievement. This collection would probably include certain sub-tests of group and individual standardized reading tests, teacher-developed checklists or tests, and classroom observations of students' behaviors. In using such instruments, it is essential that the teacher realize that the instruments are being used as criteria tests and are not for the purposes of comparing one student to another. Their value lies in the information they can provide about students' development in particular skill areas. Other measurement procedures such as psychological tests and teacher observations were reviewed in the preceding chapter.

How do these fit into a total evaluation program? First of all, there is very little evidence that psychological tests provide any useful information for diagnosing students' reading achievement. Before their use becomes accepted diagnostic practice in the classroom and clinic, their validity needs to be carefully studied. However, it should be pointed out that this research should develop from questions raised from attempts to use these tests. It is, therefore, suggested that the tests should continue to be used in controlled situations. Teacher evaluations appear to be quite valid and reliable measures of students' general reading development. In this regard, they are most comparable to standardized group reading tests and, as with the group tests, there is considerable question concerning the validity and reliability of classroom teachers' diagnosis of specific sub-skills of reading.

The past two chapters have reviewed research studies concerning the problems of measuring specific reading skills and the problems of using various procedures for assessing reading skill development. With these areas clarified to some extent, the next chapter proceeds to a consideration of the theories and research dealing with one of the major uses of measurement devices in reading—the assessment of growth.

References

Altus, Grace T. A WISC profile for retarded readers. *Journal of Consulting Psychology*, 1956, *20*, 155-57.

Artley, A. S. A study of certain relationships existing between general reading comprehension and reading comprehension in a specific subject matter area. *Journal of Educational Research*, 1944, *37*, 464-73.

Bauernfeind, R. H. Teacher preferences for types of standardized test studies in three Illinois school districts, 1964-1965. *Journal of Educational Measurement*, 1967, *4*, 11-14.

Belden, B. R., & Lee, W. D. Readability of biology text books and the reading ability of biology students. *School Science and Mathematics*, 1961, *61*, 689-93.

Betts, E. A. Reading problems at the intermediate grade level. *Elementary School Journal*, 1940, *15*, 737-46.

Bond, G. L., & Fay, L. C. A comparison of the performance of good and poor readers on the individual items of the Stanford-Binet scale. *Journal of Educational Research*, 1950, *43*, 475-79.

Brown, Sandra R. A comparison of five widely used standardized reading tests and an informal reading inventory for a selected group of elementary school children. Unpublished doctoral dissertation, University of Georgia, 1963.

Burks, H. F., & Bruce, P. The characteristics of good and poor readers as disclosed by the WISC. *Journal of Educational Psychology*, 1955, *46*, 488-93.

Burnett, R. W. The diagnostic proficiency of teachers of reading. *The Reading Teacher*, 1963, *16*, 229-34.

Buswell, G. T. Perceptual research and methods of learning. *Scientific Monthly*, 1947, *64*, 521-26.

Chall, Jeanne S. The Roswell-Chall Diagnostic Reading Test of Word Analysis Skills: evidence of reliability and validity. *The Reading Teacher*, 1958, *11*, 178-83.

Coleman, J. C., & Rasof, Beatrice. Intellectual factors in learning disorders. *Perceptual and Motor Skills*, 1963, *16*, 139-52.

Croft, J. A teacher's survey of his backward class in a secondary modern school. *British Journal of Educational Psychology*, 1951, *21*, 135-44.

Darby, C. A. Referred and self-initiated students in reading-study program. *Journal of Reading*, 1966, *9*, 186-92.

Davis, F. B. The assessment of change. In E. P. Bliesmer & A. J. Kingston (Eds.), Phases of college and other adult reading programs. *Yearbook of the National Reading Conference,* 1961, *10*, 86-95.

Deal, Margaret. A summary of research concerning patterns of WISC sub-test scores of retarded readers. *Journal of the Reading Specialist,* 1965, *4*, 101-11.

Dockrell, W. B. The use of the Wechsler Intelligence Scale for Children in the diagnosis of retarded readers. *Alberta Journal of Educational Research,* 1960, *6*, 86-91.

Dunlap, C. C. Readability of newspaper items and of basic reading material. *Elementary School Journal,* 1951, *51*, 499-501.

Eller, W. Determining reading levels for instruction. In J. A. Figurel (Ed.), Reading and inquiry. *Proceedings of the International Reading Association,* 1965, *10*, 187-88.

Eller, W., & Attea, Mary. Three diagnostic tests: some comparisons. In J. A. Figurel (Ed.), Vistas in reading. *Proceedings of the International Reading Association,* 1966, *11*, 562-66.

Emans, R. Teacher evaluations of reading skills and individualized reading. *Elementary English,* 1964, *42*, 258-60.

Fairbanks, G. The relation between eye-movements and voice in the oral reading of good and poor silent readers. *Psychological Monographs,* 1937, *48*, 78-107.

Farr, R. C. The convergent and discriminant validity of several upper level reading tests. In G. B. Schick & M. M. May (Eds.), Multidisciplinary aspects of college-adult reading. *Yearbook of the National Reading Conference,* 1968, *17*, 181-91.

Farr, R. C., & Anastasiow, N. A. *Tests of reading readiness and achievement.* Newark, Delaware: International Reading Association, 1969.

Fisher, J. A. The use of out-of-grade tests with retarded and accelerated readers. Unpublished doctoral dissertation, State University of Iowa, 1961.

Gilmore, J. V. The relation between certain oral reading habits and oral and silent reading comprehension. Unpublished doctoral dissertation, Harvard University, 1947.

Glaser, N. A. A comparison of specific reading skills of advanced and retarded readers of fifth grade reading achievement. Unpublished doctoral dissertation, University of Oregon, 1964.

Goodman, K. S. The psycholinguistic nature of the reading process.

In K. S. Goodman (Ed.), *The psycholinguistic nature of the reading process.* Detroit: Wayne State University Press, 1968. Pp. 13-26.

Graham, E. E. Wechsler-Bellevue and WISC scattergrams of unsuccessful readers. *Journal of Consulting Psychology,* 1953, *16,* 268-71.

Gray, Lillian, & Reese, Dora. *Teaching children to read.* New York: Ronald Press, 1957.

Halfter, Irma T., & Douglass, Frances M. Measurement of college level reading competence in a content area. *Journal of Educational Research,* 1960, *53,* 223-30.

Henig, M. S. Predictive value of a reading readiness test and of teachers' forecasts. *Elementary School Journal,* 1949, *50,* 41-46.

Hills, J. R. What I look for in a review of a scholastic aptitude test or battery. *Personnel and Guidance Journal,* 1964, *42,* 711-14.

Hirst, Lynne S. The usefulness of a two-way analysis of WISC subtests in the diagnosis of remedial reading. *Journal of Experimental Education,* 1960, *29,* 153-60.

Hitchcock, A. A., & Alfred, Cleo. Can teachers make accurate estimates of reading ability? *Clearinghouse,* 1955, *54,* 422-24.

Hunt, L. C. Can we measure specific factors associated with reading comprehension? *Journal of Educational Research,* 1957, *51,* 161-72.

Johnson, Marjorie S. Reading inventories for classroom use. *The Reading Teacher,* 1960, *14,* 9-14.

Johnson, Marjorie S., & Kress, R. *Informal reading inventories.* Newark, Delaware: International Reading Association, 1966.

Johnson, Mary E. The vocabulary difficulty of content subjects in grade five. *Elementary English,* 1952, *29,* 277-80.

Kallos, G. L., & Grabow, E. A. The WISC profile of disabled readers. *Personnel and Guidance Journal,* 1961, *13,* 476-78.

Keogh, Barbara K. The Bender-Gestalt as a predictive and diagnostic test of reading performance. *Journal of Consulting Psychology,* 1965, *29,* 83-84.

Kermonian, S. B. Teacher appraisal of first grade readiness. *Elementary English,* 1962, *39,* 196-201.

Killgallon, P. A. A study of relationships among certain pupil adjustments in language situations. Unpublished doctoral dissertation, Pennsylvania State University, 1942.

Knoblock, P.   A Rorschach investigation of the reading process. *Journal of Experimental Education*, 1965, *33*, 277-82.

Kottemeyer, W.   Readiness for reading. *Elementary English*, 1947, *24*, 355-66.

Krippner, S.   Diagnostic and remedial use of the Minnesota Percepto-Diagnostic Test in a reading clinic. *Psychology in the Schools*, 1966, *3*, 171-75.

Leibert, R. E.   An investigation of the differences in reading performance on two tests of reading. Unpublished doctoral dissertation, Syracuse University, 1965.

Lytton, H.   An experiment in selection for remedial education. *British Journal of Educational Psychology*, 1961, *31*, 79-84.

McClean, T. K.   A comparison of the sub-test performance of two groups of retarded readers with like groups of non-retarded readers on the Wechsler Intelligence Scale for Children. Unpublished doctoral dissertation, University of Oregon, 1968.

McCleod, J. A.   A comparison of WISC sub-test scores of pre-adolescent successful and unsuccessful readers. *Australian Journal of Psychology*, 1965, *17*, 220-28.

McCracken, R. A.   Standardized reading tests and informal reading inventories. *Education*, 1962, *82*, 366-69.

McCracken, R. A.   The development and validation of the Standard Reading Inventory for the individual appraisal of reading performance in grades 1 through 6. Unpublished doctoral dissertation, Syracuse University, 1963.

McCracken, R. A.   The development and validation of the Standard Reading Inventory for the individual appraisal of reading performance. In J. A. Figurel (Ed.), Improvement of reading through classroom practice. *Proceedings of the International Reading Association*, 1964, *9*, 310-13.

Maney, Ethel S.   Literal and critical reading in science. *Journal of Experimental Education*, 1958, *27*, 57-64.

Muir, Margaret.   The WISC test pattern of children with severe reading disabilities. *Reading Horizons*, 1962, *3*, 67-73.

Murray, Carol F., & Karlsen, B.   A concurrent validity study of the Silent Reading Tests and the Gates Reading Diagnostic Tests. *The Reading Teacher*, 1960, *13*, 293-94, 296.

Neville, D.   A comparison of the WISC patterns of male retarded and non-retarded readers. *Journal of Educational Research*, 1961, *54*, 195-97.

Olson, A. V. The Frostig Developmental Test of Visual Perception as a predictor of specific reading abilities with second grade children. *Elementary English*, 1966, *43*, 869-72.

Parrish, R. E. A study of some factors in the Bender-Gestalt reproductions of reader and non-reader children. Unpublished doctoral dissertation, University of Oklahoma, 1962.

Paterra, Mary E. A study of thirty-three WISC scattergrams of retarded readers. *Elementary English*, 1963, *40*, 394-99.

Patty, D. L. A comparison of standardized oral reading test scores and informal reading inventory scores. Unpublished doctoral dissertation, Ball State University, 1965.

Preston, R. C. The reading status of children classified by teachers as retarded readers. *Elementary English*, 1953, *30*, 225-27.

Purcell, J. W. Poor reading habits: their rank order. *The Reading Teacher*, 1963, *16*, 353-58.

Rabinovitch, R. Reading and learning disabilities. In S. Arieti (Ed.), *American handbook of psychiatry*. New York: Basic Books, 1959. Pp. 857-69.

Reid, W. R., & Schoer, L. A. Reading achievement, social class and sub-test pattern on the WISC. *Journal of Educational Research*, 1966, *59*, 469-71.

Richardson, Helen M., & Surko, Elsie F. WISC scores and status in reading and arithmetic of delinquent children. *Journal of Genetic Psychology*, 1956, *89*, 251-62.

Robeck, Mildred. Subtest patterning of problem readers on the WISC. *California Journal of Educational Research*, 1960, *11*, 110-15.

Rose, Florence C. The occurrence of short auditory memory span among school children referred for diagnosis of reading difficulties. *Journal of Educational Research*, 1958, *51*, 459-64.

Sheldon, M. S., & Garton, Jeanette. A note on a WISC profile for retarded readers. *Alberta Journal of Educational Research*, 1959, *5*, 264-67.

Sheldon, W. D., & Hatch, Shirley. Strengths and weaknesses in reading by a group of third grade children. *Elementary School Journal*, 1950, *50*, 445-52.

Sheldon, W. D., & Hatch, Shirley. Strengths and weaknesses in reading of a group of sixth grade children. *Elementary English,* 1951, *28,* 86-93.

Shores, H. J. Reading science materials for two distinct purposes. *Elementary English,* 1960, *37,* 546-53.

Shores, H. J., & Saupe, J. L. Reading for problem-solving in science. *Journal of Educational Psychology,* 1953, *44,* 149-58.

Sipay, E. R. A comparison of standardized reading test scores and functional reading levels. Unpublished doctoral dissertation, University of Connecticut, 1961.

Sipay, E. R. A comparison of standardized reading scores and functional reading levels. *The Reading Teacher,* 1964, *17,* 265-68.

Spache, G. D. A comparison of certain oral reading tests. *Journal of Educational Research,* 1950, *43,* 441-52.

Spaights, E. Accuracy of self-estimation of junior high school students. *Journal of Educational Research,* 1965, *58,* 416-19.

Weber, Rose-Marie. The study of oral reading errors: a survey of the literature. *Reading Research Quarterly,* 1968, *4,* 96-119.

Wells, C. A. The value of an oral reading test for diagnosis of the reading difficulties of college freshmen of low academic performance. *Psychological Monographs,* 1950, *64,* 1-35.

Williams, Joan L. A comparison of standardized reading test scores and informal reading inventory scores. Unpublished doctoral dissertation, Southern Illinois University, 1963.

Wyatt, Nita M., & Ridgeway, R. W. A study of the readability of selected social studies materials. *University of Kansas Bulletin of Education,* 1958, *12,* 100-05.

Test references

An asterisk after a test listing indicates the test is included in the *Guide to Tests and Measuring Instruments in Reading* which appears after Chapter 6.

Appraisal of Growth in Reading New York Public Schools. New York: Bureau of Reference, Research, and Statistics, Division of Tests and Measurement, New York Public Schools, Nov. 1941.

Bender-Gestalt Test Lauretta Bender. New York: American Orthopsychiatric Association, 1938, rev. 1946.

Brown-Holtzman Survey of Study Habits and Attitudes W. F. Brown & W. H. Holtzman. New York: Psychological Corp., 1953, rev. 1963.

California Achievement Tests E. W. Tiegs & W. W. Clark. Monterey, Calif.: California Test Bureau, 1933, rev. 1963.

California Reading Test E. W. Tiegs & W. W. Clark. Monterey, Calif.: California Test Bureau, 1957, rev. 1963*.

California Test of Mental Maturity E. T. Sullivan, W. W. Clark, & E. W. Tiegs. Monterey, Calif.: California Test Bureau, 1936, rev. 1963.

Commerce Reading Comprehension Test I. T. Halfter & R. J. McCall. Chicago: Department of Psychological Testing, De Paul University, 1956, rev. 1958*.

Developmental Reading Tests, Silent Reading Diagnostic Test G. L. Bond, T. Clymer, & C. J. Hoyt. Chicago: Lyons & Carnahan, 1958*.

Diagnostic Reading Scales G. Spache. Monterey, Calif.: California Test Bureau, 1963*.

Durrell Analysis of Reading Difficulty D. D. Durrell. N. Y.: Harcourt, Brace, & World, 1937, rev. 1955*.

Durrell-Sullivan Reading Achievement Tests D. D. Durrell & H. B. Sullivan. N. Y.: Harcourt, Brace, & World, 1937, rev. 1944.

Gates Advanced Primary Reading Test A. I. Gates. N. Y.: Bureau of Publications, Teachers College, Columbia University, 1926, rev. 1958.

Gates Primary Reading Tests A. I. Gates. N. Y.: Bureau of Publications, Teachers College, Columbia University, 1926, rev. 1958.

Gates Reading Diagnostic Tests A. I. Gates. N. Y.: Bureau of Publications, Teachers College, Columbia University, 1926, rev. 1953.

Gates Reading Survey A. I. Gates. N. Y. Bureau of Publications, Teachers College, Columbia University, 1939, rev. 1960.

Gates-McKillop Reading Diagnostic Tests   A. I. Gates & A. S. McKillop.   N. Y.: Bureau of Publications, Teachers College, Columbia University, 1926, rev. 1962*.

Gilmore Oral Reading Test   J. Gilmore and V. Gilmore.   N. Y.: Harcourt, Brace, & World, 1951, rev. 1968*.

Gray's Oral Check Test   W. S. Gray.   Bloomington, Ill.: Public School Publishing Co., n.d.

Gray Oral Reading Test   W. S. Gray.   Indianapolis: Bobbs-Merrill, 1963, rev. 1967*.

Iowa Every-Pupil Tests of Basic Skills, Test A: Silent Reading Comprehension   H. F. Spitzer, E. Horn, M. McBroom, H. A. Greene, & E. F. Lindquist.   Boston, Mass.: Houghton Mifflin, 1955, rev. 1964*.

Iowa Silent Reading Tests: Advanced   H. A. Greene, A. N. Jorgensen, & V. H. Kelley.   N. Y.: Harcourt, Brace, & World, 1927, rev. 1942*.

Kuhlmann-Anderson Intelligence Tests   F. Kuhlmann & R. G. Anderson.   Princeton, N. J.: Personnel Press, 1927, rev. 1963.

Lee-Clark Reading Readiness Test   J. M. Lee & W. W. Clark.   Monterey, Calif.: California Test Bureau, 1931, rev. 1963*.

Marianne Frostig Developmental Test of Visual Perception   M. Frostig.   Palo Alto, Calif.: Consulting Psychologists Press, 1961, rev. 1964.

Metropolitan Achievement Tests: Reading   W. N. Durost, H. H. Bixler, G. H. Hildreth, K. W. Lund, & J. W. Wrightstone.   N. Y.: Harcourt, Brace, & World, 1932, rev. 1962*.

Metropolitan Readiness Test   G. H. Hildreth, N. L. Griffiths, & M. E. McGauvran.   N. Y.: Harcourt, Brace, & World, 1933, rev. 1965*.

Minnesota Percepto-Diagnostic Test   G. B. Fuller & J. T. Laird.   Brandon, Vt.: Journal of Clinical Psychology, 1962, rev. 1963.

Nelson-Denny Reading Test   M. J. Nelson & E. Denny.   Boston: Houghton Mifflin, 1928, rev. 1960.

Ohio State University Psychological Test   H. A. Toops.   Columbus: Ohio State University, 1919, rev. 1954.

Pintner General Ability Tests   C. A. Whitman.   N. Y.: Harcourt, Brace, & World, 1923, rev. 1946.

Revised Bender-Gestalt Test   M. L. Hutt & G. S. Briskin.   N. Y.: Grune & Stratton, 1944, rev. 1960.

Rorschach Resume: Rorschach Ink Blot Personality Testing   H. Rorschach.   N. Y.: Dynamical Psychological Society Press, 1956.

Rorschach Test   H. Rorschach.   N. Y.: Grune & Stratton, 1920, rev. 1960.

Roswell-Chall Diagnostic Reading Test of Word Analysis Skills   F. G. Roswell & J. S. Chall.   N. Y.: Essay Press, 1956, rev. 1957*.

Sangren-Woody Reading Test   P. V. Sangren & C. Woody,   N. Y.: Harcourt, Brace, & World, 1928.

Standard Reading Inventory   R. A. McCracken.   Pullman, Wash.: Primer Printing Co., 1963, rev. 1966.

Stanford Achievement Test: Reading Tests   T. L. Kelley, R. Madden, E. F. Gardner, & H. C. Rudman.   N. Y.: Harcourt, Brace, & World, 1922, rev. 1966*.

Stanford-Binet Intelligence Scale   L. M. Terman & M. A. Merrill. Boston: Houghton Mifflin, 1916, rev. 1960.

Wechsler Intelligence Scale for Children   D. Wechsler.   N. Y.: The Psychological Corp., 1949.

Wepman Test of Auditory Discrimination   J. M. Wepman.   Chicago: Language Research Associates, 1958.

Wide Range Achievement Test (WRAT)   J. F. Jastak & J. R. Jastak. Austin, Tex.: Guidance Testing Associates, 1936, rev. 1965*.

4

Assessing growth

Student growth in reading skills is the single most important goal of the reading program. Probably the most valuable contribution which measuring devices can make to reading instruction is that of providing a reliable and valid assessment of this growth. The need for such assessment cannot be overemphasized: most of the elements within the reading program—the teaching procedures, the grouping practices, the curriculum structure, and even teacher capabilities—are evaluated on the basis of student growth. While it is not proposed that student growth be the *sole* basis for evaluating the reading program, nonetheless it is the single most important variable to consider in assessing reading programs. Consequently, a chapter on assessing growth in a monograph on measurement and evaluation in reading needs little justification.

Research in assessing growth has been sparse, and this in itself has been a major obstacle to improving evaluation procedures. Too often statements and suggestions are made about the value of a particular procedure when there is no research evidence to substantiate it. But the scarcity of studies in assessing growth does not prevent an intelligent discussion of current evaluation procedures and there are a number of studies which stress the need for improving present practices.

The review of research presented in this chapter deals with the problems of pre- and post-test measurement. This discussion applies to assessing student progress at all levels of instruction, from pre-school to the adult levels. Two areas have been singled out for special attention: evaluating growth in remedial reading programs and the use of readiness tests as a means for predicting performance. These two areas are given special emphasis because both require extensive use of measurement devices and because they have commanded more research attention than other facets of the reading program.

Difficulties in assessing growth

Scores on both informal and standardized tests have, for the most part, served as *the basis* for assessing growth in reading. The ways in which these scores have been used as the criterion for evaluating growth was best described by McDonald (1964). McDonald delineated three major methods for evaluating growth, all of which are comparative. The first method involves comparing scores on alternate forms of a test and using the difference in performance on the pre- and post-tests as the criteria for assessing change. A second method entails taking the average yearly gains made by a particular group and comparing them with those made by a nationwide norm. The criterion for growth in this instance is not how the student achieves individually in relation to his own past performance, but how he does, on an average, in regard to some national norm. The third method described by McDonald involves comparing test, re-test scores of a remedial group with that of a control group other than the national norm group. While the three methods for using test scores as the basis for assessing growth described by McDonald are the most commonly used ones, it does not mean that they are necessarily the most efficient or accurate means of evaluating progress. Indeed, McDonald was well aware of their limitations.

The central problem in measuring growth in reading is the validity and reliability of methods for assessing student progress. Are tests the best instruments for evaluating growth? If they are, are alternate forms (pre- and post-tests) useful? Are the alternate forms comparable, i.e., do they measure the same or different skills? Are the nationwide norms established by test publishers comparable to the group being tested so that the results, based on evaluating students' performance against that of the norm, will be meaningful? It would be both tedious and redundant to review here all those studies which have inappropriately used tests to evaluate growth; rather, it is more useful to point only to those studies which demonstrate clearly the major validity problems encountered in assessing growth in reading.

Valid measurement of the skills taught

The most important decision to be made by the practitioner in assessing reading growth is choosing the testing device. The practitioner has to be careful that the test he selects validly measures what has been taught in the instructional program, that it represents the components of reading behavior as defined by the instructional program, that the difficulty level of the test is appropriate to the group being tested, and that the evaluation includes measures of gains over longer periods of time. In other words, the practitioner must ask himself whether, given the instructional program, the estimate of growth provides the information that he needs and whether it provides that information accurately.

There are several elements which make tests appropriate to any given instructional program. The most obvious one is that the skills measured by the test be those which were taught in the reading program and that those factors deemed constituents of reading behavior by the reading program be so considered by the test in about the same proportions. No specific research studies related to this problem have been located. However, it is logical that the measurement of growth would be invalid if the testing instrument failed to measure what has been taught. For example, if one of the most important outcomes of the reading program is the development of critical reading comprehension and instruction has been organized accordingly, a test for measuring growth should be selected which places an equal emphasis on critical reading comprehension.

A test, even if it has a label which indicates that it may be measuring a skill taught in the reading program, may still be unsuitable if it is not testing that skill in the manner in which it was taught by the teacher. For example, if vocabulary improvement has been developed through using words in context, a test would not be a valid measure of vocabulary improvement if it presented words in isolation and the examinees were asked to select the "correct" synonym from a group of alternatives. Related to this is the problem of a test covering not only those abilities which have been part of the reading program, but also other abilities extraneous to its goals. The single most common error is the unconscious inclusion of a speed factor when speed of reading is not a goal of the instructional program. The speed factor enters through the use of timed tests. Results in any pre-test, post-test situation are always influenced because the student usually works harder on the post-test knowing that he is being evaluated on the basis of the difference between his initial and final performance. This Hawthorne-type effect is compounded when the post-test is a timed test; often the student does more work on it regardless of whether he has become a more powerful reader or not. The Reed (1956) study demonstrates the pitfalls of using timed tests when speed is not an integral part of the program. Reed hypothesized that intensive training in reading and study skills would yield significant gains in reading rate, vocabulary, comprehension, and grade-point averages for a group of nursing students. Students were pretested; following 27 hours of training, post-tests were given. The results indicated there was no significant growth in comprehension, vocabulary, or grade-point averages; but significant "growth" was reported for reading rate. A possible conclusion from Reed's study is that the improvement of the rate scores was not the result of the instructional program, but rather it was the result of the testing.

Once the question of the test's suitability to the *content* of instruction has been resolved, it is then necessary to turn to the test's appropriateness to the student's instructional level. While a test may validly represent the content of instruction and accurately portray growth for students at one instructional level, it may be quite inappropriate for students at another. For example, an oral reading test may be a useful measure of growth for first- or second-grade students because of the relative emphasis placed on oral reading at those grade levels and because of the need to diagnose the students' word attack skills. However, for average readers at the junior or senior high level, oral reading tests would not be useful because instructional emphasis at these levels is usually placed on silent reading and, while oral and silent reading ability are quite highly correlated at the lower grade levels, they become quite divergent at the upper grades (Gray & Reese, 1957; Wells, 1950).

Highly related to the problem of the appropriate levels of a test is the difficulty of the directions and/or design of a test for students at any given level. A test which is too easy or too hard provides little information about growth. Fisher (1961) has demonstrated that the use of tests which are suggested by the publisher for a particular grade level may not be valid for the advanced or retarded readers of that grade. For example, on the Gates Reading Survey the present author has found in classroom experiments that it is possible for students to get a raw score equivalent to a grade level of 3.0 by random guessing. If the teacher is concerned with growth, a test has to be used on which a student's score is a valid indication of his reading ability and not his chance-guessing.

One problem which is not intrinsic to test selection, but which is critical once the test has been selected, is whether the methods used in administering the test permit evaluation of long-term retention of gains. A test administered immediately after a short-term instructional reading program would reveal only limited evidence concerning the retention of any gains made by the students. Ray (1965) studied the three- and six-month retention of gains made following a thirty hour reading program for college students. No comparison groups were used, but the three- and six-month post-test scores resulted in performance which was significantly superior to pre-test performance. If the objective of the reading program is the retention of gains, then delayed post-testing procedures similar to Ray's should be adopted. However, as Ray pointed out, retention of gains may also be due, in part, to the increased reading demands at higher grade levels and the increased maturation of students. Ray's findings were supported by Smith and Wood (1955) who found that college students after a lapse of time retained and possibly improved those aspects of reading which were emphasized in the reading program.

Another procedure which might be used to measure the permanency of reading improvement is measuring general academic improvement following a remedial reading program. The relation between reading gains and academic performance is a valid estimate of reading improvement if the reading skills related to performance have been a vital part of the reading improvement program.

The use of alternate test forms

Is it desirable to select a test with alternative forms to serve as pre- and post-tests? Davis (1961) believed that it is: he argued that if the same form of a test were used more than once, a student might remember parts of it on a subsequent trial of the test or he might have even inquired about the test's content between testings. Others (Cronbach, 1960), agreeing with Davis, have specifically pointed to a "practice" effect. They have shown that a student, even if he does not remember specific items on a test or look them up during testing intervals, still performs better on that test because he has had practice on it in the form of the pre-test. Curr and Gourlay's (1960) research substantiated this practice effect. They found that when students at the 9.5 grade level were re-tested at one-, three-, and six-month intervals, their mean gains were 10.1, 18.2, and 26.9 months, respectively. Similarly, large practice effects were noted for both the mechanics of reading and reading comprehension at the 7.5 grade level. This study is limited by the small sample used, but the results are still rather amazing. If the practice effects had been compared to students' performance on alternate forms of the test and if these same large gains did not result from performance on the alternate forms, the study would have been more conclusive.

If the theory that practice affects performance if the same test is re-administered is to be accepted, the assumptions underlying this theory should be examined. The first assumption is that a student knows which items he answered incorrectly; the second is that he will recall these items after the test; another is that he will take the time to find out what the correct response is; and the fourth and final assumption is that he will recall the question and the correct response at a later testing time. It seems highly unlikely that these assumptions are valid for most elementary or secondary students. Karlin and Jolly (1965) studied the practice effect with 161 pupils in grades four to eight. In September the appropriate levels of the SRA Achievement Series: Reading, Form A, and the California Reading Test, Form W, were administered to all subjects. In May these same tests were re-administered along with their alternate forms. After a nine-month interval, there was no difference in the amount of growth reported by either the alternate forms and the same test, administered a second time. Karlin and Jolly concluded that their results raise serious doubts about the need for alternate forms of a test for measuring growth. Of course, their conclusions are limited by the nine-month period of comparison used in the study as well as by the relatively small sample of elementary school children used. Nonetheless, Karlin and Jolly's study still stresses the need for more research along the lines they used, covering varying periods of time and using different student populations.

Should research, however, prove that alternate forms are useful and necessary, the test consumer is still faced with the problem of the comparability of the alternate forms for any given test—i.e., does the post-test measure the same skills as the pre-tests? Dotson and Bliesmer (1955) examined the comparability of forms A, B, and C of the Diagnostic Reading Test: Survey Section. The forms were administered to 100 incoming freshmen at the University of Texas. It was found that the total scores on Forms A and C and the total scores on Forms B and C were not comparable. Coates (1968) reported a similar study in which Forms A, B, C, and D of the Diagnostic Reading Test: Survey Section were given to a group of 63 entering freshmen at St. Petersburg Junior College. Correlations between the test forms ranged from .53 to .87. Coates concluded that the range of these correlations cast considerable doubt on the equivalency of the four test forms. It would appear that the results of both these studies should provide a basis for a more careful examination of the comparability of test forms.

Even if the statistical equivalency of test forms could be established, there would still be unanswered questions about the content equivalency of any two forms. It would be impossible for a test developer to control all the variables on a reading test from one form to another. The difficulty of the vocabulary, the content of the material, and the sentence length and complexity are all variables which most test authors attempt to control, but for each factor that is controlled, there are several others which are uncontrolled. If two forms were exactly equivalent, the result would be that the same student getting a certain number of items correct on one form of the test would get exactly the same number correct on another form of the test. This is almost never the case since one test form is usually more difficult than another and the tests are equated through statistical procedures. With most parallel forms, the tests have been normed on the same populations or random samples from the same population, but if this has not been done the equivalency of test forms even on a statistical basis would also be void.

Validity of norms for measuring growth

If one chooses to evaluate growth in reading by comparing the performance of a particular class or group of classes with that of a national norm, it is necessary first to be sure that the population on which the test has been normed is comparable to the class which is being tested. It is always good practice to examine carefully the description of the norm population provided by the test publisher. Included in such descriptions should be all those variables which are relevant to growth in reading ability such as socio-economic class, intelligence levels, and geographic area. If these variables are not comparable to the group being tested or if the information is not supplied by the test publisher, the use of the norm data for comparing growth is not a valid procedure.

Another factor which is important for the test consumer to consider is how many times during a school year the particular test was administered in the course of being normed. In most instances, tests are administered only once and the grade norms for each month of the school year are interpolated from this single administration. The use of such grade norms obviously is based on the hypothesis that reading growth follows a fairly even pattern. Bernard (1966) examined this hypothesis by studying the applicability of published achievement test norms to testing programs taking place at different times during the school year. He concluded that children's growth in achievement does not follow a regular growth curve with progress occurring evenly throughout the school year and no growth occurring during the intervening summer. Bernard cautioned against test publisher's use of extrapolation to convert spring and fall testing to a common base. He (1966, p. 275) suggested three procedures to overcome these weaknesses: 1] schedule testing programs dictated by the norms of the tests to be used, 2] select a test normed at about the time of year testing is to be done, 3] forget the published national norms altogether and use only local norms.

Lennon (1951) also cautioned against using norms gathered at one testing period for predicting achievement at a different testing period—the procedure which must be followed if tests are normed at only one time during the year. Lennon found correlations ranging from only .51 to .69 for two adjacent grades from grades two to eight. While these correlations are fairly large, Lennon pointed out that there would be a large amount of error variance in predicting relative reading achievement in any grade from the achievement even in the next grade. For example, if the correlation between two tests given in two different grades was .60 (this is the median of the correlations reported by Lennon), only 36 per cent of the variance in the second test performance would be accounted for by the first test performance. This leaves 64 per cent of the variance unaccounted for.

The study of individual pupils' reading growth patterns has shown that this growth has been quite irregular. While the rank correlations at two different test administration times has been shown to be fairly high (Townsend, 1951), the individual growth patterns of students has been shown to be quite uneven by Traxler (1950, p. 107) who warned teachers that they "should not be disturbed when they find that their pupils fail to grow according to the average of the group. Nonconformity to the group's pattern of growth is the rule and conformity is the exception." He also pointed out, as did Lennon, that any deviations from previous testing cannot always be interpreted as a reading gain or loss because test scores always contain a certain amount of error of measurement.

Socio-economic factors are also important in the interpretation of test norms. MacArthur and Mosychuk (1966) studied the predictive validity of ninth-grade academic achievement test scores from a variety of aptitude and achievement tests administered in grades three, six, and seven. Test results were grouped on the basis of the parents' socio-economic status. The median correlations of all predictors with all criteria scores rose from grade three to grade seven for the upper status group and

fell for the lower group.   If the achievement test results of children from lower socio-economic status are compared to the expected growth from test norms based on those from a relatively
higher socio-economic status, it would seem that the comparisons will not be valid.

Procedures for assessing change

A variety of procedures have been suggested for determining
the amount of growth in reading an individual attains over any
given period.   Harris (1967) has edited a book of readings
which includes several articles on the problems of measuring
change as well as a variety of statistical models, both theoretical
and practical, which are advanced as solutions to these problems.   Most procedures for measuring change have been devised to overcome two major obstacles: 1] the fact that most
reading improvement programs are developed for the poorest
readers and 2] the relative unreliability of single measures of
reading ability.

The first obstacle—the fact that most reading improvement
programs are devised for the poorest readers in a group—
means that the procedure for measuring growth entails the following: 1] administration of a reading test to all students in a
particular grade or in several grades, 2] selection of those
scoring at the lowest end of the distribution on the test for a
reading improvement program, 3] administration of a post-test
after the reading improvement program, and 4] comparison of
post-test scores with pre-test scores (original test).   Given such
a method, significant improvement is usually noted and the
reading program is labelled a success.   But is this improvement
really significant? It is possible to find significant gains for any
group of students even if no instructional program intervened, if
their inclusion in the program was based on their having scored
at the extreme end of the distribution of test scores on the pre-
test.   This occurs because of the phenomenon known as regression toward the mean—there is a high probability that a student

who scores at one extreme of the distribution of scores on a pre-test will tend to score nearer the mean on subsequent re-tests. For a detailed discussion of the regression effect as well as suggestions for avoiding it, the reader is referred to Lord's (1967) article.

The second major obstacle involved in procedures for evaluating growth—the relative unreliability of single measures of reading ability—derives from inadequate knowledge of what sub-skills are involved in reading and how they can be measured. For this reason alone, any single measure of reading performance is limited by sampling errors (Kingston, 1965). While the reliability would seem to be higher when more than one measurement procedure is employed, there is little or no knowledge of how the various measures should be combined. The most widely accepted procedure at the present time is to change the raw scores from each test to some type of standard scores and then to combine the standard scores.

Are both these obstacles (regression effects and the unreliability of single measures) insurmountable? Davis (1961) apparently did not think so. He offered five procedures for evaluating reading growth on an individual basis and three for evaluating growth on a group basis. Davis discussed each of the procedures for estimating the reading growth on an individual basis in terms of a hypothetical case of a student who made a gain of five raw score points from a pre- to post-test. In the first procedure described, the pre-test score was subtracted from the post-test score and compared with the probability of such a change occurring by chance. This chance occurrence was based on the standard error of measurement of the test. In Davis' hypothetical case, a gain of five points was not significant at the .15 level. The second procedure Davis discussed involved using two measures in the pre-test and two measures in the post-test and averaging the results. Under these conditions, the hypothetical five point gain was considered significant because of the increased accuracy of measurement. In the third procedure, any number of pre- and post-test measures were used to increase the accuracy of measurement. Davis' fourth and fifth procedures were designed to eliminate the effects of selecting a student for a reading improvement program on the basis of extreme scores. Both methods four and five compensated for the regression effect by estimating the improvement for a student scoring at one extreme of the distribution. In addition, the fifth method increased the accuracy of estimation by considering the correlation of pre- and post-test scores for all the students tested.

Davis' three methods for estimating change on a group basis were based on the assumption that the students have been randomly selected. The first method essentially paralleled the first procedure advocated for assessing individual growth except that group averages for the pre- and post-test scores were subtracted. The second and third methods compensated for the regression effect by determining the correlation between pre- and post-test scores in the same manner that methods four and five did for individuals. These methods devised by Davis are an outstanding contribution to solving the problems of increasing the reliability of estimates of change and providing statistical techniques for removing the effects due to regression.

Tracy and Rankin (1967) applied the residual gain statistic to assessing reading improvement. They pointed out that crude gains (the subtraction of pre-test scores from post-test scores) "tend to underestimate the progress of superior 'improvers' (as measured by residual gain) and to overestimate the progress of inferior 'improvers' " (1967, p. 363). The value of using residual gain scores is that the tests that are used do not have to be expressed in equal intervals scales and, more importantly, the technique removes the regression effect from the measurement of improvement. The computational procedure for residual gain scores is relatively easy to follow:

1] Convert both pre- and post-reading test scores to z scores for each student.
2] Compute the correlation between pre- and post-test raw scores.

3] Obtain predicted post-test z scores by multiplying the correlation coefficient by the pre-test z score for each student.

4] Subtract the predicted post-test z score from the obtained post-test z score for each student.

The result of using this procedure is that a student who attained a residual gain score of 0 would have achieved exactly what was expected of him; a student with a residual gain score of $+ 1.0$ would have improved approximately one standard deviation above his *expected* progress. However, the procedure does have weaknesses: in order to use it, a large number of students must be tested and it is of no value when only one or two students have been administered pre- and post-tests. Another factor limiting the use of the residual gain statistic lies in its interpretation. Tracy and Rankin suggested a procedure for evaluating and changing residual gain scores to course grades; however, their procedure is based on the assumption that a student who scores very high on a pre-test may regress to some extent on the post-test; should he regress too much, he would be penalized. Complications in public school situations would certainly develop if such a student had scored far above the rest of the class on a pre-test and then had fallen back considerably on the post-test while still scoring among the top 25 per cent of the class. If the above procedure were used, it is possible that this student could receive a low grade despite his relatively strong standing. A thorough discussion on the reliability of residual change is presented in the works of Glass (1968) and Traub (1967).

Considerations in estimating growth

The research in measuring reading growth has not been substantial, but even the knowledge afforded by research is not having an effect on the evaluation of reading growth. There are still many problems to be solved before the valid and reliable measurement of reading growth will be possible. In the meantime, the reading practitioner is faced with the necessity of determining the effectiveness of his reading program. The five steps listed below, derived from the studies cited in this chapter, should serve as a guide in evaluating growth. While these steps do not solve all of the problems of measuring change, they will increase the reliability and validity of present assessment practices.

1] The practitioner should carefully define the reading skill or skills being taught and select a measuring instrument or several instruments that are operational definitions of these skills.

2] If test norms are used for comparisons, the test user should be sure that the norm group matches the group being tested on all important factors related to growth in reading. Developing local norms is, for most purposes, the best procedure.

3] Measurement procedures should be used under conditions as closely approximating those of the teaching situation as possible. If instruction has been designed to produce a generalization of the skills, testing should be done under those conditions to which this skill will generalize.

4] If students have been selected for a reading program on the basis of their performance on the lower extremes of test score distribution, some procedure such as the residual gain score should be applied to remove regression effects.

5] Evaluation of change scores should be interpreted cautiously. The irregular growth curves of individuals indicate that reading improvement is uneven and that measurement in reading always involves some error.

There are two areas that should be more closely examined by research. First, there is some contradiction concerning whether to use alternate forms or to reuse the same test. Secondly, the problems of combining teacher evaluations with test evaluations should be thoroughly explored. If teacher and test evaluations could be combined, it would most likely lead to more reliable measurement.

Measuring growth: two unique cases

The general problems and procedures for measuring reading growth have now been discussed and the issues raised are applicable to the measurement of growth in all areas. However, because of a concern evidenced by the large number of research studies in these two areas and because of several problems unique to these areas, the measurement of reading growth for retarded readers and the measurement of growth at the reading readiness level merit special consideration.

Assessing growth for retarded readers

Those who face the task of evaluating the reading growth for students in remedial reading programs face the same task encountered when working with students who progress at a normal rate. There are, however, a number of specific problems peculiar to assessing the progress of retarded readers, the most important of which is the selection of an appropriate test (Fisher, 1961; Glaser, 1964). A test designed for average sixth-grade students is, in all likelihood, inappropriate for sixth-grade students who are seriously retarded in reading ability. For example, a sixth-grade retarded reader might obtain a third-grade level score by chance even if he could read only at a first- or second-grade level. Upon re-testing, after a semester of intensive remedial help, he might again score at the third-grade level, but this time the score might be an accurate index of his actual reading ability. Despite rather substantial reading growth, the test results would indicate that this student had shown no improvement in reading ability. Most standardized reading tests do not indicate the score that can be achieved by chance; but the teacher should determine what a chance score might be and, if a student gets a score at or below the chance level, a different test should be administered to that student. Cronbach (1960, p. 49) provides a formula for determining a chance score which teachers might find useful.

Another problem area in measuring reading growth for retarded readers is the evaluation of change scores. Using discrepancies between mental age and reading age is a common procedure for selecting participants for remedial programs. Those students who evidence the most gain in bringing their reading ages closer to their mental ages are considered to be making the best progress. The weakness of this procedure is that the scores on intelligence tests are quite often as significantly improved as the reading tests after remedial reading instruction. Frost (1963) found significant correlations between improvement in reading test scores and group intelligence test scores for eight to ten year olds who had been in a remedial reading program. He concluded that because of the high correlations between intelligence tests and reading tests, intelligence tests are of little use in predicting reading gain. A more serious point was made by Frost: when students are excluded from a remedial reading program because of low intelligence test scores, some of the students excluded could perhaps have profited more than some students who were included. In his study, Frost found that 29 students who had made the greatest gains had the lowest intelligence test scores. Certainly, the present widespread practice of using intelligence test scores as a criteria for selecting participants for a remedial program should be carefully examined.

Woodcock (1958) attempted to resolve this problem by developing a test designed to duplicate as nearly as possible the process of learning to read so that performance on the test might be truly indicative of a student's ability to profit from remedial instruction. Woodcock concluded that his test has predictive value in selecting cases for remedial reading instruction and was of greater value than the usual procedure of selecting students for remedial programs on the basis of discrepancies between reading capacity and reading achievement. However, as Frost indicated, there are very few comparative studies which have examined predictive procedures for determining success in remedial reading.

Several authors have examined the most common method of determining growth for retarded readers—the method involves subtracting pre-test scores from post-test scores and using these as evidence of progress. Bliesmer (1962) has pointed out that an assumption underlying this procedure is that the children in remedial programs have been selected because they have not been making normal progress. He compared three methods for evaluating progress for retarded readers: 1] determining gains by the typical method of finding differences between pre- and post-test scores, 2] comparing remedial program gains with average yearly gains made by the remedial students before they were enrolled in the remedial program, and 3] finding differences between reading potential and reading achievement levels (potential-achievement gaps) at the beginning and at the end of a remedial program. The improvement shown by method one was about equivalent to what might be expected for normal readers; when the change scores were compared to yearly gains made before the remedial program (method two), the gains were from one and one-half to four times greater; the potential-achievement gap differences did not show as significant improvement as the other two methods.

Libaw, Berres, and Coleman (1962) suggested a method for evaluating the effectiveness of remedial treatment which is very similar to Bliesmer's second method. The six steps outlined by Libaw, Berres, and Coleman include: 1] obtaining measures of achievement prior to treatment, 2] computing the rate of learning prior to treatment, 3] extrapolating to predict achievement after a time interval, 4] obtaining a measure of achievement after treatment has been under way for an interval, 5] comparing the predicted measure with the actual achievement measure, 6] computing a test of significance on the difference between the predicted and obtained achievement measures. There are several weak points in this procedure. The first involves the assumption that the measures of rate of learning before remedial instruction are reliable. As was pointed out previously, the use of grade level tests for seriously retarded readers may lead to unreliable assessments of reading performance. Another shortcoming is that the procedure would probably necessitate the use of several standardized reading tests which have been normed on various populations. It would be invalid to assess growth by using one standardized test as a pretest and a different one as a post-test. The reasons for this include the differences in the skills measured by each test and the different populations used for norming each test. The problem caused by having different norming populations could be overcome if local norms were developed for each of the tests.

As in all reading evaluation, another difficulty in assessing the growth of retarded readers is the lack of means to measure the long term effects of instruction. Much short-term improvement which has appeared quite significant when tests are administered immediately following remedial instruction are found to be non-existent when students are tested at a later date. This was investigated by Shearer (1967) who compared a group of students who received follow-up remedial instruction with a group who did not. At the conclusion of the remedial program, the mean reading grades of the two groups were about equal; but the group that received follow-up instruction performed significantly higher at a later testing period. Children who did not attend the special reading classes but who had been recommended for it were also tested at follow-up testing time. These children scored at the same level of achievement as the group that had received the remedial program but did not receive follow-up instruction. Others, such as Balow and Blomquist (1965) and Preston and Yarington (1967) have studied long-range procedures evaluating the effects of remedial instruction. In these studies, however, the jobs in which subjects were employed were used as the criteria for determining the long-range success of remedial instruction.

There are two specific problems brought up earlier under the discussion of general problems in assessing reading growth which should be reiterated here in relation to retarded readers. The first involves the use of test norms. Retarded readers form an atypical population and comparing their growth with that of a normed typical population is completely inappropriate. It is questionable that standardized tests should be used for them in the first place. Secondly, in planning a remedial program the reading teacher often develops a program which is based on the specific reading problems of the students in his class. This should place a stronger emphasis on carefully selecting a test based on the objectives of the instructional program for each individual student. The best evaluation of this growth, when instruction is on such an intensive and highly individual basis, is the student's performance in the daily task of mastering reading skills. Any measurement procedures along this line would be highly related to the specific objectives of the instructional program: the norm comparisons would be quite appropriate (the student would be compared only with his own previous learning rate and to what he had learned previously) and the evaluation would be reliable and accurate since a larger than usual sampling of behavior could take place. There is only one assumption underlying this procedure: the teacher must be knowledgeable about the development of reading skills.

Reading readiness: predicting early achievement

Reading readiness tests pose unique problems for measurement. They are most commonly used to determine if a child has sufficient command of skills necessary to begin formal reading instruction. Given this function, these tests become instruments of assessing not only the child's capabilities, but also his growth in these capabilities. Thus, they enable the test user to *predict* how well a given student will progress in developing his reading skills. Another major use of reading readiness tests is diagnostic: they are used to pinpoint those skills which the student needs to develop further. The predictive validity of readiness tests has been studied quite extensively; however, the diagnostic validity of the tests has received little attention. The basic conclusion from these various research efforts seem to be that scores on readiness tests have a fair amount of predictive validity (Bremer, 1959; Henig, 1949; McCall & McCall, 1965), but there is almost no evidence that the increased teaching of these skills will ensure success in learning to read (Barrett, 1966). This is probably due to the failure of readiness tests to assess many of the more important habits and attitudes related to reading readiness.

The tests most predictive of reading ability seem to be those which are most similar to the act of reading (Barrett, 1965). This is not surprising since a test should be a sample of the behavior which it is supposed to measure; furthermore, a test which predicts best is one which is most like the behavior it is supposed to predict. The best example of this is that the consistently single best predictor of future school grades is past school grades. In comparing seven pre-reading tasks—recognition of letters, matching words, discrimination of beginning sounds in words, discrimination of vowel sounds in words, discrimination of ending sounds in words, shape completion, and copy-a-sentence—with reading test scores at the end of first grade, Barrett (1966) found that recognition of letters was the best single predictor. Of the seven tasks, the recognition of letters most closely resembles actual reading. Matching of words also seems to possess many of the components prerequisite to reading; however, in this task the child does not have to name the shape he has visually perceived as being different, as he does in naming letters. As Barrett cogently pointed out, the finding that the naming of letters is a relatively good predictor of beginning reading is not unique and student performance on this task has no validated diagnostic value. He further suggested that this skill is perhaps an indication of the child's early and broad experiences with written materials and, therefore, "it should not be inferred from this study that teaching children to recognize letters by name will necessarily ensure success in beginning reading" (1966, p. 463).

Nash (1963) also found that tests which most closely resembled reading were the most predictive. The Metropolitan Readiness Test, selected items from the Stanford-Binet Intelligence Test, a sociometric technique, the Draw-a-Man Test, Learning Rate of Words Inventory, New Gestalt Test, and the Maturity Level for Reading Readiness were administered to 132 first-grade children at the beginning of the school year. The criterion test, the Gates Primary Reading Test, was administered the last week in February. Nash concluded that the predictor tests which measured specific aspects of the reading process were the best predictors of future reading success.

Weiner and Feldman's (1963) study of the Reading Prognosis Test also provides ample evidence for predictive validity of tests resembling reading. One of the best predictors from this test was a sub-test called Beginning Reading. It appears naive not to assume that a student's performance on a sub-test called Beginning Reading is highly predictive of achievement in beginning reading. Actually Weiner and Feldman's study could be considered a concurrent validity rather than a predictive validity study.

Weintraub (1967) reviewed eighteen recent studies related to the ability of readiness measures to predict reading achievement. The readiness factors included in these studies were a numbers sub-test, a visual discrimination test, an auditory discrimination test, the Bender-Gestalt test, a test of visual-motor skills, the Draw-a-Man Test, a verbal fluency test, a measure of speech patterns, and length of attention span. The test which seemed to be the best single predictor of reading achievement according to these studies was the numbers sub-test of the Metropolitan Readiness Test. This same conclusion was reached by Abbott (1963) who found that the numbers sub-test of the Metropolitan Readiness Test was one of the best predictors of reading achievement.

The majority of the predictive validity studies, e.g., Henig (1949) and Mattick (1963), have indicated that the ability of readiness tests to predict reading achievement is better than chance and that this prediction can be improved by the inclusion of other measurement procedures including teacher observations. In the conclusion of his review, Weintraub (1967, p. 557) pleaded for the development of more highly refined readiness tests: "A survey of the literature on prediction, then, leads us to conclude that there is an urgent need for the development of better measures or batteries of measures than we now have. This development calls for creativity on the part of researchers and reading teachers in general. New directions need to be investigated." Some of the directions Weintraub suggested include measurement of attention span, oral language, and children's self-evaluations. The importance of self-evaluations for children from various sub-cultures was also stressed as being an especially important research area.

What are some of the factors which seem to affect the predictive validity of readiness tests? Those that have been reported in the research literature include socio-economic status, sex differences, and personality differences. One that has not been studied at all is the effect of the instructional program in reading. Here again, the matching of test objectives to the objectives of the instructional program constitutes a major problem neglected by research. It seems logical to conclude that readiness tests will predict reading performance better when the instructional program follows the same pattern as the test. For example, it could be hypothesized that an auditory discrimination test might predict reading success best when the instructional program is heavily oriented toward a phonics approach. Interpretation of the predictive validity studies on reading readiness would also be improved if the authors would describe the content of the reading programs which intervened between the readiness test as the pre-test and the reading achievement test as the post-test.

The particular sub-culture from which a child comes appears to be an important variable in the predictive validity of readiness tests. After administering a series of individual and group readiness tests to 105 Negro, white, Puerto Rican, and oriental first-grade pupils who were considered to be culturally different, Loper (1965) concluded that group tests did not adequately measure reading readiness for children from these backgrounds. Conflicting findings were reported by Weiner and Feldman (1963) who developed a readiness test designed to measure language, perceptual discrimination, and beginning reading skills. Comparative correlations between the readiness test and later reading achievement for low and middle-class children were found to be quite similar. The correlations between Weiner and Feldman's Reading Prognosis Test and the Paragraph Reading Test of the Gates Primary Reading Test for lower-class children was .72; for middle-class children, the correlation was .77. When the Sentence Reading Test of the Gates Primary Reading Test was the criterion test, the correlations were .68 for lower-class children and .74 for middle-class children. Another study of cultural bias in readiness tests was conducted by Standish (1959). Standish found that predictions from American readiness tests, when used with children in British schools, frequently were inadequate because the norms established on American populations rarely went as low as the age levels required for beginners in Britain.

The value of providing separate norms for each sex was discussed in Chapter 1 where it was concluded that doing so was neither useful nor necessary for reading achievement tests. The same conclusion was made in regard to readiness tests by Prescott (1955) in his study comparing the performance of 7,821 boys and 7,138 girls from 56 communities throughout the United States on the Metropolitan Readiness Test. Prescott found that the mean performance of girls was slightly superior to that of boys (2.14 raw score points) and that this difference was statistically significant.   However, this significance was probably due to the large sample sizes used—the strength of the relationship between the readiness scores for boys and girls would certainly be extremely high.   When the mean scores of average boys were compared with those of average girls and when the mean scores of under-age boys were compared with under-age girls, the mean differences in reading readiness test scores were not significant.

Personality differences could also seemingly affect the predictive validity of readiness tests. Lockhart (1965) correlated the Personal Adjustment and Social Adjustment sub-tests of the California Test of Personality with the Metropolitan Readiness Test.   The Social Adjustment sub-test correlated with reading readiness tests at a negligible level, but the Personal Adjustment sub-test and the readiness test correlations were significant at the .01 level for the total group ($r = .51$) and for boys ($r = .64$). It would have been useful if the research had gone further and performed a multiple correlation analysis between these two tests and later reading achievement.   This would have provided useful information concerning the added usefulness of administering a personality test as well as a readiness test for predicting reading achievement.

A great number of tests and test procedures have been employed as predictors of reading readiness.   Included among these have been teacher ratings, standardized reading readiness tests, intelligence tests, language development tests, perceptual-motor tests, projective tests, and tests of auditory and visual discrimination.   Because of the vast number of studies involving each of these procedures, it is impossible to note all of them. Therefore, only those studies which appear to be key to the development of the measurement of readiness skills and those which have been conducted more recently are covered in the present review.

Two studies—by Kermonian (1962) and Henig (1949)— dealing with the comparative predictive validity of teacher ratings of reading readiness were discussed earlier.   Both studies concluded that teacher forecasts and readiness tests are highly correlated and are equally valid procedures in predicting later reading achievement. Similar conclusions have been reached by other researchers. In particular, Henderson and Long (1968) found that the variance in reading readiness test scores is due to quite varied maturational-experiential factors which can only be explained through teacher ratings of students' behaviors. Most of the reported studies have discovered that teacher ratings are relatively good predictors when compared with other measurement procedures. Zaruba (1968) found that the closest relationship between reading grade placement scores given by teachers at the end of first grade was a test of letter recognition administered at the beginning of the year; a teacher evaluation given at the same time was next closest and a draw-a-man test was third closest. Lack of statistical analysis, however, limited the interpretation of Zaruba's study. Mattick (1963) compared two standardized reading readiness tests, the Metropolitan Readiness Test and the Lee-Clark Reading Readiness Test; and two standardized intelligence tests, the California Test of Mental Maturity and the Lorge-Thorndike Intelligence Test; and kindergarten teachers' predictions with teachers' assessments of first graders' early success in reading. The Metropolitan Readiness Test was the best predictor and the kindergarten teachers' ratings were the second best predictor. Alshan (1965) found that the best predictors of first-grade reading, as measured by the Word Recognition Test of Gates Primary Reading Test, in order of importance as predictors of reading, were a test of auditory blending, the Roswell-Chall Auditory Blending Test; an experimental consonant combinations test; teachers' ratings; an experimental test of visual discrimination; an experimental test of letter names and sounds; and an experimental test of oral language proficiency. Alshan factor-analyzed these measures and found that the teacher ratings loaded heavily on a single factor. This led to the conclusion that the teachers rated the children in a global fashion. A study which investigated teachers' attitudes toward ratings was carried out by Standish (1959). In research carried out in England, Standish discovered that while good teachers report reading readiness is difficult to predict, many teachers considered prediction of readiness a matter of instinct. The teachers in Standish's study, like their American counterparts, considered students' motivation high on the list of behaviors characterizing children who are ready to learn how to read.

A serious problem affecting the predictive validity of readiness tests is that the predictions seem to vary for particular populations. Savage (1959) suggested that some of these population variables include sex differences, socio-economic status, and the effects of practice in taking tests. There has also been some controversy over whether reading readiness tests are most useful as tests for predicting future reading achievement or whether their greater usefulness is in diagnosing readiness skills. A study by Karzen, Suvetor, and Thompson (1965) raised serious doubt about the predictive validity of readiness tests. They found that the Metropolitan Achievement Tests: Reading predicted reading achievement for first-grade children but it was highly correlated with the Lorge-Thorndike Intelligence test scores. They concluded that "children tend to perform in reading according to the level of the room in which they are placed, regardless of their ability as measured by conventional intelligence tests" (Karzen, Suvetor, & Thompson, 1965, p. 22). The implication of this finding is that the placement of children into groups according to their readiness scores tends to encourage them to achieve according to the expectation of the group in which they were placed. In other words, it would mean that placement, not readiness skill development, is the key to success in learning to read. Other researchers have urged caution in using readiness test scores to place students in reading groups. The relationships between the results of the Lee-Clark Reading Readiness Test administered at the beginning of first grade and the California Reading Test administered to the same pupils at the beginning of second grade were studied by Powell and Parsley (1961; Parsley & Powell, 1961). Separate correlations were computed for high, average, and low reading achievement groups. Because the correlations for the low group were negligible, the authors concluded that the Lee-Clark test is useful only as a predictor of the reading achievement for the entire group and should not be used diagnostically for placing children into reading groups.

Contradictory conclusions were reached by Bremer (1959). Bremer correlated the results of the Metropolitan Readiness Tests given at the beginning of first grade with the reading subtests of the Gray-Votaw-Rogers General Achievement Tests given at the beginning of second grade for 2,069 students. A Pearson product-moment correlation of the test scores produced a correlation of .40. A coefficient of alienation of .92 was then computed. This, Bremer said, indicated that the readiness test had an index of forecasting efficiency of eight per cent. However, the procedure in computing this correlation of alienation was never explained. Despite this shortcoming, Bremer's conclusion that the readiness tests are not very useful predictive instruments seems to be substantiated by his study. What is surprising is his conclusion that "readiness tests can be of great help in pointing out the deficiencies in the reading readiness of individual pupils" (1959, p. 224). Bremer had spent the bulk of his research report criticizing the readiness test for lack of predictive validity. Here he suggested that they can be used for diagnostic purposes, in spite of the fact that he failed to provide diagnostic or construct validity evidence to support this recommendation.

The use of intelligence tests as predictors of beginning reading achievement has been the focus of several investigations. Mattick (1963) found that group intelligence tests were poorer predictors of first-grade reading achievement than reading readiness tests or teacher ratings. A similar finding was reported by McCall and McCall (1965) when they compared the predictive validity of the Metropolitan Readiness Test (MRT) and the California Test of Mental Maturity (CTMM) with the Metropolitan Achievement Tests: Reading (MAT) and the California

Achievement Test (CAT). The CTMM correlated with CAT total score .39, while the MRT correlated with the CAT .64. The same situation resulted when the MAT was the criterion score. The CTMM correlated with the sub-tests of the MAT at significantly lower levels than the MRT.

Group intelligence tests have been shown to be relatively poor predictors of beginning reading success, but is this also true for individually administered intelligence tests? Comparisons of the relative correlations of Metropolitan Readiness Tests (MRT) and Stanford-Binet Intelligence Scale scores to Metropolitan Achievement Test (MAT) scores indicated inconclusive results (Weiser, 1965). Weiser reached this conclusion after reviewing studies by Hildreth and Griffiths (1933), Foster (1937), Wilson and Fleming (1938), Dean (1939), Keister (1941), Gavel (1958), Mitchell (1962), and Weiser (1964). In Foster's (1937) study, the Stanford-Binet scores correlated with Metropolitan Achievement Test scores .51 and the MRT correlated with the same achievement test only .38; in Wilson and Fleming's (1938) study, there were opposite results with the Stanford-Binet scores correlating with MAT scores .51 while MRT and MAT scores correlated .60. In Weiser's (1964) study with a small sample of 24 academically superior students, the MRT correlated with MAT scores .58, while Stanford-Binet scores corelated only .13. Of some surprise in Weiser's study was the additional finding that when a multiple r of MRT and Stanford-Binet scores were correlated with MAT scores, the coefficient dropped to .48.

Parsley and Powell (1961), as mentioned earlier, also found that Stanford-Binet scores were relatively poor predictors of reading readiness. They correlated Lee-Clark Reading Readiness Test scores with Stanford-Binet test scores for 169 first graders. The correlations, while positive, were fairly low— ranging from .35 to .48. It was concluded that intelligence test scores are relatively poor predictors of reading readiness. This would have been better substantiated if the tests had been correlated with later reading achievement rather than with a readiness test.

The results of the Davis-Eells Test of General Intelligence which attempts to minimize the influence of socio-economic differences, were compared to Stanford-Binet I.Q. scores in terms of its ability to predict behavior on the Gates Primary Reading Test administered at the end of the first grade (Russell, 1956). The correlations were .57 for the Stanford-Binet and .21 for the Davis-Eells test. Russell (1956, p. 270) concluded that "the Stanford-Binet test gives a better prediction of reading progress during the first year's instruction than the Davis-Eells test."

A large factor determining performance on intelligence tests is language ability. It is perhaps this aspect of intelligence tests which explains the partial correlation of intelligence tests with beginning reading. Morrison (1962) studied the relationship between maturity in the use of various types of sentence structure and children's scores on the Lee-Clark Reading Readiness Test. The children's oral language was recorded during "sharing" time and was classified according to the complexity of sentence structure. The complexity of the children's sentence structure correlated with the raw scores of the Lee-Clark .72, while the children's ability to recall incidents in a story read to them orally correlated with the Lee-Clark .79. On the basis of this study, it is certainly apparent that additional research investigating the predictive validity of oral language development is needed.

Research on the use of perception or perceptual-motor tests in predicting reading achievement have been inconclusive. In general, though, these tests do seem to be better predictors of achievement than intelligence test scores. Two studies have shown that scores on the Bender-Gestalt are adequate predictors of first-grade reading achievement. Koppitz, Mardis, and Stephens (1962) found that the Bender correlated with the Metropolitan Readiness Test – .59 and the Lee-Clark Reading Readiness Test – .61. The correlations were negative because the Bender is scored for errors; however, this does not affect the strength of relationship. The Bender was then compared to the two readiness tests in predicting end-of-first-grade achievement on the Metropolitan Achievement Test, Primary I Battery, Form R. The Bender was shown to be as good a predictor of achievement as the two readiness tests. Smith and Keogh (1962) supported this finding when they used the Bender-Gestalt on a group basis for predicting reading achievement. They concluded:

> . . . the group Bender-Gestalt, when rated with an author-developed rating scale, is an effective and useful screening instrument for evaluating the readiness level of children, comparable to our sample, who are preparing to enter a formal reading program. (Smith & Keogh, 1962, p. 645)

The importance of perception skills in predicting reading achievement was stressed by Scott (1968) who developed a seriation (perception) test. Scott administered his seriation test to 173 kindergarten children and correlated these scores with their reading scores on the California Achievement Test administered at the end of second grade. On the basis of the data, Scott concluded that a child's pre-reading capacity to process visual stimuli is an important aspect of reading readiness. The correlation between the seriation test score and the California Achievement Test reading achievement score was .59. Fox (1953) also found that perception scores were generally adequate predictors of first-grade reading achievement. He administered a tachistoscopic perception test, the Metropolitan Readiness Test, the Row-Peterson Readiness Test, and the Kuhlmann-Anderson Intelligence Tests to beginning first graders. Results of these tests were compared at the end of first grade with the Gates Primary Reading Test, a teacher rating score card, an author-constructed oral reading comprehension test, and a rating based on number of books read. The conclusions, based on these correlations, were that the ability to perceive tachistoscopically projected images is an important aspect of reading readiness. In addition,

Fox found that the tachistoscope test was slightly superior to the two readiness tests in predicting success in reading.

Robinson, Mozzi, Wittick, and Rosenbloom (1960) in a three-year longitudinal study found that the Children's Perceptual Achievement Test has only slight relationship to reading achievement in first grade. Howe (1963) also found that the author-constructed Visual Fusion Threshold Test was only moderately related to reading readiness and early reading tasks. He concluded that this test accounted only for a physical factor as one aspect of reading readiness and that the test bears no relation to the intellectual aspects of reading.

At least two studies (Meyer, 1953; Ames & Walker, 1964) have attempted to use the results of a projective test, the Rorschach, as a predictor of later reading achievement. Meyer's study revealed significant differences in the use of the diverse Rorschach variables between achieving and retarded readers at the beginning of third grade (the Rorschach tests had been given to these same children at the kindergarten level). The retarded readers were "unable to differentiate in their perceptual experiences beyond rather inaccurate, vague, and mediocre global perceptions" (1953, p. 423). Meyer concluded:

> . . . kindergarten Rorschach records may not only be used as prognostic tests of reading achievement in the primary grades, but may also be used to provide data on first grade reading readiness, particularly in the areas of intellectual and emotional readiness. (1953, pp. 424-25)

Ames and Walker (1964) correlated Rorschach scores and Wechsler Intelligence Scale for Children (WISC) scores administered in kindergarten with the reading test scores of the Stanford Achievement Test: Reading Test administered to the same children at the end of fifth grade. The WISC correlated .57 with the reading achievement scores and the Rorschach correlated .53 with the reading achievement scores. The relatively long time period between the administration of the predictor tests (the Rorschach and the WISC) and the criterion test makes these correlations even more significant. Of even greater importance is the multiple correlation (.73) between the WISC and Rorschach scores with fifth-grade reading achievement.

While visual discrimination tests have been found to be adequate predictors of reading achievement, auditory discrimination tests have been found to be less predictive. Shea (1964) found the Visual Discrimination Word Test: Schonell Reading Test administered at the beginning of first grade was superior to the Metropolitan Readiness Test in predicting word recognition ability after five months of formal instruction in reading.

Dykstra (1962) found that the use of auditory discrimination tests improved very little on the prediction of reading achievement afforded by intelligence test scores. A similar finding was reported by Thompson (1963) who concluded that auditory discrimination and intelligence are highly intercorrelated and that each is about equally predictive of success in primary reading.

Most research dealing with the validity of various tests for predicting success in beginning reading have covered only short time spans. In such studies, the predictors are usually administered at the end of kindergarten or the beginning of first grade and the criteria tests are administered at the end of first grade or the beginning of second grade. In one long-term study, Moreau (1950) found that predictions of reading achievement based on test scores on the Pintner-Cunningham Primary Test and on the Lee-Clark Reading Readiness Test were almost as reliable in predicting sixth-grade achievement on the California Basic Skills Test as they were for predicting first-grade achievement. Moreau cautioned against using the tests for individual prediction but suggested that both tests could be used as screening devices. Sutton (1960) examined the variation in reading achievement over a seven-year period for children who scored high on the Metropolitan Reading Readiness Test in kindergarten. Sutton concluded that of the 210 five-year-olds who scored at this high level, only eight were not by the sixth grade working up to capacity predicted by the test.

Using readiness tests The major conclusion from this review of the various attempts to measure reading readiness is that readiness tests generally have positive, but fairly low correlations with later reading achievement. While readiness tests have been generally the best predictors of achievement, teacher forecasts, tests of perception, and measures of language ability all appear to be somewhat valid predictors. Intelligence tests, probably because of their high correlations with these various measures, do not seem to add to the predictive validity of readiness tests. One of the most important shortcomings of the predictive studies of readiness tests is that the researchers usually fail to describe the initial reading program. Until this is done, the predictive validity of readiness tests will remain an unanswered question. The evidence regarding sub-cultural differences in predicting reading achievement are not very conclusive. On the other hand, there is fairly substantial evidence that sex differences do affect the predictive validity of reading readiness tests, but this is probably caused by the uniformity in beginning reading instruction for both boys and girls.

The lack of studies relating the predictions of readiness measures to the types of subsequent instructional programs limits the conclusions of the many researchers who indicated that readiness tests can be used diagnostically. Future research needs to focus on investigations in which the readiness test scores are used to provide information concerning the need for the development of specific readiness skills. Under ideal conditions, the eventual correlations of these readiness test scores and later reading achievement would be reduced to near zero because the effect of instruction would be designed to strengthen specific weaknesses and, therefore, lower the correlations. Of course, this direction for future study is based on the assumption that the readiness skills measured by present standardized readiness tests are the key variables related to reading achievement. The increased power of predictions when various tests of personality (Rorschach) or perception (Bender-Gestalt) are added to readiness test scores indicates that there are several important predictors which have yet to be examined. In addition, the interactions of these factors need to be examined. Yet another area in which research might well prove fruitful is that of evaluating long-term prediction of reading readiness tests, especially if evidence can be found to support the contention that the continued teaching of readiness skills is important to later reading success. The search for a non-verbal intelligence test which will be useful in predicting achievement for beginning reading is probably not a productive area for research because of the strong correlations between language factors, intelligence tests, and tests of beginning reading. Finally, in regard to predicting achievement for beginning reading, a discrimination should be made between long-term and short-term prediction. It is probable that while naming and recognizing letters of the alphabet are good short-term predictors, experiential background, motivation, and oral language development may perhaps be better long-term predictors.

Because of the need for additional research, any suggestions for using readiness tests are of necessity tentative. However, there seems to be enough evidence to warrant the following procedures for selecting and using readiness tests:

1] Select a readiness test which measures the necessary prerequisite skills to learning to read for the particular reading program that is to follow the readiness testing.
2] Develop local norms, both classroom and school, for predicting growth.
3] Use teacher judgments, skills check lists, and readiness tests to increase the validity and reliability of judgments.

A final word on the predictive validity of reading readiness tests may indicate the importance of using these tests for diagnosis rather than prediction. If a readiness test is a perfect predictor, that is if the students who score high on the readiness test also score high on the reading achievement criteria test and vice versa for the poor readers, there may be something wrong with the reading program. For example, if a student scores low on a readiness test and that test is measuring his development in the skills necessary to learn to read, the instructional program should be designed to invalidate the prediction of the readiness test.

References

Abbott, R. F. The prediction of first grade reading and numbers achievement by means of psychological tests. Unpublished doctoral dissertation, University of Tennessee, 1963.

Alshan, L. M. Reading readiness and reading achievements. In J. A. Figurel (Ed.), Reading and inquiry. *Proceedings of the International Reading Association,* 1965, *10,* 312-13.

Ames, Louise B., & Walker, R. N. Prediction of later reading ability from kindergarten Rorschach and I.Q. scores. *Journal of Educational Psychology,* 1964, *55,* 300-13.

Balow, B., & Blomquist, M. Young adults ten to fifteen years after severe reading disability. *Elementary School Journal,* 1965, *66,* 44-48.

Barrett, T. C. Visual discrimination tasks as predictors of first grade reading achievement. *The Reading Teacher,* 1965, *18,* 276-82.

Barrett, T. C. Performance on selected prereading tasks and first grade reading achievement. In J. A. Figurel (Ed.), Vistas in reading. *Proceedings of the International Reading Association,* 1966, *11,* 461-64.

Bernard, J. Achievement tests norms and time of year of testing. *Psychology in the Schools,* 1966, *3,* 273-75.

Bliesmer, E. P. Evaluating progress in remedial reading programs. *The Reading Teacher,* 1962, *15,* 344-50.

Bliesmer, E. P., & Dotson, E. J. A study of the comparability of Forms A and C and of Forms B and C of the Diagnostic Reading Tests. *Yearbook of the National Council on Measurements Used in Education Part I,* 1955, *12,* 6-9.

Bremer, N. Do readiness tests predict success in reading? *Elementary School Journal,* 1959, *59,* 222-24.

Coates, Leslie F. The enigma of the survey section of the Diagnostic Reading Test. In G. B. Schick and M. M. May (Eds.), Multidisciplinary aspects of college-adult reading. *Yearbook of the National Reading Conference,* 1968, *17,* 70-78.

Cronbach, L. F. Essentials of psychological testing. N. Y.: Harper & Row, 1960.

Curr, W., & Gourlay, N. The effects of practice and performance in scholastic tests. *British Journal of Educational Psychology,* 1960, *30,* 155-67.

Davis, F. B. The assessment of change. In E. P. Bliesmer & A. J. Kingston (Eds.), Phases of college and other adult reading programs. *Yearbook of the National Reading Conference,* 1961, *10,* 86-95.

Dean, C. D. Predicting first grade reading achievement. *Elementary School Journal*, 1939, *39*, 609-16.

Dykstra, R. The relationship between selected reading readiness measures of auditory discrimination and reading achievement at the end of first grade. Unpublished doctoral dissertation, University of Minnesota, 1962.

Fisher, J. A. The use of out-of-grade tests with retarded and accelerated readers. Unpublished doctoral dissertation, State University of Iowa, 1961.

Foster, R. The comparative value of reading readiness tests. Paper read at American Association of Applied Psychologists, Minneapolis, Minnesota, 1937.

Fox, H. C. The relationship between the perception of tachistoscopically projected images and reading readiness. *Studies in Education, Thesis Abstract Series,* 1953, *4*, 117-20.

Frost, B. P. The role of intelligence "C" in the selection of children for remedial teaching of reading. *Alberta Journal of Educational Research,* 1963, *9*, 73-78.

Gavel, Sylvia R. June reading achievements of first grade children. *Journal of Education,* 1958, *140*, 37-43.

Glaser, N. A. A comparison of specific reading skills of advanced and retarded readers of fifth grade reading achievement. Unpublished doctoral dissertation, University of Oregon, 1964.

Glass, G. V. Response to Traub's "Note on the reliability of residual change scores." *Journal of Educational Measurement,* 1968, *5*, 265-67.

Gray, Lillian, & Reese, Dora. *Teaching children to read.* New York: Ronald Press, 1957.

Guba, E. G., & Stufflebeam, D. L. *Evaluation: the process of stimulating, aiding, and abetting insightful action.* Columbus, Ohio: Evaluation Center, Ohio State University, 1968.

Harris, C. W. *Problems in measuring change.* Milwaukee, Wisconsin: University of Wisconsin Press, 1967.

Henderson, E. H., & Long, Barbara H. Correlations of reading readiness among children of varying background. *The Reading Teacher,* 1968, *22*, 40-44.

Henig, M. S. Predictive value of a reading readiness test and of teachers' forecasts. *Elementary School Journal,* 1949, *50*, 41-46.

Hildreth, Gertrude H., & Griffiths, Nellie L. *Metropolitan readiness test—manual of directions.* New York: Harcourt, Brace, & World, 1933.

Howe, J. W. The visual fusion threshold (VFT) test as a measure of perceptual efficiency in kindergarten and first grade, and as a possible predictor of later reading retardation. Unpublished doctoral dissertation, University of Southern California, 1963.

Karlin, R., & Jolly, H. The use of alternate forms of standardized reading tests. *The Reading Teacher,* 1965, *19,* 187-91.

Karzen, Judith M., Suvetor, Helene, & Thompson, G. Predicting first grade reading achievement. *Illinois School Research,* 1965, *2,* 20-22.

Keister, B. U. Reading skills acquired by five year old children. *Elementary School Journal,* 1941, *41,* 587-96.

Kermonian, S. B. Teacher appraisal of first grade readiness. *Elementary English,* 1962, *39,* 196-201.

Kingston, A. Is reading what the reading tests test? In E. L. Thurston & L. E. Hafner (Eds.), The philosophical and sociological bases of reading. *Yearbook of the National Reading Conference,* 1965, *14,* 106-09.

Koppitz, Elizabeth M., Mardis, Verilena, & Stephens, T. A note on screening school beginners with the Bender-Gestalt tests. *Journal of Educational Psychology,* 1962, *52,* 80-81.

Lennon, R. T. The stability of achievement tests results from grade to grade. *Educational and Psychological Measurement,* 1951, *11,* 121-27.

Libaw, Frieda, Berres, Frances, & Coleman, J. C. A new method for evaluating the effectiveness of treatment of learning difficulties. *Journal of Educational Research,* 1962, *55,* 582-84.

Lockhart, Hazel M. Personality and reading readiness. *Illinois School Research,* 1965, *2,* 9-11.

Loper, Doris J. Auditory discrimination, intelligence, achievement, and background of experience and information in a culturally disadvantaged first-grade population. Unpublished doctoral dissertation, Temple University, 1965.

Lord, F. M. Elementary models for measuring change. In C. W. Harris (Ed.), *Problems in measuring change.* Milwaukee: University of Wisconsin Press, 1967. Pp. 21-38.

MacArthur, R. S., & Mosychuk, H. Lower and upper socioeconomic group contrasts in long-term predictability of grade nine achievement. *Journal of Educational Measurement,* 1966, *3,* 167-68.

McCall, Rozanne A., & McCall, R. B. A comparison of first grade reading tests. *Illinois School Research,* 1965, *2,* 32-37.

McDonald, A. S. Some pitfalls in evaluating progress in reading instruction. *Phi Delta Kappan,* 1964, *46,* 336-38.

Mattick, W. E. Predicting success in first grade. *Elementary School Journal,* 1963, *63,* 273-76.

Meyer, G. Some relationships between Rorschach scores in kindergarten and reading in the primary grades. *Journal of Projective Techniques,* 1953, *17,* 414-25.

Mitchell, Blythe C. The Metropolitan Reading Readiness Tests as predictors of first grade achievement. *Educational and Psychological Measurement,* 1962, *22,* 765-72.

Moreau, Margaret. Long term prediction of reading success. *California Journal of Educational Research,* 1950, *1,* 173-76.

Morrison, Ida E. The relation of reading readiness to certain language factors. In J. A. Figurel (Ed.), Challenge and experiment in reading. *Proceedings of the International Reading Association,* 1962, *7,* 119-21.

Nash, Patt N. The effectiveness of composite predictors of reading success in the first grade. Unpublished doctoral dissertation, North Texas State University, 1963.

Parsley, K. M., Jr., & Powell, M. Relationships between the Lee-Clark Reading Readiness Test and the 1937 revision of the Stanford-Binet Intelligence Test, Form L. *Journal of Educational Research,* 1961, *54,* 304-07.

Powell, M., & Parsley, K. M., Jr. The relationships between first grade reading readiness and second grade reading achievement. *Journal of Educational Research,* 1961, *54,* 229-33.

Prescott, G. A. Sex differences in Metropolitan Readiness Test results. *Journal of Educational Research,* 1955, *48,* 605-10.

Preston, R. C., & Yarington, D. J. Status of 50 retarded readers eight years after reading clinic diagnosis. *Journal of Reading,* 1967, *11,* 122-29.

Ray, D. D. The permanency of gains made in a college reading improvement program. *Journal of Educational Research,* 1965, *59,* 17-20.

Reed, J. C. Some effects of short-term training in reading under conditions of controlled motivation. *Journal of Educational Psychology,* 1956, *47,* 257-64.

Robinson, Helen M., Mozzi, Lucille, Wittick, Mildred L., & Rosenbloom, A. A. Children's perceptual achievement forms: a three year study. *American Journal of Optometry and Archives of American Academy of Optometry*, 1960, *37*, 223-37.

Russell, I. L. The Davis-Eells test and reading success in first grade. *Journal of Educational Psychology*, 1956, *47*, 269-70.

Savage, H. W. Validity of the Dominion Group Test of Reading Readiness—short form and differences among groups of pupils tested. *Ontario Journal of Educational Research*, 1959, *2*, 63-70.

Scott, R. Perceptual readiness as a predictor of success in reading. *The Reading Teacher*, 1968, *22*, 36-39.

Shea, Carol A. Visual discrimination of words as a predictor of reading readiness. Unpublished doctoral dissertation, University of Connecticut, 1964.

Shearer, E. The long-term effects of remedial education. *Educational Research*, 1967, *9*, 219-22.

Smith, C. E., & Keogh, Barbara K. The group Bender-Gestalt as a reading readiness screening instrument. *Perceptual and Motor Skills*, 1962, *15*, 639-45.

Smith, D. E. P., & Wood, R. L. Reading improvement and college grades: a follow-up. *Journal of Educational Psychology*, 1955, *46*, 155-59.

Standish, E. J. Readiness to read. *Educational Research*, 1959, *2*, 29-38.

Sutton, Rachel S. Variations in reading achievement of selected children. *Elementary English*, 1960, *37*, 97-101.

Thompson, Bertha B. A longitudinal study of auditory discrimination. *Journal of Educational Research*, 1963, *56*, 376-78.

Townsend, Agatha. Growth of independent-school pupils in achievement on the Stanford Achievement Test. *Educational Records Bulletin*, 1951, *56*, 61-71.

Tracy, R. J., & Rankin, E. F. Methods of computing and evaluating residual gain scores in the reading program. *Journal of Reading*, 1967, *10*, 363-71.

Traub, R. E. A note on the reliability of residual change scores. *Journal of Educational Measurement*, 1967, *4*, 253-56.

Traxler, A. E. Reading growth of secondary-school pupils during a five year period. *Educational Records Bulletin*, 1950, *54*, 96-107.

Weiner, H., & Feldman, Shirley. Validation studies of a reading prognosis test for children of lower and middle socio-economic status. *Educational and Psychological Measurement*, 1963, *23*, 807-14.

Weintraub, S. What research says to the reading teacher: readiness measures for predicting reading achievement. *The Reading Teacher*, 1967, *20*, 551-58.

Weiser, Margaret G. Pre-school environmental factors and school-related competencies. *Illinois State University Journal*, 1964, *27*(2), 21-37.

Weiser, Margaret G. Three methods of appraising reading readiness. *Illinois School Research*, 1965, *2*, 23-26.

Wells, C. A. The value of an oral reading test for diagnosis of the reading difficulties of college freshmen of low academic performance. *Psychological Monographs*, 1950, *64*, 1-35.

Wilson, F. T., & Fleming, C. W. Correlation of reading progress with other abilities and traits in grade 1. *Journal of Genetic Psychology*, 1938, *35*, 33-52.

Woodcock, R. W. An experimental prognostic test for remedial readers. *Journal of Educational Psychology*, 1958, *49*, 23-27.

Zaruba, Elizabeth A. Objective and subjective evaluation at grade one. *The Reading Teacher*, 1968, *22*, 50-54.

Test references

An asterisk after a test listing indicates the test is included in the *Guide to Tests and Measuring Instruments in Reading* which appears after Chapter 6.

Bender-Gestalt Test Lauretta Bender. N.Y.: American Orthopsychiatric Press, 1938, rev. 1946.

California Achievement Tests E. W. Tiegs & W. W. Clark. Monterey, Calif.: California Test Bureau, 1933, rev. 1963.

California Basic Skills Test E. W. Tiegs & W. W. Clark. Monterey, Calif.: California Test Bureau, 1933, rev. 1954.

California Reading Test E. W. Tiegs & W. W. Clark. Monterey, Calif.: California Test Bureau, 1957, rev. 1963*.

California Test of Mental Maturity E. T. Sullivan, W. W. Clark, & E. W. Tiegs. Monterey, Calif.: California Test Bureau, 1936, rev. 1963.

California Test of Personality L. P. Thorpe, W. W. Clark, & E. W. Tiegs. Monterey, Calif.: California Test Bureau, 1939, rev. 1953.

Children's Perceptual Achievement Test Eyesight Conservation Committee. Winterhaven, Fla.: Winterhaven Lions Club, 1955, rev. 1958.

Davis-Eells Test of General Intelligence in Problem Solving Ability A. Davis & K. Eells. N.Y.: World Book Co., 1953.

Draw-a-Man Test F. L. Goodenough. N. Y.: Harcourt, Brace, & World, 1926.

Gates Primary Reading Test A. I. Gates. N. Y.: Bureau of Publications, Teachers College, Columbia University, 1926, rev. 1958.

Gates Reading Survey A. I. Gates. N. Y.: Bureau of Publications, Teachers College, Columbia University, 1939, rev. 1960.

Gray-Votaw-Rogers General Achievement Tests H. Gray, D. F. Votaw, & J. L. Rogers. Austin, Tex.: Steck Co., 1934, rev. 1965.

Kuhlmann-Anderson Intelligence Tests F. Kuhlmann & R. G. Anderson. Princeton, N. J.: Personnel Press, 1927, rev. 1963.

Lee-Clark Reading Readiness Test J. M. Lee & W. W. Clark. Monterey, Calif.: California Test Bureau, 1931, rev. 1963*.

Lorge-Thorndike Intelligence Test I. Lorge & R. Thorndike. Boston: Houghton Mifflin, 1954, rev. 1962.

Maturity Level for Reading Readiness K. Barham. *Educational and Psychological Measurement*, 1958, *18*, 371-75.

Metropolitan Achievement Tests: Reading W. N. Durost, H. H. Bixler,

G. H. Hildreth, K. W. Lund, & J. W. Wrightstone. N. Y.: Harcourt, Brace, & World, 1932, rev. 1962*.

Metropolitan Readiness Test G. H. Hildreth, N. L. Griffiths, & M. E. McGauvren. N. Y.: Harcourt, Brace, & World, 1933, rev. 1965*.

New Gestalt Test A. Brenner. Detroit: Merrill-Palmer Co., 1959.

Pintner-Cunningham Primary Test R. Pintner, B. V. Cunningham, & W. N. Durost. N. Y.: Harcourt, Brace, & World, 1923, rev. 1946.

Rorschach Test H. Rorschach. N. Y.: Grune & Stratton, 1920, rev. 1960.

Roswell-Chall Auditory Blending Test F. G. Roswell & J. Chall. N.Y.: Essay Press, 1963*.

SRA Achievement Series: Reading L. P. Thorpe, D. W. Lefever, & R. A. Naslund. Chicago: Science Research Associates, 1954, rev. 1964*.

Stanford Achievement Test: Reading Tests T. L. Kelley, R. Madden, E. F. Gardner, & H. C. Rudman. N. Y.: Harcourt, Brace, & World, 1922, rev. 1966*.

Stanford-Binet Intelligence Scale L. M. Terman & M. A. Merrill. Boston: Houghton Mifflin, 1916, rev. 1960.

Wechsler Intelligence Scale for Children D. Wechsler. N. Y.: The Psychological Corp., 1949.

Visual Word Discrimination Test: Schonell Reading Test F. Schonell. Edinburgh, Scotland: Oliver & Boyd, Ltd., 1942, rev. 1955.

5
Measurement of reading-related variables

Previous chapters of this monograph have focused almost exclusively on research dealing with specific aspects of reading behavior and their measurement. Rarely has research been mentioned which has involved the measurement of factors not considered part of the reading act, except in terms of whether sub-tests of intelligence validly measure behaviors related to reading (Chapter 3). However, research has shown that measures of psychological variables, including intelligence, and physiological variables do influence the measurement of reading. How great this influence is is still not known nor is it clear what implications it has for either the teaching or diagnosis of reading achievement. Since the relationship does exist and since reading specialists have begun to use information gained from intelligence tests and psychological and physiological measures in assessing reading achievement, no monograph on measurement and evaluation in reading would be complete without considering these measures and discussing their possible contribution to evaluating reading abilities. The review of research contained within this chapter is not comprehensive. It does not discuss the intrinsic values of measures of intelligence, psychological, and physiological variables; rather it concentrates only on the relevance their measurement has to evaluating reading achievement. The chapter is organized so that intelligence is discussed apart from other psychological measures. While intelligence is a psychological variable, intelligence tests are so extensively used to assess reading capacity that they merit special attention. Psychological factors such as social maturity, test anxiety, and motivation to achieve are discussed separately. Finally, the chapter ends with a glance at the importance of physiological measures such as lateral dominance and visual and auditory perception in analyzing reading performance.

Relation between intelligence and reading

The relationship between measures of intelligence and measures of reading achievement has long been a source of controversy. The controversy does not arise over whether intelligence is related to reading or whether intelligence test scores correlate with reading test scores (which research has shown). Rather, the controversy arises out of the explanation given for that relationship: are the correlations between reading and intelligence test scores due to a similarity between the two? If this is the case, could intelligence tests be substituted for reading tests? Or, are the correlations caused by a dependence on the part of intelligence tests on reading achievement to such an extent that the two are indistinguishable? In short, are intelligence tests in fact measuring an acquired skill (reading) rather than an innate capacity (intelligence)?

Earlier sections of this monograph have considered the value of student performance on sub-tests of intelligence in relation to assessing reading achievement (Chapter 3). There it was concluded that sub-test performance contributed little to evaluating reading achievement. Again in Chapter 4, intelligence tests were considered in terms of their helpfulness in predicting achievement at the readiness level. It was found that while intelligence tests are useful in assessing reading ability and in predicting long-term achievement, other factors such as the child's language development, self-concepts, experiential background, and beginning knowledge of reading are more closely related to immediate success in learning to read. This is not to say that intelligence does not underlie language development or initial reading skill development, it is merely to point out that intelligence is not the only factor in learning to read and it may not be the most important one.

Probably the key to understanding the nature of the relationship between reading test performance and intelligence test performance is in studying the variables which affect the correlation between the two. For instance, research has shown that achievement on reading tests is more highly correlated with verbal intelligence tests scores than it is with non-verbal intelligence test scores. Hage and Stroud (1959) reported this in their study using the verbal and non-verbal sub-tests of the Lorge-Thorndike Intelligence Test, the Pressey Diagnostic Reading Tests, and the Iowa Every-Pupil Tests of Basic Skills. Triggs, Cantee, Binks, Foster, and Adams (1954) reported similar findings when the Wechsler Intelligence Scale for Children was used as the intelligence measure.

Another variable affecting the correlation between intelligence and reading test scores appears to be the ages of the subjects tested (Lennon, 1950; Triggs, Cantee, Binks, Foster, & Adams, 1954; Gates, 1921). As chronological age increases, the correlations between intelligence and reading increase. This can be accounted for, in part, by the fact that at the higher levels, those who are still in school are either brighter and/or better readers: those who are bright but could not master reading have dropped out of school, especially by the college level. Thus, despite the fact that the relation between reading and intelligence test scores is quite high at the college level, it is still fallacious to interpret this as an identity between intelligence and reading achievement. Even correlations of .80 leave approximately 36 per cent of the variance unaccounted for.

The correlation between reading and intelligence test scores has been found to be influenced by opportunity to learn. This was demonstrated by Wheeler's (1949) study in which scores on reading, intelligence, and general academic achievement tests were analyzed for Negro and white children in Tennessee. While intelligence test scores of Negro children were 9 per cent lower than those of the white children, their reading test scores were 28 per cent lower and their general academic achievement was 65 per cent lower. This meant, of course, that the correlation between reading test scores and intelligence test scores was significantly lower for Negro children than for white children.

Another approach to understanding the nature of the correlation between performance on reading tests and intelligence tests is in the effect that reading has on intelligence test performance. Research has strongly suggested that reading is key to performance on intelligence tests and tests of general academic achievement (Durrell, 1933; Jones, 1953; Fitzgerald, 1960). This is especially true of group intelligence tests which are primarily paper and pencil tests requiring a great deal of reading. It is fairly well known that poor readers do not perform as well on group intelligence tests as do good readers. For instance, Durrell (1933) found that sixth-graders were penalized on group intelligence tests in direct proportion to their degree of reading retardation.

The strong influence reading has on intelligence test performance was emphasized by Jones (1953) who compared a group of monoglot English children with 51 Welsh bilingual children who had learned English as a second language. Group non-verbal and verbal tests of intelligence as well as a silent reading test in English were given to both groups. The non-verbal test was administered in Welsh to the bilingual group and in English to the monoglot group. The other tests were given in English to both groups. No differences between the two groups were found in the means and variances on the non-verbal tests, but there was a significant difference in favor of the monoglot group on both the verbal intelligence test and the silent reading test.

Underscoring the point made by Jones' study, Fitzgerald (1960) used WISC scores as measures of the true intelligence for students in grades four, five, and six. He then examined the effects of reading on group intelligence tests by administering the Gates Reading Survey and the verbal battery of the Lorge-Thorndike Intelligence Test. Fitzgerald discovered that children retarded in reading scored even lower on group intelligence tests than their achievement levels, as indicated by the individual intelligence test scores, would have led one to believe. A similar finding was reported by Plattor, Plattor, Sherwood, and Sherwood (1959) with junior high students. Having compared the performance of average readers and retarded readers on the Pintner Verbal Tests of General Ability and the Pintner Non-Language Primary Mental Test, they concluded that reading disability invalidated the Pintner Verbal test as a measure of intelligence.

Neville (1965) attempted to find out not only if reading achievement negatively influences group verbal intelligence test scores, but also the level at which the inability to read affects group verbal intelligence test performance to such an extent as to invalidate their use. The measure of reading achievement used by Neville was the Metropolitan Achievement Tests: Reading, the group verbal intelligence test used was the verbal battery of Lorge-Thorndike Intelligence Tests, Form A, and the individual intelligence tests used as criteria tests were the Wechsler Intelligence Scale for Children and the Peabody Picture Vocabulary Test. Neville did find that poor reading negatively affects group verbal intelligence test scores. As to whether the inability to read invalidates the use of group verbal intelligence test scores, Neville (1965, p. 260) concluded that "a grade 4.0 achievement level in reading is a critical minimum for obtaining reasonably valid I.Q.'s for children in intermediate grades." One limitation of Neville's study is that the grade score of 4.0 would not represent the same level of performance on all reading achievement tests. If a researcher or teacher wanted to determine such a minimum level for a particular test, he would have to replicate the pertinent aspects of Neville's experiment, using the tests the teacher himself chooses with the particular students whose intelligence he is concerned with assessing.

Grade level differences seem important in determining the effect of reading achievement on intelligence test performance.

For instance, Shein (1961) demonstrated that with college students removing the effect of reading comprehension from group intelligence test scores did not affect the correlation of group intelligence tests with individual intelligence tests.

The question of whether reading ability influences performance on individual intelligence tests has received relatively little attention because individual intelligence tests are usually used as criterion measures for assessing group intelligence test validity. Researchers have not developed other criterion measures which could be used to measure true intelligence and serve as a basis for assessing the individual intelligence tests themselves. Tanyzer (1962) developed an unusual procedure to overcome this problem. He hypothesized that the average gain per month in reading achievement would be significantly related to improvement on the Wechsler Intelligence Scale for Children. This hypothesis was rejected when Tanyzer found that significant improvement in reading achievement for retarded readers had little effect on change in WISC scores.

Some researchers have focused their attention on the effects of reading ability on sub-tests scores, rather than total test scores, on individual intelligence tests. There is some evidence that poor readers are penalized on certain sub-tests of the WISC such as Information, Arithmetic, Digit Span, Coding, and Vocabulary. In several studies reviewed in Chapter 3 (Coleman & Rasof, 1963; Graham, 1952; Muir, 1962; Dockrell, 1960), it was found that poor readers tended to perform poorly on those sub-tests which would seem to involve reading; these same students had scored higher on non-verbal tests. The researchers in most of these studies had attempted to compare WISC performance only for students of equal intelligence. However, because of the possible penalty imposed if the student was deficient in reading, average readers of average intelligence may have ended up being compared with poor readers of above average intelligence who scored at an average intelligence level because of poor performance on those sub-tests affected by reading. The study carried out by Bond and Fay (1950) also collaborated this: they discovered that poor readers are penalized on the verbal items on the Stanford-Binet Intelligence Scale.

A different approach to exploring the relation between measured intelligence and reading was undertaken by Bliesmer (1954). Bliesmer compared the reading abilities of "bright" children and "dull" children having the same mental ages. The group of "bright" children consisted of 28 third and fourth graders who had Stanford-Binet scores of 116 or above; the "dull" group consisted of 28 eighth and ninth graders with Stanford-Binet scores of 84 or below. Both groups had comparable ranges of mental ages; the mean mental age for both groups was 11.3. In terms of reading achievement, the children in the "bright" group were superior in total reading comprehension, locating or recognizing factual details, recognizing main ideas, drawing inferences and conclusions, memory of factual details, and perception of relationships among definitely stated ideas. "Bright" children and "dull" children appeared to be comparable in reading rate, word recognition, and word meaning. From Bliesmer's study, it is apparent that individual intelligence test performance is only one factor affecting reading test performance. Even when comparing children of the same mental ages, factors such as chronological age, amount of education, experiential background, motivation, and self-concept affect reading test performance.

If poor reading negatively affects performance on group and perhaps individual intelligence tests, it can also be hypothesized that poor reading will negatively affect performance on other achievement and aptitude tests. Johnson and Bond (1950) examined the readability of ten vocational aptitude and personality tests and five group intelligence tests. They concluded that many of the tests were too difficult for the level at which their use was recommended. They pointed out that if the reading achievement of students in those grades where these tests are used are below average for that grade, the tests are probably not validly measuring the skills or other factors that they were intended to measure. Johnson and Bond also noted the variations in readability among test directions as well as test items.

Another approach to the study of the influence of reading on achievement test scores is to administer the same test both as a listening test and a reading test and examine the differences in performance. Lundsteen (1966) found that the correlation between a problem-listening test and a problem-reading test was only .39 for a group of sixth-grade students. Lundsteen did not indicate if the poor readers scored better on the listening than the reading test. Contradictory results were reported by Westover (1958) who compared the achievement of a group of college students on listening tests to reading tests. No mean differences were found in test performance or in student preference for one type of test over another. However, Westover reported that some students consistently performed better on one type of test.

Studies of the effects of reading on achievement and intelligence test performance indicate that the degree of the effect depends on the test used as the criteria of "true" performance. The use of individual intelligence tests as measures of "true" intelligence level is restricted because they may be affected by reading ability. Any studies which use listening test performance as the "true" level of ability penalize the poor reader because he has had only limited opportunities to gain through reading the knowledge required by the test. In addition, there is evidence to indicate that as a student progresses through school, reading achievement becomes less and less a factor in test performance because most students tend to achieve the minimum levels of reading ability necessary to comprehend most aptitude or achievement tests or they leave school; those who do not, the poorest readers, are often pushed out of schools (Penty, 1956). Therefore, at the upper high school and college levels, the poorest readers are not included in studies which examine the influence of poor reading on test performance. However, when the effects of reading achievement are removed from these tests, they become poor predictors of future academic success. Because of the great amount of learning which takes place through reading in the schools, it is important to remember that poor reading not only penalizes achievement test performance, but it also affects performance in most school learning activities.

The use of intelligence tests to estimate reading achievement

The research reviewed on the relationship between performance on intelligence and on reading tests has led to the conclusion that reading negatively affects performance on intelligence tests. This finding raises problems for the remedial reading teacher who is accustomed to labelling as "remedial reading cases," those students whose reading capacity as measured by intelligence tests is found to exceed achievement on reading tests. If the performance on intelligence tests upon which the evaluation of the student's capacity is based has been distorted by reading disability, the student may in fact be a remedial reading case even if the intelligence measure would seem to indicate that he is reading up to capacity—in simple terms, his capacity has been misestimated by a test adversely affected by reading disability. There have been a variety of attempts to overcome this problem, some of which have used intelligence tests which do not involve reading and which are supposedly culture-free.

Neville (1965) compared performance on an individually-administered non-reading intelligence test—the Peabody Picture Vocabulary Test (PPVT)—to scores on the WISC for good, average, and poor readers. The correlations were .42, .65, and .66, respectively. On this basis, Neville tentatively suggested that the PPVT could be substituted for the WISC with poor readers. However, the correlation of .66 still leaves over fifty per cent of the variance in the WISC test unaccounted for and would make any substitution of one test for the other very tenuous. Ivanoff and Tempero (1965) did not recommend the

PPVT for use with poor readers. Using a normal seventh-grade population, they examined the correlations of the PPVT with two group tests of mental ability—Henmon-Nelson Test of Mental Ability and the California Test of Mental Maturity (CTMM). The correlations of the PPVT with the language sub-tests of the CTMM were significantly higher (.82) than they were with the non-language sub-tests (.59). This seems to raise serious questions about the use of the PPVT with the poor readers because of its apparent reliance on language functions. Another picture vocabulary test recommended for use with poor readers is The Quick Test. Otto and McMenemy (1965) found significant but low correlations between The Quick Test and WISC scores with retarded readers. However, Otto and McMenemy concluded that while The Quick Test should not be considered a substitute for the WISC, "it appears to be a worthwhile device for use by remedial reading teachers—even with minimal training—in obtaining quick estimates of poor readers' I.Q.'s (1965, p. 197). It should be noted that no evidence regarding the usefulness of The Quick Test as a capacity measure was provided by the authors; the only evidence supplied was that the test correlated positively but at a low level with WISC scores.

Culture-free tests have also been suggested for use with retarded readers, many of whom have different cultural backgrounds. Justman and Aronow (1955) studied whether the Davis-Eells Test of General Intelligence in Problem Solving Ability, an intelligence test which does not require reading ability and is also designed to be free of cultural bias, was a more satisfactory measure of intelligence of poor readers than the Pintner Intermediate Test. It was hypothesized that poor readers might achieve higher I.Q.'s on the Davis-Eells test because of its limited reading demands. The results indicated that the two tests produced quite comparable results. For sixth-grade students with reading grades below 4.0, the mean score for the Davis-Eells test was only 4.5 raw score points higher than the mean Pintner I.Q. For those students with reading grades between 4.0 and 4.9, the mean of the Davis-Eells test was only 2.5 raw score points higher.

A usual procedure in using intelligence tests scores to determine reading potential is to subtract a student's mental grade from his reading grade. Typical of these procedures is one described by Ravenette (1961). To identify retarded readers, Ravenette used students' ability to define words orally as a capacity measure. The weakness of this procedure is that many children who are poor readers have limited oral vocabularies, although they may have the potential to learn to read. Included among such cases would be students with limited or different experiential backgrounds (such as foreign-born students) and those with hearing deficiencies. Several authors have suggested that years in school should also be part of any formula for estimating reading capacity (Bond & Tinker, 1967; Winkley, 1962). Another method was advocated by Woodbury (1963) who developed a differential index for identifying poor readers. Woodbury's index takes into account the inequality of distances between raw scores points, the variances of aptitude and achievement tests, and the correlation of one test with another. While Woodbury's index may be somewhat complex to apply, it certainly demonstrates the weakness of using the typical age to age or grade to grade comparisons in identifying retarded readers.

A system of computing multiple regression equations for predicting reading age from chronological age and WISC verbal scores was devised by Fransella and Gerver (1965). Their system is limited to the Schonell Reading Tests and to the atypical population of British children used in their study; however, employing the multiple regression equation does allow the researcher to take into account several factors and assign them appropriate emphasis in predicting reading potential. Bliesmer (1956) compared four tests for determining capacity levels for retarded readers. The measures included the Stanford-Binet, Kuhlmann-Anderson Intelligence Test, California Short-Form

Test of Mental Maturity, and the Durrell-Sullivan Reading Capacity Test. The tests were administered to eighty retarded readers in grades four through seven who were enrolled in a reading clinic. Bliesmer reached three conclusions: 1] the Durrell-Sullivan test provides the highest estimate of reading capacity, followed by the Stanford-Binet; 2] utilizing median values of Kuhlmann-Anderson, Durrell-Sullivan, and California total scores does not aid greatly in approximating Stanford-Binet estimates; and 3] none of the group tests yield estimates which are adequate approximations of Stanford-Binet estimates.

The various procedures for determining reading capacity which have been developed are quite limited in their usefulness because the research on which they are based has failed to relate the estimates of capacity to actual reading improvement programs. If a measure of capacity is valid, then a student in a remedial reading program with only a small gap between his achievement and capacity scores would be expected not to make any reading gains other than those expected in normal development. On the other hand, students with a large discrepancy between achievement and capacity would be expected to make much greater gains. Studies along this line should supply evidence concerning the "usefulness" of capacity measures.

Until research does develop some accurate efficient means for assessing capacity, what is the practitioner to do? For one thing, research does tend to indicate that if one were to predict reading potential, a variety of measures, rather than one kind of device, is more accurate. However, it is important to bear in mind that the estimates of accuracy of potential measures almost always rely on an individual intelligence test as the validity criterion. McDonald suggested that the best estimates of potential include perceptive observations by classroom teachers:

The willingness of teachers to leave the "safe, familiar" level of "objective" tests to undertake the greater challenge laid down by Kingston of making tentative assessments involving observation and study of the background, nature of thought processes, personality structure and other attributes acquired in the course of living is a promising sign. (1964, p. 118)

The use of other psychological measures in assessing reading achievement

Up to this point, research concerned only with the relation between measures of reading and measures of one psychological factor, intelligence, has been discussed. But there are other psychological factors whose measurement may or may not contribute to assessing reading skills. These include assessments of social maturity, impulsivity and compulsion, interpersonal skills, test anxiety, and motivation to achieve. There is little research evidence concerning the best way to use information gathered from the measurement of such factors. The most research has indicated is that these factors are somewhat related to reading achievement and, as yet, there is little information on how they affect reading. A complete review of research on problems and procedures in measuring all psychological variables thought to be related to reading is beyond the scope of this monograph. Those studies reviewed here are only those which have attempted to develop new methods for measuring some of the variables related to reading and/or which have compared methods for measuring them.

Although the relationship between reading and personality seems to be well established (Strang, McCullough, & Traxler, 1961; Wiksell, 1948), the attempts to determine a relationship between personality patterns and reading achievement have been inconsistent (Holmes, 1961). Tabarlet (1958) studied whether the Mental Health Analysis would differentiate poor readers from average readers at the fifth-grade level. Immature behavior, lack of interpersonal skills, and failure to participate in social affairs were found to be characteristic of poor readers. Joseph and McDonald (1964) correlated performance on the Edwards Personal Preference Schedule with scores on the

Diagnostic Reading Test for 1,475 college freshmen and concluded that good readers scored higher on such personality factors as the need to achieve and the need for change and affiliation while poor readers exhibited greater aggression, order, and abasement needs.

Robinson (1953) reviewed a number of studies delineating procedures for relating measures of personality to measures of reading under three main categories, according to the following measurement procedures: 1] informal observations or rating scales, 2] psychiatric evaluations, and 3] projective tests. Research in the field, Robinson noted, has been inconclusive, perhaps because:

> . . . first, different concepts of what constitutes reading may be held; second, divergent theories of learning place different emphases on the role of personal adjustment in learning to read; and finally divergent theories of personality stress varying parameters, appraised and interpreted in different ways. (1953, p. 98)

If group standardized personality tests are used as indicators of personality, several problems arise. It is always possible that some examinees are unable to read the questions because of poor reading and, therefore, are invalidly assessed on the particular trait being studied. Substantiating this point, Hanes (1953) found that the Minnesota Multiphasic Personality Inventory (MMPI) communicates different amounts of and not necessarily the identical information to poor readers.

Projective tests for assessing personality characteristics have also been correlated with reading achievement in several studies. Zimmerman and Allebrand (1965) compared scores on the Thematic Apperception Test (TAT) and the California Test of Personality to performance on two reading achievement tests, the California Reading Test and the Wide Range Reading Achievement Test. The results indicate significant differences in TAT and California Test of Personality results for good readers when compared to poor readers. Spache (1954) found the

Rosenzweig Picture Frustration Test to be a valid measure for differentiating the personality characteristics of good versus poor readers.

The use of these projective tests for aiding in the diagnosis of retarded readers is limited by several problems. First, while there seems to be some evidence that projective measures are able to distinguish groups of good and poor readers for certain personality characteristics, most of the studies (Zimmerman & Allebrand, 1965; Spache, 1954) fail to indicate any validity evidence for the instructional use of the test results. In addition, the projective tests are limited by a lack of precise criteria for interpreting examinee responses. Reliabilities for most projective tests have been shown to be quite inconsistent for different examiners and even for the same examiners in test, re-test situations (Cronbach, 1960, Chapter 19). Because of the need for sophisticated interpretation, most of the projective tests should be administered and interpreted only by specially trained personnel. A final problem in the use of projective techniques is the amount of rapport necessary to achieve valid results. The examinee should know what the test is attempting to measure and he should have confidence that accurate responses from him will provide a reliable measure of his status on the particular trait and that this information will aid in planning a useful educational program for him.

The predictive validity of personality tests for forecasting reading improvement has been studied by several researchers. For one, Kagan (1965) found that measures of reflection-impulsivity gathered in the first grade were predictive of reading improvement one year later. In general, children classified as impulsive in the first grade had the highest reading error scores at the end of second grade.

Pre- and post-test reading improvement scores were predicted with the Brown-Holtzman Survey of Study Habits and Attitudes, the American Council on Education Psychological Examination for College Freshmen (a verbal intelligence test), and the hysteria and psychasthenia scores of the MMPI (Chansky

& Bregman, 1957). Of the four predictors, the psychasthenia score of the MMPI, a measure of the examinees' obsessions, compulsions, and phobias, was the best predictor of reading improvement. It should be noted that the correlation was negative, but this, of course, did not affect the predictive validity. Neville, Pfost, and Dobbs (1967) found that high scores on the Test Anxiety Scale for Children were inversely related to improvement in reading comprehension, but not to vocabulary gain. Their subjects were 54 boys, seven to fourteen years of age, who were enrolled in a summer remedial reading program.

The effect of personality variables on the reliability and validity of reading test scores has received some attention by researchers. Rankin (1963) found that for a group of college students, reading test reliability and validity indexes were higher for introverted than for extroverted examinees. Chansky (1964) found that two validity scores of the MMPI correlated quite high with reading achievement for a group of 56 college freshmen. He suggested that this correlation indicated "that diagnoses of reading behavior based on standardized tests may be in error unless carelessness and test-taking attitudes are controlled" (Chansky, 1964, p. 90). A study investigating reader attitudes toward topics on a comprehension test was undertaken with a group of high school students by McKillop (1952). McKillop found that for reading comprehension questions of specific fact and detail, the relationship of test performance to students' attitudes regarding the topic was negligible. However, on questions of judgment, evaluation, and prediction, the relation was significant.

The general conclusion from these studies is that personality tests are valid measures for distinguishing good readers from poor readers on certain personality characteristics. Good readers seem to possess a higher need to achieve, higher anxiety, and compulsion; poor readers tend to interact less often with others and exhibit immature behaviors. The major limitations of the measures of personality include the reading difficulty of group tests, the interpretation of projective tests, and the rapport needed between examiners and examinees for adequate assessment. The validity of personality tests for assessing individuals is quite inconclusive. There also appears to be some indication that personality variables may be affecting the reading test performance of students. Finally, one of the most consistent findings is that certain personality tests seem to be valid predictors of reading growth, but much more research is needed on this topic. Robinson (1953, p. 98) stated that no conclusive relationships between personality variables and reading achievement have been established and indicated that future research, "if carefully organized and controlled, may identify the most acceptable measures of personality and reading, and may clarify these controversial issues."

The use of physiological measures to estimate reading capacity

Measures of physiological variables such as visual and auditory acuity, visual and auditory perception, eye movements, lateral dominance, blood cell hemoglobin counts, muscle tension, and kinesthetic recognition have *sometimes* been shown to make a valuable contribution to the assessment of reading capabilities. However, for every study which shows a relation between a particular physiological measure and estimates of reading achievement, there are other studies demonstrating that no relationship exists. Therefore, it is questionable that the measurement of physiological factors has any validity for diagnosing reading achievement. However, many reading clinicians do measure physical abilities to determine whether some physical disability could be impeding reading development.

As was the case with research on psychological variables, a complete review of the research on problems and procedures for measuring physiological variables is not possible in this monograph. The short review included here only attempts to draw attention to the problems involved in measuring those factors which appear most closely related to reading measurement and which hold the most interest for the practitioner.

Studies dealing with the validity of procedures for measuring visual acuity have been inconclusive due to the lack of consensus as to what constitutes the minimum amount of vision necessary for reading. Research in visual acuity has also suffered from contradictory findings regarding the relation between poor reading and poor vision. For instance, Kelley (1954) found no relationship between the Massachusetts Vision Test and any of several school achievement measures, including reading achievement. Kelley's population consisted of 553 children in grades one to six. Edson, Bond, and Cook (1953) also found no relationship between poor reading and poor vision. Their study, which utilized 188 fourth-grade children, involved comparing the relation of each of ten measures of silent reading skills with each of thirteen tests of visual characteristics. The vision tests included the American Optical Company E Chart, the Eames Eye Tests, the Keystone Ophthalmic Telebinocular, and slides from the Betts Visual Sensation and Perception Tests. Robinson (1951), confirming these findings, discovered no differences in monocular or binocular reading for randomly selected intermediate-grade pupils. Still more confirmation for lack of a solid relationship between visual acuity and poor reading is given in Deady's (1952) review of 17 studies in which reading disability was related to various visual anomalies. Deady concluded that myopia was not related to reading disability—Eames (1948), for example, had reported only four per cent of 1,000 poor readers were myopic; hypermetropia, however, was found in 43 per cent of the cases. Similar findings were also reported by other researchers (Farris, 1936; Fendrick, 1935). Astigmatism was found not to be closely related to poor reading, but among the few cases of poor readers who had astigmatic conditions the problems were quite severe (Eames, 1948). Other vision problems, such as binocular incoordination, strabismus, and aniseikonia were reviewed and their relation to reading disability were discussed by Deady. Deady also suggested that the Eames Eye Test or the Massachusetts Vision Test is a much better screening device for vision than the Snellen Chart. When visual anomalies are noted, Deady recommended that an examination by an ophthalmologist or optometrist should be conducted in cooperation with a trained reading clinician.

Eames (1955), in the conclusion to his study on the influence of hypermetropia and myopia on reading achievement, suggested that reading disability cases should have complete eye examinations by a vision specialist. Where this is not possible, Eames advised that any one of the following tests could be used: the Eames Eye Test, Keystone Visual Survey, or the Massachusetts Vision Test. Checklists based on classroom observations are sometimes used as a screening procedure for vision problems. Knox (1953) found that an observation checklist of symptoms of poor vision did not agree with the results of a battery of vision screening tests. Knox used a checklist in observing each of 126 third graders on three different occasions during the school day. It was concluded that "the number of different symptoms exhibited by a pupil in third grade is not a good criterion for referral to a refractionist" (Knox, 1953, p. 100). Smith (1955) compared stereoscopic instruments with clinical observations and concluded that stereoscopic tests are not sufficient for determining the status and functional performance of the oculomotor apparatus of students with reading disabilities. Robinson and Huelsman (1953) developed a visual screening battery for use with poor readers by comparing a list of visual anomalies to what existing vision tests identified and by developing new tests when existing tests were not available.

Visual and auditory perception are dependent on both physical and psychological factors. Perception involves acuity, discrimination, and memory or organizational functions. The measurement of visual perception has received a great deal of research attention within the past decade, but the reliability and validity of the measurement devices are still subject to much criticism. For example, while McAninch (1966) suggested that the measurement of visual perception performance is necessary to accurately diagnose reading disability cases, she seriously questioned whether present visual perception tests measure skills which are relevant to the reading process. McAninch urged future research to investigate which aspects of the visual perceptual process are related to reading. Olson (1966) supported this conclusion in his study of the relationship between scores on the Marianne Frostig Developmental Test of Visual Perception and reading ability. Further support was supplied by Alexander and Money (1965) who found that patients with Turner's syndrome, a cyto-genetic deficit characterized by deficits of form perception and of directional sense, did not exhibit atypical reading behavior. They concluded that if "space form and directional sense deficits are involved in the etiology of reading retardation, they must be specifically related to the language function and its symbolic representation rather than to general cognitional function" (Alexander & Money, 1965, p. 984). They did not, however, include any suggestions for measuring this specific perceptual handicap.

If visual and auditory perception were related to reading disability, how might one use a test of visual disability as a diagnostic tool in reading disability and which test should be used? Maslow, Frostig, Lefever, and Whittlesey (1964) suggested that the Marianne Frostig Developmental Test of Visual Perception is a valid indicator of learning disability and should serve as an integral part in diagnosis. The validity evidence they presented, however, is quite limited: references are only made to studies in which the correlation between the visual perception test and reading scores range from .4 to .5. Coleman (1953) used the non-verbal section of the Otis Quick-Scoring Mental Ability Test as a measure of visual perception and concluded that a majority of the subjects who were retarded in reading also showed slow development in perceptual differentiation. Several new tests for measuring visual perception have also been examined in the research. Of particular interest are

Weiner, Wepman, and Morency's (1965) study of the Chicago Test of Visual Discrimination and Edwards' (1960) study of three different methods of establishing thresholds for tachistoscopically presented words.

Attempts to measure auditory perception have met with conflicting results. For instance, Wheeler and Wheeler (1954) administered the musical tone pitch test from the Seashore Measures of Musical Talents, a test designed by the authors to measure auditory discrimination in oral language, and the vocabulary and reading comprehension sub-tests of the Metropolitan Achievement Tests to 629 fourth, fifth, and sixth graders. They concluded that while there is some correlation between the musical tone test and their oral language discrimination test with the reading sub-tests, the relationship is probably too low to be of educational value. Wepman (1960), in another study of this sort, administered the Wepman Test of Auditory Discrimination and a group reading test to 156 first- and second-grade children. Wepman found that the reading grade test score differences of the first graders scoring at high, average, and low levels on the auditory discrimination test were significantly different. The second graders who scored high on the discrimination test did not, however, score significantly higher on the reading test than did the low scorers. Clark and Richards (1966) studied the Wepman test and found that it indicated a significant deficiency in auditory discrimination for disadvantaged pre-school children. They recommended it as a diagnostic tool with similar populations.

Eye movements have also been related to reading achievement. Several attempts to measure eye movements were reviewed by Tinker (1958). Those procedures discussed by Tinker included electrical devices, which seem to be superior for measurements which are needed over longer periods, and photographic procedures, which involve using corneal reflections and recording the movement of the edge of the iris. A study relating eye movements to reading achievement was initiated by Taylor, Frackenpohl, and Pettee (1960). In order to develop grade norms for various kinds of eye movements, they administered the ophthalmograph to 12,143 subjects in the first grade through college levels. Differences in eye movements were found at various grade levels. The average span or intake unit at the first-grade level was .45 of a word; by the college level, this average increased to only 1.11 words. In the entire study, not one subject was found to have an eye-span intake reaching three words.

Measures of lateral dominance have been found to be invalid as diagnostic tools in assessing reading disability. Balow and Balow (1964) and Balow (1963) found the correlation between the Harris Tests of Lateral Dominance and various reading tests—the Gates Advanced Reading Tests and the Gates Primary Reading Test—for first and second graders was quite low. Both studies demonstrated that having the dominant hand and eye on the same side of the body, on the opposite side of the body, or having mixed hand dominance has no significant effect on reading achievement. Similar results have been reported by others (Belmont & Birch, 1965; Capabianco, 1966).

Various other physical factors, such as blood cell and hemoglobin changes, muscle tension, and kinesthetic recognition, have been measured and related to reading achievement. Eames (1953) studied the blood cells of thirty reading failures and concluded that while blood cell and hemoglobin changes would not differentiate good from poor readers, they do merit attention in the individual case study since the blood count variations may actually be one of the many causes contributing to reading failure. Wilhelm (1966) attempted to measure muscle tension and concluded that measurement of this kind significantly distinguished good readers from poor readers. Hughes, Leander, and Ketchum (1945) discovered abnormal electroencephalographic measurements in 75 per cent of reading disability cases. French (1953) devised a test of kinesthetic recognition and found that while it did discriminate between groups of good and poor readers, it was too unreliable for individual use.

From this brief overview of the research, it appears that, with the possible exception of visual acuity, physiological measures are neither valid nor dependable tools for diagnosing reading ability. While the measurement of eye movements has been quite reliable, validity studies have clearly demonstrated that it is a result rather than a cause of reading performance. Furthermore, attempts to alter eye movements have not resulted in improved reading achievement. The major research needed in measuring physiological factors lies in the area of validity studies that are based on procedures other than correlation techniques. In many of the studies conducted to date, correlations of .4 or .6 have been reported between various factors and reading ability. This has led researchers to conclude that while the correlations are not too high, it does appear that a particular factor is important to measure because it is related in some way to reading achievement. Such a conclusion is unwarranted—the importance or usefulness of these measurements has certainly not been substantiated by research.

For the reading practitioner, this means that, with the possible exception of visual acuity, the measurement of physical factors is not relevant to the diagnosis of reading achievement. The validity of the measurement of these factors for assessing reading is so limited that the reading teacher will certainly find that the diagnosis of reading achievement would be markedly improved by emphasizing the valid and reliable measurement of reading behaviors.

A note to the practitioner

Based on the review of research presented in this chapter on the measurement of variables related to reading, the practitioner may well be left in a considerable confusion as to the implications which this has for the teaching of reading and the planning of instruction. Therefore, it appears worthwhile to review the usefulness of measures of intelligence, psychological variables, and physiological variables in terms of how a teacher can use these measures in the classroom profitably.

In applying measures of intelligence to the diagnosis of reading achievement, the practitioner should:

1] Use a variety of procedures as well as a variety of tests to estimate reading capacity—language development tests, intelligence tests (both verbal and performance), and measures of experiential background.

2] Recognize the effect reading achievement has on most reading capacity estimates and try to compensate for these effects through the use of additional measures which do not confound reading skills and reading capacity.

3] Remember that the relation between intelligence test performance and reading test performance becomes stronger at the older chronological ages and, therefore, that the use of reading capacity minus reading achievement scores for selecting remedial readers becomes a less valid procedure as chronological age increases.

In using measures of psychological variables other than those of intelligence, the practitioner should bear in mind that most of these variables have only a very limited relation to reading achievement. Research has not yet begun to explore the nature of this relationship and the contribution it can make to diagnosing reading achievement. Therefore, it seems reasonable to conclude that at the present time the practitioner should view this area as one which is in need of further research and which offers little in terms of practical application at the classroom level.

The relation of physiological factors such as visual acuity, auditory acuity, and general physical *status* to reading is very limited. However, it is important for the teacher to be aware that these may impede reading skills and that physiological measures can be useful only in this sense. Otherwise, the measurement of other physiological factors such as laterality, does not, at the present time, appear to be of any value to the practitioner and he should not attempt to use such measurement until research is able to show how these measures can be applied to the planning of a reading program.

References

Alexander, D., & Money, J. Reading ability, object constancy, and Turner's syndrome. *Perceptual and Motor Skills,* 1965, *20,* 981-84.

Balow, I. H. Lateral dominance characteristics and reading achievement in the first grade. *Journal of Psychology,* 1963, *55,* 323-28.

Balow, I. H., & Balow, B. Lateral dominance and reading achievement in the second grade. *American Educational Research Journal,* 1964, *1,* 139-43.

Bliesmer, E. P. Reading abilities of bright and dull children of comparable mental ages. *Journal of Educational Psychology,* 1954, *55,* 321-31.

Bliesmer, E. P. A comparison of results of various capacity tests used with retarded readers. *Elementary School Journal,* 1956, *56,* 400-02.

Belmont, Lillian, & Birch, H. G. Lateral dominance, lateral awareness, and reading disability. *Child Development,* 1965, *36,* 57-71.

Bond, G. L., & Fay, L. C. A comparison of the performance of good and poor readers on the individual items of the Stanford-Binet scale. *Journal of Educational Research,* 1950, *43,* 475-79.

Bond, G. L., & Tinker, M. A. *Reading difficulties: their diagnosis and correction.* New York: Appleton-Century-Crofts, 1967.

Capabianco, R. J. Ocular-manual laterality and reading in adolescent mental retardates. *American Journal of Mental Deficiency,* 1966, *70,* 781-85.

Chansky, N. M. A note on the validity of reading test scores. *Journal of Educational Research,* 1964, *58,* 90.

Chansky, N. M., & Bregman, M. Improvement of reading in college. *Journal of Educational Research,* 1957, *51,* 313-17.

Clark, A. B., & Richards, C. J. Auditory discrimination among economically disadvantaged and non-disadvantaged pre-school children. *Exceptional Children,* 1966, *33,* 259-62.

Coleman, J. C. Perceptual retardation in reading disability cases. *Journal of Educational Psychology,* 1953, *54,* 497-503.

Coleman, J. C., & Rasof, Beatrice. Intellectual factors in learning disorders. *Perceptual and Motor Skills,* 1963, *16,* 139-52.

Cronbach, L. J. *Essentials of psychological testing.* N.Y.: Harper & Row, 1960.

Deady, Marion C. Visual factors in reading disability. *Columbia Optometrist,* 1952, *26,* 5-7.

Dockrell, W. B. The use of the Wechsler Intelligence Scale for Children in the diagnosis of retarded readers. *Alberta Journal of Educational Research,* 1960, *6,* 86-91.

Durrell, D. D. The influence of reading ability on intelligence measures. *Journal of Educational Psychology,* 1933, *24,* 412-16.

Eames, T. H. Comparison of eye conditions among 1,000 reading failures, 500 opthalmic patients, and 150 unselected children. *American Journal of Ophthalmology,* 1948, *31,* 713-17.

Eames, T. H. The blood picture in reading failures. *Journal of Educational Psychology,* 1953, *44,* 372-75.

Eames, T. H. The influence of hypermetropia and myopia on reading achievement. *American Journal of Ophthalmology,* 1955, *39,* 375-77.

Edson, W. H., Bond, G. L., & Cook, W. W. Relationships between visual characteristics and specific silent reading abilities. *Journal of Educational Research,* 1953, *46,* 451-57.

Edwards, A. E. Subliminal tachistoscopic perception as a function of threshold method. *Journal of Psychology,* 1960, *50,* 139-44.

Farris, L. P. Visual defects as factors influencing achievement in reading. *Journal of Experimental Education,* 1936, *5,* 58-60.

Fendrick, P. Visual characteristics of poor readers. *Contributions to Education: Bureau of Publications, Columbia University,* No. 656, 1935, 1-86.

Fitzgerald, L. A. Some effects of reading ability on group intelligence test scores in the intermediate grades. Unpublished doctoral dissertation, State University of Iowa, 1960.

Fransella, Fay, & Gerver, D. Multiple regression equations for predicting reading age from chronological age and WISC verbal I.Q. *British Journal of Educational Psychology,* 1965, *35,* 86-89.

French, E. L. Kinesthetic recognition in retarded readers. *Educational and Psychological Measurement,* 1953, *13,* 536-54.

Gates, A. I. An experimental and statistical study of reading and reading tests. *Journal of Educational Psychology,* 1921, *12,* 303-12, 378-91.

Graham, E. E. Wechsler-Bellevue and WISC scattergrams of unsuccessful readers. *Journal of Consulting Psychology,* 1952, *16,* 268-71.

Hage, D. S., & Stroud, J. B. Reading proficiency and intelligence scores, verbal and non-verbal. *Journal of Educational Research,* 1959, *52,* 258-62.

Hanes, B. Reading ease and MMPI results. *Journal of Clinical Psychology*, 1953, *9*, 83-85.

Holmes, J. A. Personality characteristics of the disabled reader. *Journal of Developmental Reading*, 1961, *4*, 111-22.

Hughes, J., Leander, R., & Ketchum, G. Electroencephalographic study of special reading disabilities. *Electroencephalography and Clinical Neurophysiology*, 1949, *1*, 377-78.

Ivanoff, J. M., & Tempero, H. E. Effectiveness of the Peabody Picture Vocabulary Test with seventh-grade pupils. *Journal of Educational Research*, 1965, *58*, 412-15.

Johnson, R. H., & Bond, G. L. Reading ease of commonly used tests. *Journal of Applied Psychology*, 1950, *34*, 319-24.

Jones, W. R. The influence of reading ability in English on the intelligence test scores of Welsh speaking children. *British Journal of Educational Psychology*, 1953, *23*, 114-20.

Joseph, M. P., & McDonald, A. S. Psychological needs and reading achievement. In E. L. Thurston & L. E. Hafner (Eds.), New concepts in college-adult reading. *Yearbook of the National Reading Conference*, 1964, *13*, 150-57.

Justman, J., & Aronow, M. The Davis-Eells Games as a measure of the intelligence of poor readers. *Journal of Educational Psychology*, 1955, *46*, 418-22.

Kagan, J. Reflection-impulsivity and reading ability in primary grade children. *Child Development*, 1965, *36*, 609-28.

Kelley, Dorothy J. Using children's atypicalities to indicate ocular defects. *Journal of Educational Research*, 1954, *47*, 455-65.

Knox, Gertrude E. Classroom symptoms of visual efficiency. In Helen M. Robinson (Ed.), Clinical studies in reading. *Supplementary Educational Monographs*, 1953, *77*, 97-101.

Lennon, R. T. The relation between intelligence and achievement test results for a group of communities. *Journal of Educational Psychology*, 1950, *41*, 301-08.

Lundsteen, Sara. Listening, reading and qualitative levels of thinking in problem solving. In J. A. Figurel (Ed.), Vistas in reading. *Proceedings of the International Reading Association*, 1966, *11*, 450-54.

Maslow, Phyllis, Frostig, Marianne, Lefever, D. W., & Whittlesey, J. R. B. The Marianne Frostig developmental test of visual perception, 1963 standardization. *Perceptual and Motor Skills*, 1964, *19*, 463-99.

McAninch, Myrene. Identification of visual perceptual errors in young children. In J. A. Figurel (Ed.), Vistas in reading. *Proceedings of the International Reading Association,* 1966, *11,* 507-12.

McDonald, A. S. Research for a classroom: reading potential: appraisal or prediction? *Journal of Reading,* 1964, *8,* 115-19.

McKillop, Anne S. The relationship between the reader's attitude and certain types of reading response. New York: Bureau of Publications, Teachers College, Columbia University, 1952.

Muir, Margaret. The WISC test pattern of children with severe reading disabilities. *Reading Horizons,* 1962, *3,* 67-73.

Neville, D. The relationships between reading skills and intelligence test scores. *The Reading Teacher,* 1965, *18,* 257-62.

Neville, D., Pfost, P., & Dobbs, Virginia. The relationship between test anxiety and silent reading gain. *American Educational Research Journal,* 1967, *4,* 45-50.

Olson, A. V. The Frostig Developmental Test of Visual Perception as a predictor of specific reading abilities with second grade children. *Elementary English,* 1966, *43,* 869-72.

Otto, W., & McMenemy, R. A. An appraisal of the Ammons Quick Test in a remedial reading program. *Journal of Educational Measurement,* 1965, *2,* 193-98.

Penty, Ruth C. *Reading ability and high school drop-outs.* New York: Bureau of Publications, Teachers College, Columbia University, 1956.

Plattor, Emma E., Plattor, S. D., Sherwood, C., & Sherwood, Sylvia. Relationships between reading retardation and the measurement of intelligence. *Personnel and Guidance Journal,* 1959, *38,* 49-51.

Rankin, E. F. Reading test reliability and validity as a function of introversion-extroversion. *Journal of Developmental Reading,* 1963 *6,* 106-17.

Ravenette, A. T. An empirical approach to the assessment of reading retardation: vocabulary level and reading attainment. *British Journal of Educational Psychology,* 1961, *31,* 96-103

Robinson, Helen M. Factors related to monocular and binocular reading efficiency. *Americal Journal of Optometry,* 1951, *28,* 337-46.

Robinson, Helen M. Personality and reading. In A. E. Traxler (Ed.), Modern educational problems. *Proceedings of the Conference of the Educational Records Bureau,* 1953, *17,* 87-99.

Robinson, Helen M., & Huelsman, C. B., Jr. Visual efficiency and progress in learning to read. In Helen M. Robinson (Ed.), Clinical studies in reading, *Supplementary Educational Monographs*, 1953, *77*, 31-63.

Shein, B. T. The influence of reading and time variables on group intelligence tests at the college level. Unpublished doctoral dissertation, New York University, 1961.

Smith, W. Report of vision screening tests in a group of ten reading problem cases. *American Journal of Optometry and Archives of American Academy of Optometry*, 1955, *32*, 295-303.

Spache, G. D. Personality characteristics of retarded readers as measured by the picture-frustration study. *Educational and Psychological Measurement*, 1954, *14*, 186-92.

Strang, Ruth, McCullough, Constance M., & Traxler, A. E. *The improvement of reading*. New York: McGraw-Hill Book Co., 1961.

Tabarlet, B. E. Poor readers and mental health. *Elementary English*, 1958, *35*, 522-25.

Tanyzer, H. J. The relationship of change in reading achievement to change in intelligence among retarded readers. Unpublished doctoral dissertation, University of Connecticut, 1962.

Taylor, S. E., Frackenpohl, H., & Pettee, J. L. Grade level norms for the components of the fundamental reading skill. *Educational Developmental Laboratories Research and Information Bulletin*, 1960, *3*.

Tinker, M. A. Recent studies of eye-movements in reading. *Psychological Bulletin*, 1958, *54*, 215-31.

Triggs, Frances O., Cantee, J. K., Binks, Virginia, Foster, D., & Adams, N. A. The relationship between specific reading skills and general ability at the elementary and junior-senior high school levels. *Educational and Psychological Measurement*, 1954, *14*, 176-85.

Weiner, P. S., Wepman, J. M., & Morency, A. S. A test of visual discrimination. *Elementary School Journal*, 1965, *65*, 330-37.

Wepman, J. M. Auditory discrimination, speech and reading. *Elementary School Journal*, 1960, *60*, 325-33.

Westover, F. L. A comparison of listening and reading as a means of testing. *Journal of Educational Research*, 1958, *52*, 23-26.

Wheeler, L. R. The relation of reading to intelligence. *School and Society*, 1949, *70*, 225-27.

Wheeler, L. R., & Wheeler, Viola D. A study of the relationship of auditory discrimination to silent reading abilities. *Journal of Educational Research*, 1954, *48* 103-13.

Wikesell, W. The relationship between reading difficulties and psychological adjustment. *Journal of Educational Research*, 1948, *41*, 557-58.

Wilhelm, Rowena. Diagnostic value of test score differentials found between measure of visual and auditory memory in severely disabled readers. *Academic Therapy Quarterly*, 1966, *2*, 42-44, 58.

Winkley, Carol K. Building staff competence in identifying underachievers. In H. A. Robinson (Ed.), The underachiever in reading. *University of Chicago Supplementary Educational Monographs*, 1962, *92*, 155-62.

Woodbury, C. A. The identification of underachieving readers. *The Reading Teacher*, 1963, *16*, 218-23.

Zimmerman, Irla L., & Allebrand, G. N. Personality characteristics and attitudes toward achievement of good and poor readers. *Journal of Educational Research*, 1965, *59*, 28-30.

Test references

An asterisk after a test listing indicates the test is included in the *Guide to Tests and Measuring Instruments in Reading* which appears after Chapter 6.

American Council on Education Psychological Examination for College Freshmen L. Thurstone & T. Thurstone. Princeton: Cooperative Test Division, 1924, rev. 1954.

Betts Visual Sensation and Perception Tests E. A. Betts. Meadville, Pa.: Keystone View Co., 1936.

Brown-Holtzman Survey of Study Habits and Attitudes W. F. Brown & W. H. Holtzman. N. Y.: Psychological Corp., 1953, rev. 1963.

California Reading Test E. W. Tiegs & W. W. Clark. Monterey, Calif.: California Test Bureau, 1957, rev. 1963*.

California Short-Form Test of Mental Maturity E. T. Sullivan, W. W. Clark, & E. W. Tiegs. Monterey, Calif.: California Test Bureau, 1938, rev. 1964.

California Test of Mental Maturity E. T. Sullivan, W. W. Clark, & E. W. Tiegs. Monterey, Calif.: California Test Bureau, 1936, rev. 1963.

California Test of Personality L. P. Thorpe, W. W. Clark, & E. W. Tiegs. Monterey, Calif.: California Test Bureau, 1939, rev. 1953.

Davis-Eells Test of General Intelligence in Problem Solving Ability. A. Davis & K. Eells. N. Y.: World Book Co., 1953.

Diagnostic Reading Tests F. Triggs. Mountain Home, N. C.: Committee on Diagnostic Reading Tests, 1947, rev. 1963*.

Durrell-Sullivan Reading Capacity Tests D. D. Durrell & H. B. Sullivan. N. Y.: World Book Co., 1937, rev. 1945.

Edwards Personal Preference Schedule N.Y.: Psychological Corp., 1953, rev. 1959.

Gates Advanced Primary Reading Test A. I. Gates. N. Y.: Bureau of Publications, Teachers College, Columbia University, 1926, rev. 1958.

Gates Primary Reading Test A. I. Gates. N.Y.: Bureau of Publications, Teachers College, Columbia University, 1926, rev. 1958.

Gates Reading Readiness Tests A. I. Gates. N.Y.: Bureau of Publications, Teachers College, Columbia University, 1939, rev. 1942.

Gates Reading Survey A. I. Gates. N.Y.: Bureau of Publications, Teachers College, Columbia University, 1939, rev. 1960.

Harris Tests of Lateral Dominance   A. Harris.   N.Y.: Psychological Corp., 1947.

Henmon-Nelson Tests of Mental Ability   V. Henmon & M. Nelson. Boston: Houghton Mifflin, 1931, rev. 1950.

Iowa Every-Pupil Tests of Basic Skills, Test A: Silent Reading Comprehension   H. F. Spitzer, E. Horn, M. McBroom, H. A. Greene, & E. F. Lindquist.   Boston: Houghton Mifflin, 1955, rev. 1956*.

Kuhlmann-Anderson Intelligence Tests   F. Kuhlmann & R. G. Anderson.   Princeton: Personnel Press, 1927, rev. 1963.

Lorge-Thorndike Intelligence Test   I. Lorge & R. Thorndike.   Boston: Houghton Mifflin, 1954, rev. 1962.

Marianne Frostig Developmental Test of Visual Perception   M. Frostig. Palo Alto, Calif.: Consulting Psychologists Press, 1961, rev. 1964.

Massachusetts Vision Test   H. M. Leverett & E. A. Barker.   Danbury, Conn.: American Optical Co., 1955.

Mental Health Analysis   L. Thorpe.   Monterey, Calif.: California Test Bureau, 1946, rev. 1959.

Metropolitan Achievement Tests: Reading   W. N. Durost, H. H. Bixler, G. H. Hildreth, K. W. Lund, & J. W. Wrightstone.   N.Y.: Harcourt, Brace, & World, 1932, rev. 1962*.

Minnesota Multiphasic Personality Inventory   S. Hathaway & J. McKinley.   N.Y.: Psychological Corp., 1942, rev. 1951.

Otis Quick Scoring Mental Ability Test   A. S. Otis.   N.Y.: World Book Co., 1939.

Peabody Picture Vocabulary Test   L. M. Dunn.   Washington, D.C.: American Guidance Service, 1959.

Pintner Intermediate Test   R. Pintner.   N.Y.: Bureau of Publications, Teachers College, Columbia University, 1931, rev. 1939.

Pintner Non-Language Primary Mental Test   R. Pintner.   N.Y.: Bureau of Publications, Teachers College, Columbia University, 1929, rev. 1930.

Pintner Verbal Tests of General Ability   R. Pintner.   N. Y.: World Book Co., 1923, rev. 1946.

Pressey Diagnostic Reading Tests   S. L. Pressey & L. C. Pressey. Indianapolis: Bobbs-Merrill, 1929*.

The Quick Test   R. B. Ammons & C. H. Ammons.   Missoula, Mon.: Psychological Test Specialists, 1958, rev. 1962.

Rosenzweig Picture Frustration Test S. Rosenzweig. St. Louis, Mo.: Saul Rosenzweig, 1944.

Schonell Reading Tests F. J. Schonell. Edinburgh, Scotland: Oliver & Boyd, 1942.

Seashore Measures of Musical Talents C. Seashore, D. Lewis, & J. G. Saetneit. N. Y.: The Psychological Corporation, 1919, rev. 1960.

Stanford-Binet Intelligence Scale L. M. Terman & M. A. Merrill. Boston: Houghton Mifflin, 1916, rev. 1960.

Test Anxiety Scale for Children S. B. Sarason, *et al. Child Development*, 1959, *29*, 105-13.

Thematic Apperception Test S. Tomkins. N.Y.: Grune-Stratton, 1949.

Wechsler Intelligence Scale for Children D. Wechsler. N. Y.: Psychological Corp., 1949.

Wepman Test of Auditory Discrimination J. M. Wepman. Chicago: Language Research Associates, 1958.

Wide Range Achievement Test (WRAT) J. F. Jastak & J. R. Jastak. Austin, Tex.: Guidance Testing Associates, 1936, rev. 1965*.

6
Summary: test usage and research needs

This monograph has focused on the contribution which various procedures for measurement can make to the teaching of reading. Much of the research reviewed in the monograph has cast considerable doubt on the validity and reliability of all testing instruments in general and group standardized tests in particular. This is not to say that measuring devices have no value in reading instruction. On the contrary, the preceding chapters have stressed that tests can make a valuable contribution to classroom practice if they are used with caution and if the test user is well aware of their limitations: the test consumer should know *why* he wants to use tests and *for what* he is testing. In addition, the objectives of the tests used and the objectives of the instructional program should be closely related. Because testing instruments have limited reliability and validity, a variety of devices should be used.

This monograph does not provide detailed procedures for using tests in the school program; it does provide guidelines. Some major uses of testing in the reading program center around the following four points: 1] determining students' instructional reading levels, 2] diagnosing reading skills, 3] estimating reading growth, and 4] evaluating the instructional program. The latter point was not treated extensively in this monograph. These test uses are discussed individually in the following paragraphs in terms of the kinds of devices which can be most effectively used in each of the areas.

Determining instructional levels Informal reading inventories based on classroom instructional reading materials provide the most valid estimate for determining functional reading levels, both in general reading and in reading in the content areas. Standardized group tests are not accurate in determining students' instructional reading levels as they tend to overestimate them by significant amounts (although this is dependent on the particular test used). Standardized reading tests are valid for ranking students, but they should not be used for determining instructional levels.

Diagnosing reading skills Reading diagnosis should be an integral, continuous part of reading instruction. In diagnosis, it is particularly important to select a test which defines reading in the same manner as the reading program does. Sub-tests of standardized reading tests have consistently been shown to have limited validity as measures of reading sub-skills when used on a group basis; their validity when used on an individual basis has not been studied extensively. Therefore, sub-tests of standardized reading tests should be used cautiously for diagnostic purposes. Informal means of assessment such as teachers' observations and skills check lists when combined with standardized tests tend to be more valid for diagnosis. Physiological and psychological tests have limited value in assessing reading skills and determining instructional programs.

Estimating growth Growth in reading ability should be measured as it relates to specific goals of the reading program. In fact, it is impossible to evaluate growth unless these goals are specified. In addition, the tests used should measure skills in the same manner in which they were taught in the instructional program. Many times it is more efficient not to test all students if the estimate of

growth desired is for the entire class. Instead, students
can be selected at random for testing or test items can be
assigned at random to students. For many reasons delineated in Chapter 4, it is not good practice to evaluate
growth on the basis of standardized test norms. If standardized test scores are used as the basis for measuring
growth in a remedial program and if any of the pre-test
scores are extremely low, a correction for regression
should be used. Also, any assessment of change should
take into account the error of measurement of the instruments used.

Evaluating the instructional program Program evaluation
should be continuous and should provide feedback for improving the instructional program. Informal observations
are most useful in evaluating the program; however, the
behaviors that are to be observed should be clearly specified.

If the guidelines presented above seem sparse, it is because
the state of knowledge in the field of testing and evaluation in
reading is so limited. In fact, present measurement practices
and instruments often are not as helpful as they could be in
teaching reading. This is not the fault of either test consumers
or test producers. Test users have been naive about the value
of tests in the classroom. This has led to gross misuse of tests
and situations where important stated objectives of reading programs have been consistently unevaluated. Compounding the
problem is the fact that tests have been produced which do not
meet the needs of the instructional program. More often than
not tests fail to provide teachers with information about students' instructional reading levels, basic reading skills development, and attitudes toward reading. Most reputable test publishers do not claim that tests can supply such knowledge, but
they do imply that they do provide diagnostic information by including reading sub-test profiles and grade level norms.

Standardized reading tests are the instruments teachers most often rely on to determine students' instructional needs. However, these tests are not very helpful to the teaching of reading for several basic reasons. First of all, the sub-tests of these tests are of questionable validity for determining students' specific reading strengths and weaknesses. The research examining the sub-tests of present standardized reading tests for diagnosing individuals has been almost wholly neglected. This validity problem is certainly the result of the focus of reading tests, reading teachers, and reading research on the product of reading rather than on the reading process. Most tests are designed to reveal *what* a student can do and not *how* he does it. Only recently have reading researchers begun to focus on the reading process.

One of the major shortcomings in the classroom measurement and evaluation of reading ability stems from incomplete knowledge as to the nature of the reading process and the factors that influence it. Tests are often developed, interpreted, and administered, as if reading ability was a skill which had no relation to the individual's experiential background, environmental factors both within school and society, the classroom setting, instructional materials, etc. As was pointed out in earlier chapters, if the subject content of the reading material, the purpose for reading, the reading conditions, the difficulty of the reading material, or any factors related to the reading situation were altered, reading performance would certainly be changed.

Much research remains to be done before tests can begin to make their full contribution to reading instruction. The major obstacle in testing and measurement today is the lack of a clear understanding of what the reading process entails. Until a theoretical construct of reading is developed and substantiated, the value of testing devices will remain extremely limited. However, once reading is defined, the avenues for test development will broaden: it will be possible to develop criterion tests geared to assess how well an individual reads on the basis of what reading is rather than on the basis of how others perform (which current tests do). The development of such criteria should itself be a major step forward in terms of classroom practice; for once the goal for reading instruction is established, one can begin to determine what skills an individual should possess in order to read and how instruction can be organized to teach these skills. Certainly, a clearer conception of the reading process will facilitate the development of more valid and reliable sub-tests of reading. Another area which has suffered because of the lack of knowledge about the reading process has been procedures for determining reading capacity. One of the pressing needs in estimating capacity is the development of measures of reading potential which are not dependent on acquired reading. Perhaps once reading is defined, the capacity to read can be isolated from reading achievement in the tests themselves.

The need for a sound definition of reading cannot be overemphasized: the validity of reading measures depends upon the validity of their theoretical basis. Once a sound foundation has been established and tests developed, then research can proceed in the direction of determining *how best* to use these tests in the reading program. Certainly, the problem of the validity of using equivalent forms of tests should be probed, as should methods for measuring growth over short time periods. Also, much work would need to be done in attempting to combine various procedures to measure growth. Perhaps another important avenue for further research would be the development of tests which measure qualitative as well as quantitative levels of response. Current tests measure only the quantitative levels, even though they contain items which could be used to assess depth and variety of understanding on items such as vocabulary and comprehension. This is because the test scores are based only on a total number of correct answers and supply no indication of how correct or incorrect the responses were.

An important function of tests, as mentioned earlier in this chapter, is in the evaluation of the school program. The development of a clear definition of reading would certainly open research up in this area. Variables such as instructional materials, curriculum, teacher effectiveness, and teaching procedures could be investigated in the context of how each contributes to developing reading skills. The interaction of these variables should also be studied to determine the most effective combination for promoting reading development.

Answers to these research questions should provide a basis for the improvement of the measurement and evaluation of reading. However, there are a number of new (and several rediscovered) procedures which are being tried out and studied. These procedures are closely related to the research questions posed earlier in this chapter and while their use is generally limited, the very fact that they have been developed is encouraging.

One of the newer approaches to measuring reading behavior which seems to hold some promise for improving the analysis of reading ability is the greater emphasis on defining purposes for reading. This should not only aid in assessing reading ability, but also, it might help in improving the teaching of reading. Ample evidence is now available that students do not alter their reading patterns to achieve particular purposes unless they have had guided practice in doing so. If teachers discover that students can improve their reading test scores and, more importantly, their reading in content subjects if they establish specific purposes for reading, tests which use this procedure will have provided a springboard to improved instruction.

A second procedure which is being developed on some reading vocabulary and comprehension tests is the use of qualitative levels of responses for multiple-choice questions. The attempts thus far have been in the direction of developing a more diagnostic utilization of student responses. The usual patterns of one correct response and four incorrect responses may be replaced by levels of correct responses.

A third development is a tendency to measure reading skills as they are actually used in classroom situations. The development of reading vocabulary tests in which the words to be defined are imbedded in the reading text is not an innovation.

However, more test producers are using this procedure because it provides a more realistic appraisal of reading ability than do tests in which vocabulary items are presented in isolation and examinees are to select the best synonym for a group of alternatives.

The cloze procedure, which was discussed in earlier sections of this monograph, also seems to be a testing method which more closely resembles actual reading behavior. However, cloze techniques do not seem to allow the test developer to examine the inferential reading-thinking abilities of examinees as well as multiple-choice techniques. Additional research is needed to learn more about the construct validity of this measurement approach.

The technical procedures in developing reading tests also are improving. Test publishers, and more importantly, test consumers are becoming increasingly aware of the American Psychological Association's *Standards for Educational and Psychological Tests and Manuals* (available from the American Psychological Association, 1200 Seventeenth Street, N.W., Washington, D.C. 20036). Many test publishers have improved their tests and manuals to meet these specifications. Perhaps the most notable technical improvement in the development of standardized reading tests has been improved sampling procedures for securing representative national norms. Not only are these norm populations selected with better care, but the description of the norm groups is more complete and, therefore, more useful to the test user. Some of the needed improvements in the development of standardized reading tests are being withheld because of outdated word lists, questionable readability formulas, and lack of information about the basic skills of reading.

Future research and development in testing will, in time, provide answers to some of the more fundamental questions of what reading is. In the meantime, research will have to concentrate on how to use current testing instruments more effectively. Hopefully, this monograph is a step in that direction.

Glossary

Achievement test—a measure of the degree to which a person has attained objectives of instruction or education.

Age Equivalent—the chronological age for which a given score is the real or estimated average score.

Cloze procedure—the method for determining a student's reading comprehension on a particular selection. The procedure involves eliminating every fifth word (or some other number may be chosen) and asking the examinee to supply the missing word.

Coefficient of correlation—a measure of the degree of relationship between two sets of measures either for the same group of individuals or for paired individuals (e.g., twins). The Pearson product-moment coefficient is r; the Spearman rank coefficient is rho (ρ).

Coefficient of equivalence—the type of reliability coefficient obtained when parallel or equivalent forms of the same test are administered to the same individuals.

Concurrent validity—the degree to which an individual's test performance predicts performance on some criterion external to that test.

Construct validity—the degree to which an individual's performance on a particular test is predictive of the degree to which the individual possesses some trait or quality.

Content validity—the degree to which the results of a particular test represent an individual's performance on a given universal content of which the test is a sample.

Convergent validity—the degree to which a particular test shows agreement with the measurement of variables that are the same or quite similar.

Criterion—a standard by which a test may be judged or evaluated; a set of scores, measures, ratings, products, etc., that a test is designed to predict or correlate with as a test of its validity. A set of concepts or ideas used in judging the content of a test, in estimating its content or logical validity.

This glossary has been taken, with some revision and some additions, from H. Remmers, N. L. Gage, and J. F. Rummel, *A Practical Introduction to Measurement and Evaluation* (N.Y.: Harper & Row, 1965); R. T. Lennon, *A Glossary of 100 Measurement Terms* (N.Y.: Harcourt, Brace, & World); and H. B. English and A. C. English, *A Comprehensive Dictionary of Psychological and Psychoanalytical Terms* (N.Y.: Longmans, Green, 1958). This material is presented here by permission of David McKay Company, Inc.; Harcourt, Brace, & World; and Harper & Row.

Criterion test—a test whose primary purpose is to determine the extent to which individuals in a group have learned or mastered a given unit of instruction. This type of test is intended not to differentiate widely among individuals, but to determine whether or not a group of students has achieved a certain level of proficiency. It is used primarily to determine whether or not the group is ready to advance to another unit of instruction.

Culture-free test—a test devised to rule out the effects of an individual's previous environment on his score. No such test is actually possible. A "culture-free" test does not rule out such effects but merely makes them equivalent for the persons to be compared.

Diagnostic test—a test used to diagnose or to show an individual's strengths and weaknesses in a specific area of study. It yields measures of the components, or subparts, of some larger body of information or skill.

Discriminant validity—the degree to which a particular test does not overlap with measurement of variables from which it should differ.

Equivalent form—any of two or more forms of a test that are closely parallel in content and in difficulty of items, and that yield very similar average scores, measures of variability, and reliability estimates for a given group.

Error of measurement—See Standard error.

Face validity—the apparent validity of a test that seems fair to and appropriate for the individual being measured. The extent to which a test is made up of items that seem related to the variable being tested. See Validity.

Factor—a hypothetical trait derived by factor analysis.

Factor analysis—a method of computing for determining factors from the intercorrelations among a set of variables, usually tests.

Grade equivalent—the grade level for which a given score is the real or estimated average.

Grade norm—the average score obtained by pupils of a given grade placement. Also referred to as the modal grade age.

Group test—a test that can be administered to a number of individuals at the same time by one examiner.

Hawthorne effect—any effect which causes an experimental group to perform differently from expectant levels as a result of their knowledge of their inclusion in the experiment.

Individual test—a test that can be administered to only one individual at a time.

Instructional level—the level at which it is expected the student will make the maximal amount of growth.

Intelligence quotient (I.Q.)—the ratio obtained by dividing mental age by chronological age, i.e., $(MA \div CA)$ 100. A measure of brightness that takes into consideration both score on an intelligence test and age.

Inventory—an instrument used for cataloging or listing all or a sample of behaviors, interests, attitudes, etc., regarded as useful or relevant for a given purpose. It is not a "test" or a measure in the usual sense and has no right or wrong answers.

Local norms—norms that have been made by collecting data in a certain school or school system and using them, instead of national or regional norms, to evaluate student performance.

Mental age (M.A.)—the age for which a given score on an intelligence or scholastic ability test is average. It is the average age of individuals making the average score on the test.

National norm—a norm based on nation-wide sampling.

Non-verbal test—a paper-and-pencil test, usually used with children in the primary grades, in which the test items are symbols, figures, and pictures rather than words; instructions are given orally.

Norming population—the population which was utilized to establish average performance for various age or grade groups.

Norms—values that describe the performance of various groups on a test or inventory. Norms are only descriptive of existing types of performance and are not to be regarded as standards or as desirable levels of attainment.

Parallel tests—see Equivalent form.

Percentile rank—the percentage of scores in a distribution equal to or lower than the score corresponding to the given rank.

Physiological measures—any set of procedures or instruments which are used to assess physical development, ability, or capacity.

Power test—a test intended to measure level of performance rather than speed of response; hence, one in which there is either no time limit or a very generous one.

Practice effect—the influence of previous experience with a test on the later administration on the same or a similar test. The term is usually employed when the practice effect is not itself what is at issue, but is something to be eliminated or allowed for.

Predictive validity—the degree to which the results of a particular test have been shown to be predictive of the examinee's future performance.

Product-moment coefficient—the most widely used correlation coefficient for linear relationships. Also called Pearson product-moment coefficient or correlation; symbolized by r.

Profile—a graphic presentation of the results of an individual's performance on a group of tests.

Psycholinguistic—a term applied to the analysis of language based on an understanding of both cognitive development and language structure.

Psychological measures—any set of procedures or instruments which are used to assess mental ability and personality structure.

r—see Coefficient of correlation.

Rank-order correlation (rho, ρ)—a method of obtaining a correlation coefficient by assigning ranks to each score of all individuals, and determining the relationship between them. Also called rank-difference coefficient of correlation.

Raw score—the original, untreated result obtained from a test or other measuring instrument. Usually the number of right answers, or points on a point scale.

Readiness test—a test that measures the extent to which an individual has achieved a degree of maturity or acquired certain skills or information needed for beginning some new learning activity. Most frequently used with pre-school children to determine their readiness for entering school.

Reading age—an age-equivalent score assigned to the average score on a reading test for individuals at a given age.

Reliability—the extent to which a test is consistent with itself in measuring whatever it does measure.

Reliability coefficient—the coefficient of correlation obtained between two forms of a test (alternate-form or parallel-form reliability); between scores on repeated administrations of the same test (test-retest reliability); between halves of a test properly corrected (split-half reliability); or by using the Kuder-Richardson formulas.

Standard deviation (SD, s, σ)—a measure of the variability or dispersion of a set of scores. The more the scores cluster about the mean, the smaller the standard deviation. In a normal distribution, approximately 68 per cent of the scores fall within the range of one SD above and below the mean; approximately 95 per cent fall within a range of two SD's; and practically all the scores fall within a range of three SD's.

Standard error (SE)—an estimate of the magnitude of the "error of measurement" in a score, i.e., the amount by which an obtained score differs from a hypothetically true score. The standard error is an amount such that in approximately two-thirds of the cases the obtained score does not differ more than one SE from the true score.

Standard score, z score—a score in which each individual's score is expressed in terms of the number of standard deviation units of the score from the mean.

Standardized test, standard test—a test that has been given to various samples or groups under standardized conditions and for which norms have been established.

Sub-tests—a set of sub-groups of items which are developed to supposedly measure specific sub-areas of a more general ability.

Survey test—a test that measures general achievement in a given subject or area and is more generally concerned with breadth of coverage than with specific details or discovery of causal factors. It is most frequently used for screening large groups of persons.

T score—a standard score with a mean of fifty and a standard deviation of ten; usually used to convert raw scores on two or more tests into comparable scores for ease in interpretation.

True score—the score that would be obtained if we had a perfectly reliable measuring instrument. If it were possible to measure an individual over and over again with the same test, without any changes in the individual, the average of all his test scores would be an estimate of his true score. True scores are never obtained, but rather are considered hypothetical values.

Validity—the extent to which a test measures what it is supposed to measure. Validity is defined on the basis of different purposes; different kinds of evidence are used in defining types of validity. The most common types of validity are: *content validity*, which describes how well the content of the test samples the class of situations or subject-matter about which conclusions are to be drawn; *concurrent validity*, which describes how well test scores correspond to measures of concurrent criterion performance or status; *predictive validity*, which indicates how well predictions made from the test are confirmed by evidence gathered at some later time; and *construct validity*, which indicates the degree to which certain explanatory constructs or conceptualizations account for performance on the test.

Verbal test—a test in which results depend to some extent on the use and comprehension of words, as in most paper-and-pencil tests.

z score—see Standard score.

Guide to tests and measuring instruments in reading

Roger Farr
Indiana University

Edward G. Summers
University of British Columbia

The purpose of the *Guide to Tests and Measuring Instruments in Reading* is to provide researchers and practitioners with a reference tool for quickly identifying those reading tests which meet their particular needs. Test consumers often want to locate a number of tests which could be used at a particular grade level or those which contain certain sub-tests. This Guide should aid in that type of search. For example, if a test consumer wanted to identify a number of reading tests that could be used with fifth-grade children, he could quickly look down the column labelled *Grade* and find several possible choices. After identifying the alternative choices, he could then carefully examine copies of the actual test. Test publishers are often quite willing to supply sample tests to prospective test users. For the readers' convenience, a list of publishers' addresses follows the Guide.

Following the Guide are two indexes which will supply the test user with the means for conducting a more critical study of the tests. The first index is to Buros' *Reading Tests and Reviews* (Highland Park, N.J.; Gryphon Press, 1968) and Buros' *Mental Measurement Yearbooks*. By consulting these reviews, the test consumer can learn more about the strengths, weaknesses, and uses of any of the tests he is interested in. A second index provides references to those documents in the six ERIC/CRIER basic references which reported use of the test in reading research. These basic references include materials which have been reported in the published journal literature. These references provide valuable information to the researcher or test consumer interested in an indepth study of a particular test.

The Guide contains only those tests which are currently published in the United States. Therefore, those reading tests which are either out of print or have been published abroad are not included. The tests are organized alphabetically by test name. In most cases, the information supplied was taken directly from the test or the test manual provided by the publisher. Descriptive information for each test includes the data listed below.

1] **Test title** The title listed on the front cover of the test booklet. The date of first publication and most recent revision are listed in parentheses after the test title. If an asterisk appears following the entry, it indicates that the test is an individual test; the absence of any notation indicates that the test is a group test.

2] **Grade or age level** The suggested grade level for using the test is listed as indicated by the publisher. In several instances, the test publisher supplied only age levels. These have been converted to grade level equivalencies. A dagger (†) has been placed after those which were originally given in age levels.

3] **Sub-tests** The names of the sub-tests are as indicated in the test booklet.

4] **Number of forms** The number of forms is listed so the potential test user will know if alternative forms are available for pre- and post-testing.

5] **Time in minutes** The approximate time needed for administering the tests is based on information provided by the publisher.

6] **Authors** The names are listed as they appear on the front of the test booklet.

7] **Publisher** The publishing company is listed as indicated on the front of the test booklet.

Test	Grade	Sub-tests	Number of forms	Time in min.	Author(s)	Publisher
ABC Inventory to Determine Kindergarten and School Readiness (1965)	K-1		1		N. Adair & G. Blesch	Research Concepts
Academic Promise Tests (1959, rev. 1961)	6-9	Verbal; numerical; abstract reasoning; language usage	2	90	G. K. Bennett, M. K. Bennett, D. M. Clendenin, J. E. Doppelt, J. H. Ricks, Jr., H. G. Seashore, & A. G. Wesman	Psychological Corp.
Adult Basic Reading Inventory (1966)	Functionally illiterate adolescents or adults	Sight words; sound and letter discrimination; word meaning (reading); word meaning (listening); context reading	1		R. W. Burnett	Scholastic Testing Service
American School Achievement Tests						
Part I, Reading, Primary Battery (1941, rev. 1955)	2-3	Sentence and word meaning; paragraph meaning	4	35	W. E. Pratt, R. V. Young, & C. E. Cockerville	Bobbs-Merrill
Part I, Reading, Intermediate Battery (1941, rev. 1958)	4-6	Sentence and word meaning; paragraph meaning	4	35	W. E. Pratt, R. V. Young, & C. E. Cockerville	Bobbs-Merrill
Part I, Reading, Advanced Battery	7-9	Sentence and word meaning; paragraph meaning	4	40	W. E. Pratt, R. V. Young, & C. E. Cockerville	Bobbs-Merrill

Test	Grade	Skills			Author	Publisher
American School Reading Readiness Test (1941, rev. 1955)	K-1†	Vocabulary; discrimination of letter forms; discrimination of letter combinations; word selection; word matching; discrimination of geometric forms; following directions; memory of geometric forms.	1	45	W. E. Pratt, R. V. Young, & C. A. Whitmer	Bobbs-Merrill
American School Reading Tests (1955)	10-13	Vocabulary; reading rate; comprehension	2	80	W. E. Pratt & S. W. Love	Bobbs-Merrill
Anton Brenner Development Gestalt Test of School Readiness (1964)*	K-1†	Number producing; number recognition; ten-dot gestalt; sentence gestalt; draw-a-man	1	3-10	A. Brenner	Western Psychological Services
Binion-Beck Reading Readiness Test for Kindergarten and First Grade (1945)	K-1	Picture vocabulary; ability to follow directions; memory for a story; motor control	1	40	H. S. Binion & R. L. Beck	Acorn Publishing Co.
Botel Reading Inventory (1961, 1966)*	1-12	Phonetics mastery (consonants, vowels, syllabication, nonsense words); word recognition; word opposites	2		M. Botel, C. L. Holsclaw, & G. C. Cammarata	Follett Publishing Co.
Buffalo Reading Test for Speed and Comprehension (1933, rev. 1965)	9-16	Speed; comprehension	2	35	M. E. Wagner	Foster & Stewart Publishing Corp.

Test	Grade	Sub-tests	Number of forms	Time in min.	Author(s)	Publisher
Burnett Reading Series: Survey Test						
Primary 1 (1966, rev. 1967)	1.5-2.4	Word identification; word meaning; comprehension	1	47	R. W. Burnett	Scholastic Testing Service
Primary II (1966)	2.5-3.9	Word identification; word meaning; comprehension	1	55	R. W. Burnett	Scholastic Testing Service
Intermediate (1967)	4.0-6.9	Word identification; word meaning; comprehension	1	45	R. W. Burnett	Scholastic Testing Service
Advanced (1967)	7.0-9.9	Vocabulary; rate and accuracy; comprehension	1	38	R. W. Burnett	Scholastic Testing Service
Senior (1968)	10.0-12.9	Vocabulary; rate and accuracy; comprehension	1		R. W. Burnett	Scholastic Testing Service
California Phonics Survey (1956, rev. 1963)	7-16	Long-short vowel confusion; other vowel confusion; consonants—confusion with blends and digraphs; consonant-vowel reversals; configuration; endings; negatives—opposites—sight words; rigidity	2	40-45	G. M. Brown & A. B. Cottrell	California Test Bureau
California Reading Test						
Lower Primary (1957, rev. 1963)	1-2	Vocabulary; comprehension	2	35	E. W. Tiegs & W. W. Clark	California Test Bureau
Upper Primary (1957, rev. 1963)	2.5-4.5	Vocabulary; comprehension	2	50	E. W. Tiegs & W. W. Clark	California Test Bureau

Test	Grade	Areas		Time (min.)	Author(s)	Publisher
Elementary (1957, rev. 1963)	4-6	Vocabulary; comprehension	4	60	E. W. Tiegs & W. W. Clark	California Test Bureau
Junior High Level (1957, rev. 1963)	7-9	Vocabulary; comprehension	4	80	E. W. Tiegs & W. W. Clark	California Test Bureau
Advanced (1957, rev. 1963)	9-14	Vocabulary; comprehension	3	80	E. W. Tiegs & W. W. Clark	California Test Bureau
California Study Methods Survey (1958)	7-13	Attitudes toward school; mechanics of study; planning and system; verification	1	35-50	H. D. Carter	California Test Bureau
California Survey Series: Survey of Reading Achievement						
Junior High Level (1959)	7-9		2	45	E. W. Tiegs & W. W. Clark	California Test Bureau
Advanced	9-12		2	45	E. W. Tiegs & W. W. Clark	California Test Bureau
Classroom Reading Inventory (1965)	2-8	Word recognition; independent reading level; instructional reading level; frustration level; hearing capacity level; spelling	2		N. J. Silvaroli	William C. Brown Book Co.
Clymer-Barrett Pre-reading Battery (1966, rev. 1967)	K-1	Visual discrimination; auditory discrimination; visual motor performance	2		T. Clymer & T. C. Barrett	Personnel Press

Test	Grade	Sub-tests	Number of forms	Time in min.	Author(s)	Publisher
Commerce Reading Comprehension Test (1956, rev. 1958)	12-16+		1	65	I. T. Halfter & R. J. McCall	Department of Psychological Testing, DePaul University
Comprehensive Primary Reading Scales (1956, rev. 1960)	1	Reading comprehension; picture reading vocabulary; meaning reading vocabulary; word recognition vocabulary	1		M. J. Van Wagenen, M. A. Van Wagenen, & M. Klaeger	Van Wagenen Psycho-Educational Research Laboratories
Comprehensive Reading Scales (1948, rev. 1953)	4-12		1		M. J. Van Wagenen	Van Wagenen Psycho-Educational Research Laboratories
Cooperative English Tests: Reading Comprehension (1940, rev. 1960)	9-14	Vocabulary; level of comprehension; speed of comprehension	3	45	C. Derrick, D. P. Harris, & B. Walker	Cooperative Test Division, Educational Testing Service
Cooperative Inter-American Tests Tests of Natural Sciences (1950)	8-13	Vocabulary; interpretation of reading materials	4	45	Committee on Modern Languages of American Council on Education	Cooperative Test Division, Educational Testing Service
Tests of Reading (1950)	1-13	Vocabulary; comprehension (level and speed)	4		Committee on Modern Languages of American Council on Education	Cooperative Test Division, Educational Testing Service

Tests of Social Studies (1950)	8-13	Vocabulary; interpretation of reading materials	4	45	Committee on Modern Languages of American Council on Education[2]	Cooperative Test Division, Educational Testing Service
Cumulative Reading Record (1933, rev. 1956)	9-12		1		M. M. Skinner	National Council of Teachers of English
Davis Reading Test						
Series I (1956, rev. 1962)	11-13	Level of comprehension; speed of comprehension	4	40	F. B. Davis & C. C. Davis	Psychological Corp.
Series II (1956, rev. 1962)	8-11	Level of comprehension; speed of comprehension	4	40	F. B. Davis & C. C. Davis	Psychological Corp.
Delaware County Silent Reading Test (1965)	1.5-8	Interpretation; organization; vocabulary; structural analysis	1		J. E. Newburg & N. A. Spennato	Delaware County Reading Consultants Assn.
Developmental Reading Tests						
Primer Reading (1955, rev. 1968)	1.5	Basic vocabulary; general comprehension; specific comprehension	1	55	G. L. Bond, B. Balow, & C. J. Hoyt	Lyons & Carnahan
Lower Primary Reading (1955, rev. 1968)	1.5-2.5	Basic vocabulary; general comprehension; specific comprehension	1	55	G. L. Bond, B. Balow, & C. J. Hoyt	Lyons & Carnahan
Upper Primary Reading (1955, rev. 1968)	2.5-3	Basic vocabulary; general comprehension; specific comprehension	1	55	G. L. Bond, B. Balow, & C. J. Hoyt	Lyons & Carnahan

Test	Grade	Sub-tests	Number of forms	Time in min.	Author(s)	Publisher
Developmental Reading Tests (cont'd) Intermediate Reading (1959, rev. 1968)	4-6	Basic vocabulary; reading to retain information; reading to organize; reading to evaluate-interpret; reading to appreciate; average comprehension	2	50	G. L. Bond, B. Balow, & C. J. Hoyt	Lyons & Carnahan
Developmental Reading Tests: Silent Reading Diagnostic Tests (1958)	3-8	Recognition of words in isolation; recognition of words in context; recognition of reversible words in context; locating elements; syllabication; locating the root word; word elements; beginning sounds; rhyming sounds; letter sounds; word synthesis	1	90	G. L. Bond, T. Clymer, & C. J. Hoyt	Lyons & Carnahan
Diagnostic Examination of Silent Reading Abilities (1939, rev. 1954)	4-16	Rate of comprehension; perception of relations; vocabulary in context; vocabulary-isolated words; general information; ability to grasp the central thought; ability to note clearly stated details; interpretation; integration of dispersed ideas; ability to draw inferences	1	140-150	A. Dvorak & M. J. Van Wagenen	Educational Test Bureau

Test	Grade	Content	No.	Time/Age	Author	Publisher
Diagnostic Reading Scales (1963)*	1-8	Word recognition; oral reading; silent reading; auditory comprehension	1	45	G. D. Spache	California Test Bureau
Diagnostic Reading Tests						
Diagnostic Reading Test (1957, rev. 1963)	K-4	Survey; word attack	2		F. Triggs	Committee on Diagnostic Reading Tests
Lower Level (1947, rev. 1963)	4-8	Survey; word attack	2		F. Triggs	Committee on Diagnostic Reading Tests
Upper Level (1947, rev. 1963)	7-13	Survey; vocabulary; comprehension (silent and auditory); rate of reading; word attack	2		F. Triggs	Committee on Diagnostic Reading Tests
Diagnostic Reading Test, Pupil Progress Series						
Primary Level I (1956, rev. 1957)	1.9-2.1	Word recognition; word-content relation; words in use; rate of reading for meaning; comprehension; recalling information; reading to locate information; reading for descriptions	2	40-60	O. F. Anderhalter, R. S. Gawkowski, & R. Colestock	Scholastic Testing Service
Primary Level II (1956, rev. 1957)	2.2-3	Words in use; word meaning; rate of reading for meaning; recalling information; locating information; reading for descriptions; following directions; reading for meaning	2	40-60	O. F. Anderhalter, R. S. Gawkowski, & R. Colestock	Scholastic Testing Service

Test	Grade	Sub-tests	Number of forms	Time in min.	Author(s)	Publisher
Diagnostic Reading Test, Pupil Progress Series (cont'd)						
Elementary Level (1956, rev. 1957)	4-6	Functions of common sources; use selection of best source; use of the index; use of table of contents; rate of reading for meaning; recalling information; locating information; reading for descriptions; word meaning; reading for meaning; reading for directions or procedures	2	65	O. F. Anderhalter, R. S. Gawkowski, & R. Colestock	Scholastic Testing Service
Advanced Level (1956, rev. 1960)	7-8	Functions of common sources; selection of best source; use of index; use of table of contents; rate of reading for meaning; recalling information; locating information; reading for descriptions; word meaning; reading for meaning; reading for directions or procedures	2	65	O. F. Anderhalter, R. S. Gawkowski, & R. Colestock	Scholastic Testing Service
Digest-Diagnostic Inventory Group Evaluation Tests (1967)	4-5, 7-9	Computation; reading; attitude inventory	1	65	L. Lepore, H. C. Beaman, P. Miner, & D. R. Phillips	Science Research Associates

Test	Grade	Skills	Forms	Time (min.)	Author	Publisher
Dolch Basic Sight Word Test (1942)	1-2		1	35	E. W. Dolch	Garrard Publishing Co.
Doren Diagnostic Reading Test of Word Recognition Skills (1956, rev. 1964)	1-9	Letter recognition; beginning sounds; whole word recognition; words within words; speech consonants; ending sounds; blending; rhyming; vowels; sight words; discriminate guessing	1	180	M. Doren	American Guidance Service
Durrell Analysis of Reading Difficulty (1937, rev. 1955)*	1-6	Oral reading; silent reading; listening comprehension; word recognition and analysis; naming letters; identifying letters; matching letters; visual memory of words—primary; hearing sounds in words—primary; learning to hear sounds in words; sounds of letters; learning rate; visual memory of words—intermediate; phonic spelling; spelling test; handwriting	1	30-90	D. D. Durrell	Harcourt, Brace, & World
Durrell Listening-Reading Series						
Primary Level (1969)	1-2	Vocabulary listening; vocabulary reading; sentence listening; sentence reading	1	80	D. D. Durrell	Harcourt, Brace, & World
Intermediate Level (1969)	3-6	Vocabulary listening; vocabulary reading; paragraph listening; paragraph reading	1	80	D. D. Durrell	Harcourt, Brace, & World

Test	Grade	Sub-tests	Number of forms	Time in min.	Author(s)	Publisher
Durrell Listening-Reading Series (cont'd) Advanced Level (1969)	7-9	Vocabulary listening; vocabulary reading; paragraph listening; paragraph reading	1	80	D. D. Durrell	Harcourt, Brace, & World
Early Detection Inventory (1967)	Pre-K	School readiness tasks; social-emotional behavior responses; motor performance	1		F. E. McGahan & C. McGahan	Follett Publishing Co.
Emporia Reading Tests Primary Reading Test (1964)	1	Word recognition; word matching; matching like words; matching similar objects; auditory word recognition; phonetic recognition; word meaning	4	36	M. Barnett & M. W. Sanders	Bureau of Educational Measurements
Elementary Reading Test (1964)	2-3	Word reading; sentence reading; paragraph reading	4	20	M. Barnett & M. W. Sanders	Bureau of Educational Measurements
Intermediate Reading Test (1964)*	4-6	Paragraph reading	4	30	D. Carline, A. Seybold, E. L. Eaton, & M. W. Sanders	Bureau of Educational Measurements

Test	Grade	Content	Forms	Time (min.)	Author	Publisher
Junior High School Reading Test (1964)	7-8	Paragraph reading; word meaning	4	55	D. Carline, A. Seybold, E. L. Eaton, & M. W. Sanders	Bureau of Educational Measurements
Emporia Silent Reading Test (1933, rev. 1935)	3-8		4	20	H. E. Schrammel & W. H. Gray	Bureau of Educational Measurements
Evaluation Aptitude Test (1951, rev. 1952)	12+, 16+	Neutral syllogisms; emotionally toned syllogisms; emotional bias; indecision	1	55	D. E. Sell	Psychometric Affiliates
Every Pupil Achievement Test Primary Reading (1935, rev. 1967)	1	Word recognition; comprehension; listening; sentence completion; matching	1	40-60	M. Barnett	Bureau of Educational Measurements
Primary Reading (1935, rev. 1967)	2-3	Testing knowledge of environment through reading; sentence completion; comprehension	1	20	M. Barnett	Bureau of Educational Measurements,
Flash-X Sight Vocabulary Test (1961)*	1-2	Sight vocabulary; experience vocabulary	1	10	G. D. Spache & S. E. Taylor	Educational Developmental Laboratories

Test	Grade	Sub-tests	Number of forms	Time in min.	Author(s)	Publisher
Functional Readiness Questionnaire for School and College Students (1957)*	1-16	Physical readiness; emotional readiness	1	5	E. A. Taylor & H. A. Sloan	Reading and Study Skills Center
Gates-MacGinitie Reading Tests						
Primary A (1926, rev. 1965)	1	Vocabulary; comprehension	2	45	A. I. Gates & W. MacGinitie	Teachers College Press, Columbia University
Primary B (1926, rev. 1965)	2	Vocabulary; comprehension	2	45	A. I. Gates & W. MacGinitie	Teachers College Press, Columbia University
Primary C (1938, rev. 1965)	3	Vocabulary; comprehension	2	55	A. I. Gates & W. MacGinitie	Teachers College Press, Columbia University
Primary Cs (1926, rev. 1965)	2-3	Speed and accuracy	3	12	A. I. Gates & W. MacGinitie	Teachers College Press, Columbia University
Survey D (1939, rev. 1965)	4-6	Speed and accuracy; vocabulary; comprehension	6	50	A. I. Gates & W. MacGinitie	Teachers College Press, Columbia University
Survey E (1964, rev. 1965)	7-9	Speed and accuracy; vocabulary; comprehension	6	49	A. I. Gates & W. MacGinitie	Teachers College Press, Columbia University

Test	Grade	Forms	Time	Skills	Author	Publisher
Gates-MacGinitie Reading Tests—Readiness Skills (1939, rev. 1968)	K-1	1		Listening; comprehension; auditory discrimination; visual discrimination; following directions; letter recognition; visual-motor coordination; auditory blending; word recognition	A. I. Gates & W. MacGinitie	Teachers College Press, Columbia University
Gates-McKillop Reading Diagnostic Tests (1926, rev. 1962)*	2-6	2	30-60	tions; mispronunciation; Omissions; additions; repetitions; words—flash presentation; words—untimed presentation; phrases—flash presentation; recognizing and blending common word parts; giving letter sounds; naming capital letters; naming lower case letters; recognizing the visual form of sounds; auditory blending; spelling; oral vocabulary; syllabication; auditory discrimination	A. I. Gates & A. McKillop	Teachers College Press, Columbia University
Gilliland Learning Potential Examination (1966)	K+	1		Nonreading and noncultural; predicted comprehension; visual memory	H. Gilliland	Montana Reading Clinic Publications
Gilmore Oral Reading Test: New Edition (1951, rev. 1968)*	1-8	2	15-20	Accuracy; comprehension; rate	J. Gilmore & V. Gilmore	Harcourt, Brace, & World

Test	Grade	Sub-tests	Number of forms	Time in min.	Author(s)	Publisher
Gray Oral Reading Test (1963, rev. 1967)*	1-16+		4		W. S. Gray	Bobbs-Merrill
Gray-Votaw-Rogers General Achievement Test						
Level I (1934, rev. 1963)	1-3	Reading comprehension; reading vocabulary; spelling; arithmetic reasoning; arithmetic computation	4	70-80	H. Gray, D. F. Votaw, & J. L. Rogers	Steck Co.
Level II (1934, rev. 1963)	4-9	Reading comprehension; reading vocabulary; spelling; arithmetic reasoning; arithmetic computation; elementary science; language; literature (optional); social studies; health and safety	4	170	H. Gray, D. F. Votaw, & J. L. Rogers	Steck Co.
Group Diagnostic Reading Aptitude and Achievement Tests—Intermediate Form (1939)	3-9	Reading; word discrimination; spelling; visual arithmetic; auditory ability; motor ability; vocabulary	1	60-70	M. Monroe & E. E. Sherman	C. H. Nevins Printing Co.
Harrison-Stroud Reading Readiness Profiles (1949, rev. 1956)	K-1	Using symbols; making visual discriminations; using the context; making auditory discriminations; using context and auditory clues; giving names of letters	1	80-90	M. L. Harrison & J. B. Stroud	Houghton Mifflin

Test	Grade	Skills measured	No. of forms	Time	Author	Publisher
individual Placement Series—Reading Adequacy "READ" Test (1961, rev. 1966)	12+	Reading rate; per cent of comprehension; corrected reading rate	1	10-15	J. H. Norman	Personnel Research Associates
Iowa Every-Pupil Tests of Basic Skills, Test A: Silent Reading Comprehension						
Elementary Battery (1955, rev. 1964)	3-5	Reading comprehension; vocabulary	4	60	H. F. Spitzer, E. Horn, M. McBroom, H. A. Greene, & E. F. Lindquist	Houghton Mifflin
Advanced Battery (1955, rev. 1964)	5-9	Reading comprehension; vocabulary	4	85	H. F. Spitzer, E. Horn, M. McBroom, H. A. Greene, & E. F. Lindquist	Houghton Mifflin
Iowa Every-Pupil Tests of Basic Skills, Test B						
Elementary Battery (1940, rev. 1947)	3-5	Map reading; use of references; use of index; use of dictionary; alphabetizing	4	55	H. F. Spitzer, E. Horn, M. McBroom, H. A. Greene, & E. F. Lindquist	Houghton Mifflin
Advanced Battery (1940, rev. 1947)	5-9	Map reading; use of references; use of index; use of dictionary; graphing	4	90	H. F. Spitzer, E. Horn, M. McBroom, H. A. Greene, & E. F. Lindquist	Houghton Mifflin

Test	Grade	Sub-tests	Number of forms	Time in min.	Author(s)	Publisher
Iowa Silent Reading Tests						
Elementary (1933, rev. 1942)	Pre-K-3†	Rate; comprehension; directed reading; word meaning; paragraph comprehension; sentence meaning; alphabetizing; use of index	4	60	H. A. Greene & V. H. Kelley	Harcourt, Brace, & World
Advanced (1927, rev. 1942)	9-14	Rate; comprehension; directed reading; poetry comprehension; word meaning; sentence meaning; paragraph comprehension; use of index; selection of key words	4	60	H. A. Greene, A. N. Jorgensen, & V. H. Kelley	Harcourt, Brace, & World
Iowa Tests of Educational Development						
Test 5: Ability to Interpret Reading Materials in the Social Studies (1942, rev. 1961)	9-12		2	70	E. F. Lindquist	Science Research Associates
Test 6: Ability to Interpret Reading Materials in the Natural Sciences (1942, rev. 1961)	9-12		2	70	E. F. Lindquist	Science Research Associates
Test 9: Use of Sources of Information	9-12		2	35	E. F. Lindquist	Science Research Associates
Kelley-Greene Reading Comprehension Test	9-13	Paragraph comprehension; directed reading; retention of details; reading rate	1	75	V. H. Kelley & H. A. Greene	Harcourt, Brace, & World

Test	Grade	Description			Author	Publisher
Keystone Ready to Read Tests (1954)	K		1			Keystone View Co.
Learning Methods Test (1954, rev. 1955)*	K-3	Word recognition; learning methods training and testing	1	85-100	R. E. Mills	Mills Center Inc.
Lee-Clark Reading Readiness Test (1931, rev. 1962)	K-1	Letter symbols; concepts; word symbols	1	20	J. M. Lee & W. W. Clark	California Test Bureau
Lee-Clark Reading Test						
Primer (1931, rev. 1958)	1	Auditory stimuli; visual stimuli; following directions	2	20-30	J. M. Lee & W. W. Clark	California Test Bureau
First Reader (1931, rev. 1958)	1-2	Auditory stimuli; visual stimuli; following directions; completion; inference	2	20-30	J. M. Lee & W. W. Clark	California Test Bureau
Library Tests						
Library Survey Test (Test I) (1967)	7-8	General information: periodicals; oral and written reports; Dewey Decimal system; dictionary; reference books	1		Perfection Form Co.	Perfection Form Co.
Library Sources and Skills (Test II) (1967)	9-10	Readers guide to periodicals; terms scholars use; terms used in discussing books and manuscripts; Dewey Decimal classification; research organization; reference material; Webster's Third International Dictionary; encyclopedia; periodicals; card catalog	1		Perfection Form Co.	Perfection Form Co.

Test	Grade	Sub-tests	Number of forms	Time in min.	Author(s)	Publisher
Library Tests (cont'd)						
Library Sources and Uses of Information (Test III) (1967)	11-12	Alphabetizing; Dewey Decimal classification; periodicals; card catalog; reference books; Readers Guide; identifying resources; using sources of information	1		Perfection Form Co.	Perfection Form Co.
Lippincott Reading Readiness Test (Including Readiness Checklist) (1965)	K-1		1		P. H. McLeod	J. B. Lippincott
Logical Reasoning (1955)	9-16+		1	25	A. F. Hertzka & J. P. Guilford	Sheridan Psychological Services
Los Angeles Elementary Reading Test (1926, rev. 1931)	3-8		4	35	J. E. Ingraham	California Test Bureau
McCullough Word Analysis Tests (1960, rev. 1963)	4-6	Initial blends and digraphs; phonetic discrimination; matching letters to vowel sounds; sounding whole words; interpreting phonetic symbols; dividing words into syllables; root words in affixed forms	1	70	C. M. McCullough	Personnel Press

Test	Level	Skills			Author	Publisher
McGrath Test of Reading Skills, Second Edition (1965, rev. 1967)	1-13	Word recognition; oral reading; vocabulary; oral reading rate		1	J. E. McGrath	McGrath Reading Clinic
McHugh-McParland Reading Readiness Test (1966, rev. 1968)	K-1	Rhyming words; beginning sounds; visual discrimination; identifying letters		1	W. J. McHugh & M. McParland	Cal-State Bookstore
McMenemy Measure of Reading Ability						
Primary (1965, rev. 1968)	3			1	R. A. McMenemy	R. A. McMenemy
Intermediate (1965, rev. 1968)	5-6			1	R. A. McMenemy	R. A. McMenemy
Advanced (1965, rev. 1968)	7-8			1	R. A. McMenemy	R. A. McMenemy
Maintaining Reading Efficiency Tests (1966)	9-16	Rate; comprehension accuracy; reading efficiency		2	W. E. Peeples & J. K. Taylor	Developmental Reading Distributors
Maturity Level for School Entrance and Reading Readiness (1950, rev. 1959)*	K-1	Maturity level; reading readiness	20	1	K. M. Banham	American Guidance Service
Metropolitan Achievement Tests: Reading						
Upper Primary Reading Test (1932, rev. 1962)	2	Word knowledge; word discrimination; reading	79-84	2	W. N. Durost, H. H. Bixler, G. H. Hildreth, K. W. Lund, & J. W. Wrightstone	Harcourt, Brace, & World

Test	Grade	Sub-tests	Number of forms	Time in min.	Author(s)	Publisher
Metropolitan Achievement Tests: Reading (cont'd)						
Elementary Reading Test (1932, rev. 1962)	3-4	Word knowledge; reading	3	43	W. N. Durost, H. H. Bixler, G. H. Hildreth, K. W. Lund, & J. W. Wrightstone	Harcourt, Brace, & World
Intermediate Reading Test (1933, rev. 1962)	5-6	Word knowledge; reading	3	46	W. N. Durost, H. H. Bixler, G. H. Hildreth, K. W. Lund, & J. W. Wrightstone	Harcourt, Brace, & World
Advanced Reading Test (1933, rev. 1962)	7-9	Word knowledge; reading	3	46	W. N. Durost, H. H. Bixler, G. H. Hildreth, K. W. Lund, & J. W. Wrightstone	Harcourt, Brace, & World
Metropolitan Readiness Tests (1933, rev. 1965)	K-1	Word meaning; listening; matching; alphabet; numbers; copying; drawing a man (optional)	2	65-75	G. H. Hildreth, N. L. Griffiths, & M. E. McGauvran	Harcourt, Brace, & World
Minnesota Reading Examinations for College Students (1930, rev. 1935)	9-16	Vocabulary; paragraph reading	2	55	M. E. Haggerty & A. C. Eurich	University of Minnesota Press

Test	Grade	Skills Measured	Forms	Time (min.)	Author	Publisher
Minnesota Speed of Reading Test for College Students (1936)	12-16	History; geography; economics; government; psychology; education; science	2	15	A. C. Eurich	University of Minnesota Press
Monroe Reading Aptitude Tests (1935)	K-1	Visual; auditory; motor; articulation; language	1	30	M. Monroe	Houghton Mifflin
Monroe's Standardized Silent Reading Test (1919, rev. 1954)	3-12	Rate; comprehension	8	10	W. S. Monroe	Bobbs-Merrill
Mott Basic Language Skills Placement Test (1967)*	1-3†	Initial consonant recognition; word meaning; sentence completion; comprehension	1	15		Allied Education Council
Murphy-Durrell Reading Readiness Analysis (1949, rev. 1965)	K-1	Sound recognition; letter meaning; learning words	1	80	H. A. Murphy & D. D. Durrell	Harcourt, Brace, & World
National Achievement Tests: High School Reading Test (1939, rev. 1952)	7-12	Vocabulary; word discrimination; sentence meaning; noting details; interpreting paragraphs	2	40	R. K. Speer & S. Smith	Acorn Publishing Co., Psychometric Affiliates
National Achievement Tests: Municipal Tests: Reading Test (Comprehension and Speed) (1938, rev. 1957)	3-8	Following directions; sentence meaning; paragraph meaning; reading speed	2	37-38	R. K. Speer & S. Smith	Acorn Publishing Co., Psychometric Affiliates
National Achievement Tests: Reading Comprehension Test (1938, rev. 1957)	3-8	Following directions; sentence meaning; paragraph meaning	2	30	R. K. Speer & S. Smith	Acorn Publishing Co., Psychometric Affiliates

Test	Grade	Sub-tests	Number of forms	Time in min.	Author(s)	Publisher
National Achievement Tests: Reading Comprehension Test (1953, rev. 1957)	4-9		1	35	L. D. Crow, M. J. Kuhlmann, & A. Crow	Acorn Publishing Co., Psychometric Affiliates
Neale Analysis of Reading Ability (1957, rev. 1958)*	1-7†	Accuracy; comprehension; rate of reading; names and sounds of letters (optional); auditory discrimination through simple spelling (optional); blending and recognition of syllables (optional)	3	10-15	M. D. Neale	St. Martins Press
Nelson-Denny Reading Test: Vocabulary-Comprehension-Rate (1924, rev. 1960)	9-16+	Vocabulary; comprehension; rate	2	35	M. J. Nelson, E. Denny, & J. Brown	Houghton Mifflin
Nelson Reading Test (1931, rev. 1962)	3-9	Vocabulary; paragraph comprehension	2	35	M. J. Nelson	Houghton Mifflin
OC Diagnostic Dictionary Test (1960)	5-8		1	20	K. O'Connor	O'Connor Reading Clinic Publishing Co.
OC Diagnostic Syllabizing Test (1960, rev. 1962)	4-6		1	15-20	K. O'Connor	O'Connor Reading Clinic Publishing Co.
Ohio Diagnostic Reading Test[1] Level I (1966)	2.5-8.5	Reading comprehension; vocabulary; auditory discrimination; syllabication; beginning and ending sounds; sound discrimination; blending	1	133	B. Karlsen, R. Madden, & E. F. Gardner	Ohio Testing Services

Test	Grade/Level	Content	Forms	Time	Author	Publisher
Level II (1966)	4.5-8.5	Reading comprehension; vocabulary; syllabication; sound discrimination; blending; rate of reading	1	100	B. Karlsen, R. Madden, & E. F. Gardner	Ohio Testing Services
Peabody Library Information Test						
Elementary Level (1940)	4-8		1	35	L. Shores & J. E. Moore	Educational Test Bureau
High School Level (1940)	9-12		1	35	L. Shores & J. E. Moore	Educational Test Bureau
College Level (1938, rev. 1940)	13-16	The book; arrangement of books; catalog; dictionary; encyclopedia; periodicals and indexes; special reference books; bibliography	1	37	L. Shores & J. E. Moore	Educational Test Bureau
Perceptual Forms Test (1955, rev. 1967)	6-8.5		1	10	Publication Committee, Winter Haven Lions Club	Winter Haven Lions Research Foundation
Perceptual Test of Complete Copy Forms (1966)	K-3	Perceptual forms; incomplete forms	2		Publication Committee, Winter Haven Lions Club	Winter Haven Lions Research Foundation
Phonics Knowledge Survey (1964)*	1-6	Names of letters; consonant and vowel sounds; syllabication	1	10-30	D. Durkin & L. Meshover	Teachers College Press, Columbia University
Phonovisual Diagnostic Test (1949, rev. 1958)	3-12	Phonetic weaknesses	1	15	L. D. Schoolfield & J. G. Timberlake	Phonovisual Products

¹ A special form of the Stanford Diagnostic Reading Test.

Test	Grade	Sub-tests	Number of forms	Time in min.	Author(s)	Publisher
Pictographic Self Rating Scale (1955, rev. 1957)	9-16		1	35	E. R. Ryden	Acorn Publishing Co., Psychometric Affiliates
Pressey Diagnostic Reading Tests (1929)	3-9	Speed; vocabulary; paragraph meaning	1		S. L. Pressey & L. C. Pressey	Bobbs-Merrill
Primary Academic Sentiment Scale (1968)	4.4-7.3	Sentiment; dependency	1		G. R. Thompson	Priority Innovations
Primary Reading Profiles (1953, rev. 1968)	1-2	Reading aptitude; auditory association; word recognition; word attack; reading comprehension	1	95-100	J. B. Stroud, A. N. Hieronymous, & P. McKee	Houghton Mifflin
Primary Reading Test: Acorn Achievement Tests (1943, rev. 1957)	2-3	Word recognition; words-similar meaning; word meaning-opposites; story-paragraph-sentence meaning	2	40	W. E. Stayton, F. C. Ransom, & R. L. Beck	Acorn Publishing Co., Psychometric Affiliates
Public School Achievement Tests: Reading (1928, rev. 1959)	3-8		2	45	J. S. Orleans	Bobbs-Merrill
Purdue Reading Test (1928, rev. 1953)	7-16		2	45	H. H. Remmers, J. M. Stalnaker, & P. C. Baker	State High School Testing Service for Indiana
Purdue Reading Test for Industrial Supervisors: Purdue Personnel Tests (1955)	12+		1	35	J. Tiffin & R. Dunlap	Purdue Research Foundation

Test	Level	Skills/Content			Author	Publisher
RBH Reading Comprehension Test (1951, rev. 1963)	12+		1	25		Richardson, Bellows, Henry, & Co.
RBH Scientific Reading Test (1950, rev. 1962)	12+		1			Richardson, Bellows, Henry, & Co.
Reader's Inventory (1963)	9-16+		1		G. D. Spache & S. Taylor	Educational Developmental Laboratories
Reader Rater with Self-Scoring Profile (1959, rev. 1965)*	10-12+†	Speed; comprehension; reading habits; reading for details; reading for inferences; reading for main ideas and adjusting speed; summarizing; skimming; recall of information read; unspeeded vocabulary; speeded vocabulary	1	60-120		Better Reading Program
Reading: Adult Basic Education Survey, Parts 1 and 2 (1966, rev. 1967)	Poorly educated adults	Comprehension; vocabulary	1		E. Rasof & M. C. Neff	Follett Publishing Co.
Reading Eye (1959, rev. 1960)*	1-16+	Fixations; regressions; average span of recognition; average duration of fixation; rate with comprehension; grade level of fundamental reading skill; relative efficiency; directional attack; visual adjustment; general adjustment to reading	8	4	S. E. Taylor & H. Frackenpohl	Educational Developmental Laboratories

Test	Grade	Sub-tests	Number of forms	Time in min.	Author(s)	Publisher
Reading Readiness—Form A (1953, rev. 1960)	K-1	Uses of things; likenesses; likenesses in words; listening for **c** sound; listening for **d** sound	1	30-45	O. F. Anderhalter & R. Colestock	Scholastic Testing Service
Reading Skills Diagnostic Test (1967)	2-8	Letter identification; letter-sound identification; phonetic sounds; phonetic words; inconsistent words; consistent phrases; inconsistent phrases; letters in context; words in context	1		R. H. Bloomer	Brador Publications
Reading for Understanding Placement Test						
Junior and General Edition (1959, rev. 1965)	3-16		1		T. G. Thurstone	Science Research Associates
Senior Edition (1963, rev. 1965)	8-12		1		T. G. Thurstone	Science Research Associates
Reading Versatility Test						
Paper and Pencil Edition (1961, rev. 1967)	5-8	Rate of reading; comprehension; skimming (rate, comprehension); scanning (rate, comprehension)	4	30	A. S. McDonald & M. Alodia	Educational Developmental Laboratories
Basic, Reading Eye Edition (1961, rev. 1962)*	6-10	Comprehension; rate; fixation per 100 words; duration of fixation; apparent number of lines; regressions per 100 words; span of recognition	2	35	A. S. McDonald, M. Alodia, & S. E. Taylor	Educational Developmental Laboratories

Test	Grade	Description			Authors	Publisher
Intermediate (1961, rev. 1962)	8-12	Rate of reading; comprehension; skimming (rate, comprehension); scanning (rate, comprehension)	1		A. S. McDonald, M. Alodia, & H. S. Nason	Educational Developmental Laboratories
Advanced (1961, rev. 1962)	12-16	Rate of reading; comprehension; skimming (rate, comprehension); scanning (rate, comprehension)	4	30	G. Zimny & J. Byrne	Educational Developmental Laboratories
Road Map Test of Direction Sense (1965)*	2-12		1		J. Money	Johns Hopkins Press
Robinson-Hall Reading Tests (1940, rev. 1949)	13-16	Reading ability for art, geology, history, and fiction: rate and comprehension	5		F. P. Robinson & P. Hall	University Publications Sales, Ohio State University
Roswell-Chall Auditory Blending Test (1963)*	1-4		1		F. G. Roswell & J. S. Chall	Essay Press
Roswell-Chall Diagnostic Reading Test of Word Analysis Skills (1956, rev. 1959)*	2-6	Simple consonants and combinations; short vowel sounds; rule to- silent e; vowel combinations; syllabication	2	510	F. G. Roswell & J. S. Chall	Essay Press
Scholastic Tests—Educational Development Series Elementary (1965)	4-6		1	360	O. F. Anderhalter, R. H. Bauernfiend, W. Moore, J. Walden, G. Mallinson, J. Mallinson, J. C. McLendon, & V. M. Cashen	Scholastic Testing Service

Test	Grade	Sub-tests	Number of forms	Time in min.	Author(s)	Publisher
Scholastic Tests—Educational Development Series (cont'd)						
Advanced (1965)	6-9		2	360	O. F. Anderhalter, R. H. Bauernfiend, W. Moore, J. Walden, G. Mallinson, J. Mallinson, J. C. McLendon, & V. M. Cashen	Scholastic Testing Service
Senior (1965)	9-12		2	360	O. F. Anderhalter, R. H. Bauernfiend, W. Moore, J. Walden, G. Mallinson, J. Mallinson, J. C. McLendon, & V. M. Cashen	Scholastic Testing Service
School Readiness Behavior Tests Used at the Gesell Institute (1964, rev. 1965)	K-5	Readiness to start school	1		F. L. Ilg & L. B. Ames	Programs for Education
School Readiness Checklist, Research Edition (1963)	K-1		1		J. J. Austin & J. C. Lafferty	Research Concepts
School Readiness Survey (1967)	K-1		1		F. L. Jordan & J. Massey	Consulting Psychologists Press
Schrammel-Gray High School and College Reading Test (1940, rev. 1942)	7-16	Gross-comprehension; comprehension-efficiency; rate	2	30	H. E. Schrammel & W. H. Gray	Bobbs-Merrill

Test	Grade	Description			Author	Publisher
Screening Test of Academic Readiness (1966)	K-1	Picture vocabulary; letters; picture completion; copying; picture description; human figure drawings; relationships; numbers	1		A. E. Ahr	Priority Innovations
Screening Test for the Assignment of Remedial Treatments (1968)	K-1	Visual memory; auditory memory; visual copying; visual discrimination	1		A. E. Ahr	Priority Innovations
Screening Tests for Identifying Children with Specific Language Disability (1962, rev. 1967)	1-4	Visual copying (far point and near point); visual perception memory for words; visual discrimination; visual perception memory in association with kinesthetic memory; auditory recall; auditory perception of beginning and ending sounds; auditory association; Echolalia Test (individual and optional)	1		B. H. Slingerland	Educators Publishing Service
Sequential Tests of Educational Progress—Reading Level 1 (1956, rev. 1963)	13-14	Ability to recall ideas; ability to translate ideas and make inferences; ability to analyze motivation; ability to analyze presentation; ability to criticize	2	90-100		Cooperative Test Division, Educational Testing Service

Test	Grade	Sub-tests	Number of forms	Time in min.	Author(s)	Publisher
Sequential Tests of Educational Progress—Reading (cont'd)						
Level 2 (1956, rev. 1963)	10-12	Ability to recall ideas; ability to translate ideas and make inferences; ability to analyze motivation; ability to analyze presentation; ability to criticize	2	90-100		Cooperative Test Division, Educational Testing Service
Level 3 (1956, rev. 1963)	7-9	Ability to recall ideas; ability to translate ideas and make inferences; ability to analyze motivation; ability to analyze presentation; ability to criticize	2	90-100		Cooperative Test Division, Educational Testing Service
Level 4 (1956, rev. 1963)	4-6	Ability to recall ideas; ability to translate ideas and make inferences; ability to analyze motivation; ability to analyze presentation; ability to criticize	2	90-100		Cooperative Test Division, Educational Testing Service
Slosson Oral Reading Test (SORT) (1963)*	1-12		1	3	R. L. Slosson	Slosson Educational Publications
SRA Achievement Series: Reading (1954, rev. 1964)	1-9	Comprehension; vocabulary; verbal-pictorial association; language perception	4	185 130 80 80	L. P. Thorpe, D. W. Lefever, & R. A. Naslund	Science Research Associates

Test	Grades	Areas	No.	Author	Publisher
SRA Reading Checklist (1966)*	1-8	Preparation for reading; values in reading; mechanics of reading	1		Science Research Associates
SRA Reading Progress Test (1962, rev. 1963)	12+	Vocabulary; logical thinking reading for information; rate	1		Science Research Associates
SRA Reading Record (1947, rev. 1954)	6-12	Reading rate; comprehension; everyday reading scales; vocabulary	1	30	G. T. Buswell	Science Research Associates
SRA Tests of Educational Ability					
Level I (1958, rev. 1962)	4-6	Language; reasoning; quantitative	1	52	L. L. Thurstone & T. G. Thurstone	Science Research Associates
Level II (1958, rev. 1962)	6-9	Language; reasoning; quantitative	1	67	T. G. Thurstone	Science Research Associates
Level III (1957, rev. 1962)	9-12	Language; reasoning; quantitative	1	45	T. G. Thurstone	Science Research Associates
SRA Tests of General Ability (1957, rev. 1960)	4-6	Information; non-cultural reasoning	1	35-45	J. C. Flanagan	Science Research Associates
SRA Youth Inventory (1949, rev. 1960)	9-12	My school; looking ahead; about myself; getting along with others; my home and family; boy meets girl; health; things in general	1	30-45	H. H. Remmers, A. J. Drucher, & B. Shimberg	Science Research Associates
Standardized Oral Reading Check Tests (1923, rev. 1955)	1-8	Rate; accuracy	5	1-3	W. S. Gray	Bobbs-Merrill

Test	Grade	Sub-tests	Number of forms	Time in min.	Author(s)	Publisher
Standardized Oral Reading Paragraphs (1915)*	1-8		1	5-15	W. S. Gray	Bobbs-Merrill
Stanford Achievement Test: High School Reading Test (1965)	9-12				E. F. Gardner, J. C. Merwin, R. Callis, & R. Madden	Harcourt, Brace, & World
Stanford Achievement Test: Reading Tests						
Primary 1 (1922, rev. 1966)	1.5-2.4	Word reading; paragraph meaning; vocabulary; word study skills	1	95	T. L. Kelley, R. Madden, E. F. Gardner, & H. C. Rudman	Harcourt, Brace, & World
Primary 2 (1922, rev. 1966)	2.5-3.9	Word meaning; paragraph meaning; word study skills	1	85	T. L. Kelley, R. Madden, E. F. Gardner, & H. C. Rudman	Harcourt, Brace, & World
Intermediate 1 (1922, rev. 1966)	4-5.5	Word meaning; paragraph meaning	1	48	T. L. Kelley, R. Madden, E. F. Gardner, & H. C. Rudman	Harcourt, Brace, & World
Intermediate 2 (1922, rev. 1966)	5.5-6.9	Word meaning; paragraph meaning	1	50	T. L. Kelley, R. Madden, E. F. Gardner, & H. C. Rudman	Harcourt, Brace, & World
Advanced Paragraph Meaning (1922, rev. 1966)	7-9	Paragraph meaning	1	35	T. L. Kelley, R. Madden, E. F. Gardner, & H. C. Rudman	Harcourt, Brace, & World

Test	Grade	Areas measured	Forms	Time	Authors	Publisher
Stanford Diagnostic Reading Test						
Level 1 (1966)	2.4-4.5	Comprehension; vocabulary; auditory discrimination; syllabication; beginning and ending sounds; blending; sound discrimination	2		B. Karlsen, R. Madden, & E. F. Gardner	Harcourt, Brace, & World
Level 2 (1966)	4.5-8.5	Comprehension; vocabulary; syllabication; sound discrimination; blending; rate	2		B. Karlsen, R. Madden, & E. F. Gardner	Harcourt, Brace, & World
Steinbach Test of Reading Readiness (1963)	K-1	Identifying capital letters; identifying lower case letters; memory of word forms; auditory discrimination; language ability	1	45	M. N. Steinbach	Scholastic Testing Service
Study Habits Checklist (1957, rev. 1967)	9-16		1		R. C. Preston & M. Botel	Science Research Associates
Study Habits Inventory (1934, rev. 1941)	12-16		1	10-20	C. G. Wrenn	Consulting Psychologists Press
Study Performance Test (1934, rev. 1943)	9-16		1		H. A. Toops & G. Shover	Wilbur L. Layton
Study Skills Counseling Evaluation (1962)	7-16	Study time distribution; study conditions; taking notes; preparing and taking examinations; habits and attitudes	1	10-20	G. Demos	Western Psychological Services
Survey of Primary Reading Development (1957, rev. 1964)	1-4		4		J. R. Harsh & D. Soeberg	Educational Testing Service

Test	Grade	Sub-tests	Number of forms	Time in min.	Author(s)	Publisher
Survey of Study Habits and Attitudes (SSHA) (1953, rev. 1965, 1967)	7-14	Study habits (efficiency, promptness); study attitudes (toward teachers, coeducational objectives)	2	25-35	W. F. Brown & W. H. Holtzman	Psychological Corp.
Survey of Study Habits, Experimental Edition (1944)	8-14		1	30	A. E. Traxler	Educational Records Bureau
Survey Tests of Reading (1931, rev. 1932)	3-13	Central thought; power	2		L. J. O'Rourke	Psychological Institute
Test of Individual Needs in Reading (1961, rev. 1966)	1-6	Oral reading; comprehension; rate; word analysis	1		H. Gilliland	Montana Reading Clinic Publications
Test on the Use of the Dictionary (1955, rev. 1963)	9-16	Pronunciation; meaning; spelling; derivation; usage	1	30-40	G. D. Spache	Reading Laboratory and Clinic, University of Florida
Tests of Academic Progress: Reading (1964, rev. 1965)	9-12		1		H. P. Smith & D. P. Scannell	Houghton Mifflin
Tests of General Educational Development						
Test 2: Interpretation of Reading Materials in the Social Studies (1944, rev. 1968)	9-16		1	120	Examination Staff of the United States Armed Forces Institute	Veterans Testing Service, American Council on Education
Test 3: Interpretation of Reading Materials in the Natural Sciences	9-16		1	120	Examination Staff of the United States Armed Forces Institute	Veterans Testing Service, American Council on Education

263

Test	Grade/Age	Levels	Minutes	Author	Publisher	Content
Tinker Speed of Reading Test (1947, rev. 1955)	7-16+	2	15-40	M. A. Tinker	University of Minnesota Press	
Traxler High School Reading Test (1938, rev. 1967)	10-12	2	55	A. E. Traxler	Bobbs-Merrill	Reading rate; story comprehension; main ideas; total comprehension
Traxler Silent Reading Test (1934, rev. 1942)	7-10	4	55	A. E. Traxler	Bobbs-Merrill	Reading rate; story comprehension; word meaning; paragraph meaning
Tyler-Kimber Study Skills Test (1937)	9-16	1	60-90	H. T. Tyler & G. C. Kimber	Consulting Psychologists Press	Finding what you want in a book; using an index; using general reference books; recognizing common abbreviations; using the library card catalog; interpreting maps; current periodical literature; interpreting graphs
Understanding Communication (Verbal Comprehension) (1956, rev. 1959)	12+	1	20	T. G. Thurstone	Education-Industry Service	
Valett Developmental Survey of Basic Learning Abilities (1966)	Pre-K-2	1		R. E. Valett	Consulting Psychologists Press	Motor integration and physical development; tactile discrimination; auditory discrimination; visual-motor coordination; visual discrimination; language development and verbal fluency; conceptual development

Test	Grade	Sub-tests	Number of forms	Time in min.	Author(s)	Publisher
Van Wagenen Reading Readiness Scales (1933, rev. 1958)*	K-1	Listening vocabulary; range of information; perception of information; opposites; memory span for ideas; word discrimination; word learning; verbal I.Q.	2	30	M. J. Van Wagenen	Van Wagenen Psycho-Educational Research Laboratories
Watson-Glaser Critical Thinking Appraisal (1942, rev. 1964)	9-16+	Inference; recognition of assumptions; deductions; interpretation; evaluation of arguments	3	50-60	G. Watson & E. M. Glaser	Harcourt, Brace, & World
Watson Reading Readiness Test (1960)	K-1	Subjective (teacher's ratings physical, social, emotional and psychological readiness); objective	1	50-60	G. M. Watson	C. S. Hammond & Co.
Wide Range Achievement Test (WRAT)						
Level I (1936, rev. 1965)	1-6	Reading; spelling; arithmetic	1	20-30	J. F. Jastak & J. R. Jastak	Guidance Testing Associates
Level II (1936, rev. 1965)	7-12+	Reading; spelling; arithmetic	1	20-30	J. F. Jastak & J. R. Jastak	Guidance Testing Associates
Wide Range Vocabulary Test (1945)	3-12+	Reading vocabulary	2	10	C. R. Atwell & . F. L. Wells	Psychological Corp.

Williams Primary Reading Test				
Primary I (1926, rev. 1955)	1	2	25-35	A. J. Williams	Bobbs-Merrill
Primary II (1926, rev. 1955)	2-3	2	25-35	A. J. Williams	Bobbs-Merrill
Williams Reading Test for Grades 4-9 (1929)	4-9	1		A. J. Williams	Bobbs-Merrill

List of publishers

Acorn Publishing Company
Psychometric Affiliates
1743 Monterey Ave.
Chicago, Illinois 60643

American Guidance Service, Inc.
Publishers' Building
Circle Pines, Minnesota 55014

Allied Education Council
P. O. Box 78
Galien, Michigan 49113

Better Reading Program, Inc.
230 East Ohio Street
Chicago, Illinois 60611

The Bobbs-Merrill Company, Inc.
4300 West 62nd Street
Indianapolis, Indiana 46206

Brador Publications, Inc.
Livonia,
New York 14487

William C. Brown Book Company
135 South Locust Street
Dubuque, Iowa 52001

Bureau of Educational Measurements

Kansas State Teachers College
Emporia, Kansas 66801

California Test Bureau
Del Monte Research Park
Monterey, California 93940

Cal-State Bookstore
25776 Hillary Street
Hayward, California 92542

Committee on Diagnostic Reading Tests, Inc.
Mountain Home,
North Carolina 28758

Consulting Psychologists Press, Inc.
577 College Avenue
Palo Alto, California 94306

Cooperative Test Division
Educational Testing Service
20 Nassau Street
Princeton, New Jersey 08540

Delaware County Reading Consultants Association
c/o Nicholas A. Spennato
Delaware County Public Schools
Court House Annex
Media, Pennsylvania 19063

Department of Psychological
Testing
DePaul University
25 East Jackson Boulevard
Chicago, Illinois 60604

Developmental Reading Dis-
tributors
1944 Sheridan Avenue
Laramie, Wyoming 82070

Educational Developmental
Laboratories, Inc.
294 Pulaski Road
Huntington, New York 11744

Educational Records Bureau
21 Audubon Avenue
New York, New York 10032

Educational Test Bureau
Publishers' Building
Circle Pines, Minnesota 55014

Educational Testing Service
20 Nassau Street
Princeton, New Jersey 08540

Educators Publishing Service
301 Vassar Street
Cambridge, Massachusetts
02139

Essay Press

P. O. Box 5
Planetarium Station
New York, New York 10024

Follett Publishing Company
1010 West Washington Blvd.
Chicago, Illinois 60607

Foster & Stewart Publishing
Corporation
c/o M. E. Wagner
500 Klein Road
Buffalo, New York 14221

Garrard Publishing Company
1607 North Market Street
Champaign, Illinois 61820

Guidance Testing Associates
6516 Shirley Avenue
Austin, Texas 78756

C. S. Hammond and Company
515 Valley Street
Maplewood, New Jersey 07040

Harcourt, Brace & World, Inc.
757 Third Avenue
New York, New York 15017

Houghton Mifflin Company
110 Tremont Street
Boston, Massachusetts 02107

Johns Hopkins Press
Homewood
Baltimore, Maryland 21218

Keystone View Company
Meadville,
Pennsylvania 16335

Wilbur L. Layton
3604 Ross Road
Ames, Iowa 50010

J. B. Lippincott Company
East Washington Square
Philadelphia, Pennsylvania
19105

Lyons and Carnahan, Inc.
407 East 25th Street
Chicago, Illinois 60616

McGrath Reading Clinic
15944 West McNichols Road
Detroit, Michigan 48235

R. A. McMenemy
3028 N. E. Brazee Street
Portland, Oregon 97212

Mills Center, Inc.
1512 East Broward Blvd.
Fort Lauderdale, Florida
33301

Montana Reading Clinic Publications
517 Rimrock Road
Billings, Montana 59102

National Council of Teachers
of English
508 South Sixth Street
Champaign, Illinois 61820

C. H. Nevins Printing Company
311 Bryn Mawr Island
Bradenton, Florida 33505

O'Connor Reading Clinic Pub-
lishing Company
Box 447
Roscommon, Michigan 48653

Ohio Testing Service
Division of Guidance and
Testing
State Department of Educa-
tion
751 Northwest Boulevard
Columbus, Ohio 43212

Perfection Form Company
214 West 8th Street
Logan, Iowa 51546

Personnel Press, Inc.
20 Nassau Street
Princeton, New Jersey 08540

Personnel Research Associates, Inc.
1435 South La Cienega Blvd.
Los Angeles, Calif. 90035

Phonovisual Products, Inc.
4708 Wisconsin Avenue N.W.
Washington, D. C. 20007

Priority Innovations, Inc.
P. O. Box 792
Skokie, Illinois 60076

Programs for Education
Box 85
Lumberville, Pennsylvania 18933

The Psychological Corporation
304 East 45th Street
New York, New York 10017

Psychological Institute
P. O. Box 1118
Lake Alfred, Florida 33850

Psychometric Affiliates
1743 Monterey Avenue
Chicago, Illinois 60643

Purdue Research Foundation
Personnel Evaluation Research Service

Division of Educational Reference
Purdue University
Lafayette, Indiana 47907

Reading and Study Skills Center, Inc.
c/o Taylor Center for Controlled Reading and Research
75 Prospect Street
Huntington, New York 11744

Reading Laboratory and Clinic
University of Florida
Gainesville, Florida 32601

Research Concepts
1368 East Airport Road
Muskegon, Michigan 49444

Richardson, Bellows, Henry & Co.
355 Lexington Avenue
New York, New York 10017

St. Martins Press, Inc.
175 Fifth Avenue
New York, New York 10010

Scholastic Testing Service, Inc.
480 Meyer Road
Bensenville, Illinois 60106

Science Research Associates, Inc.
259 East Erie Street
Chicago, Illinois 60611

Sheridan Supply Company
c/o Sheridan Psychological Services, Inc.
P. O. Box 837
Beverly Hills, California 90213

Slosson Educational Publications
140 Pine Street
East Aurora, New York 14052

State High School Testing Service for Indiana
Purdue University
Lafayette, Indiana 47907

The Steck Company
P. O. Box 16
Ninth and Lavaca
Austin, Texas 78767

Teachers College Press
Teachers College, Columbia University
525 West 120th Street
New York, New York 10027

University of Minnesota Press
2037 University Avenue S.E.
Minneapolis, Minnesota 55455

University Publications Sales
Ohio State University
242 West 18th Street
Columbus, Ohio 43210

Van Wagenen Psycho-Educational Research Laboratories
1729 Irving Avenue South
Minneapolis, Minnesota 55411

Veterans' Testing Service
c/o General Educational Development Testing Service of the American Council on Education
1785 Massachusetts Avenue N.W.
Washington, D.C. 20036

Western Psychological Services
Box 775
Beverly Hills, California 90213

Winter Haven Lions Research Foundation, Inc.
P. O. Box 1045
Winter Haven, Florida 33881

Index to Reading Tests and Reviews and Mental Measurement Yearbooks

This index provides a quick reference to the critiques of reading tests appearing in Buros' *Reading Tests and Reviews* (Highland Park, New Jersey: Gryphon Press, 1968) and to Buros' *Mental Measurement Yearbooks* (Highland Park, New Jersey: Gryphon Press, 1938, 1940, 1949, 1953, 1959, 1965). These excellent test reviews should be studied before a test consumer makes a final test selection.

Within the index, tests are arranged alphabetically by test name. The first column after the test name gives the volume number of the *Mental Measurements Yearbook* (MMY) which includes the most recent review of each test. Following this MMY number is the test's number in that yearbook. The second column supplies the page number on which there is a descriptive listing and/or a critical review of the test in *Reading Tests and Reviews*. Only those tests in the Guide which have been reviewed or described in Buros are included in the index. For those tests which have been described, but not reviewed in Buros, the first column is left blank.

For example, the column entries for the *American School Achievement Tests* are 6:783 and 290. The first number indicates that the tests are listed in Buros' *Sixth Mental Measurement Yearbook* and are the 783rd test listing in that book. The second number indicates that the tests are also reviewed on page 290 of *Reading Tests and Reviews*.

It should be noted that the reviews in *Reading Tests and Reviews* are the same ones which have appeared in the MMY's. The reason why both references are listed here is that a test consumer may have access to only one of these references.

Test	Volume and test number in Mental Measurement Yearbooks	Page in Reading Tests and Reviews
ABC Inventory to Determine Kindergarten and School Readiness		15
Adult Basic Reading Inventory		17
American School Achievement Tests		
Part I, Reading, Primary Battery	6:783	290
Part I, Reading, Intermediate Battery	6:783	290
Part I, Reading, Advanced Battery	6:783	290
American School Reading Readiness Test	5:675	262
American School Reading Tests	5:621	219
Anton Brenner Development Gestalt Test of School Readiness	6:844a	373
Binion-Beck Reading Readiness Test for Kindergarten and First Grade	3:514	128
Botel Reading Inventory	6:834	359
Buffalo Reading Test for Speed and Comprehension	3:477	86
Burnett Reading Series: Survey Test		
Primary I		2
Primary II		2
Intermediate		2
Advanced		2
Senior		2
California Phonics Survey	6:820	338
California Reading Test		
Lower Primary	6:784	290

Test	Volume and test number in Mental Measurement Yearbooks	Page in Reading Tests and Reviews
California Reading Test (cont'd)		
Upper Primary	6:784	290
Elementary	6:784	290
Junior High Level	6:784	290
Advanced	6:784	290
California Study Methods Survey	6:857	379
California Survey Series: Survey of Reading Achievement		
Junior High Level	6:815	334
Advanced	6:815	334
Classroom Reading Inventory		9
Clymer-Barrett Prereading Battery		15
Commerce Reading Comprehension Test	5:624	221
Comprehensive Primary Reading Scales		2
Comprehensive Reading Scales		2
Cooperative English Tests: Reading Comprehension	6:806	321
Cooperative Inter-American Tests		
Tests of Natural Sciences	4:576	198
Tests of Reading	6:818	337
Tests of Social Studies	4:577	199
Cumulative Reading Record		12
Davis Reading Test		
Series I	6:786	291
Series II	6:786	291

Test	Volume and test number in Mental Measurement Yearbooks	Page in Reading Tests and Reviews
Delaware County Silent Reading Test		3
Developmental Reading Tests		
Primer Reading	6:787	293
Lower Primary Reading	6:787	293
Upper Primary Reading	6:787	293
Intermediate Reading	6:787	293
Developmental Reading Tests:	6:832	355
Silent Reading Diagnostic Tests		
Diagnostic Examination of Silent Reading Abilities	3:480	89
Diagnostic Reading Scales	6:821	339
Diagnostic Reading Test		
Lower Level	6:823	342
Upper Level	6:823	342
Diagnostic Reading Test, Pupil Progress Series		
Primary Level I	6:822	340
Primary Level II	6:822	340
Elementary Level	6:822	340
Advanced Level	6:822	340
Dolch Basic Sight Word Test		12
Doren Diagnostic Reading Test of Word Recognition Skills	5:659	246
Durrell Analysis of Reading Difficulty	5:660	248
Early Detection Inventory		15

Test	Volume and test number in Mental Measurement Yearbooks	Page in Reading Tests and Reviews
Emporia Reading Tests		
Primary Reading Test		3
Elementary Reading Test		3
Intermediate Reading Test		3
Junior High School Reading Test		3
Emporia Silent Reading Test	2:1534	46
Evaluation Aptitude Test	5:691	275
Every Pupil Achievement Test		
Primary Reading (Grade 1)	6:803	320
Primary Reading (Grades 2-3)	6:803	320
Flash-X Sight Vocabulary Test	6:841	367
Functional Readiness Questionnaire for School and College Students	6:835	360
Gates-MacGinitie Reading Tests		
Primary A	6:792	301
Primary B	6:792	301
Primary C	6:792	301
Primary Cs	6:792	301
Survey D	6:792	301
Survey E	6:792	301
Gates-MacGinitie Reading Tests— Readiness Skills		15
Gates-McKillop Reading Diagnostic Tests	6:824	345
Gilliland Learning Potential Examination		13
Gilmore Oral Reading Test	5:671	257
Gray Oral Reading Test	6:842	367

Test	Volume and test number in Mental Measurement Yearbooks	Page in Reading Tests and Reviews
Group Diagnostic Reading Aptitude and Achievement Tests—Intermediate Form	6:825	348
Harrison-Stroud Reading Readiness Profiles	5:677	265
Individual Placement Series—Reading Adequacy "READ" Test	6:805	321
Iowa Every-Pupil Tests of Basic Skills, Test A: Silent Reading Comprehension		
Elementary Battery	4:554	182
Advanced Battery	4:554	182
Iowa Every-Pupil Tests of Basic Skills, Test B		
Elementary Battery	4:588	210
Advanced Battery	4:588	210
Iowa Silent Reading Tests		
Elementary	6:794	307
Advanced	6:794	307
Iowa Tests of Educational Development		
Test 5: Ability to Interpret Reading Materials in the Social Studies	6:852	378
Test 6: Ability to Interpret Reading Materials in the Natural Sciences	6:853	378
Test 9: Use of Sources of Information	6:858	381
Kelley-Greene Reading Comprehension Test	5:636	226
Keystone Ready to Read Tests		15
Learning Methods Test	6:836	340

Test	Volume and test number in Mental Measurement Yearbooks	Page in Reading Tests and Reviews
Lee-Clark Reading Readiness Test	6:846	373
Lee-Clark Reading Test		
Primer	6:795	308
First Reader	6:795	308
Lippincott Reading Readiness Test (Including Readiness Checklist)		15
Logical Reasoning	5:694	279
Los Angeles Elementary Reading Test	4:541	171
McCullough Word Analysis Tests	6:826	348
McGrath Test of Reading Skills, Second Edition		4
McHugh-McParland Reading Readiness Test		15
McMenemy Measure of Reading Ability		
Primary		4
Intermediate		4
Advanced		4
Maintaining Reading Efficiency Tests		4
Maturity Level for School Entrance and Reading Readiness	6:847	374
Metropolitan Achievement Tests: Reading		
Upper Primary Reading Test	6:797	311
Elementary Reading Test	6:797	311
Intermediate Reading Test	6:797	311
Advanced Reading Test	6:797	311

Test	Volume and test number in Mental Measurement Yearbooks	Page in Reading Tests and Reviews
Metropolitan Readiness Tests	4:570	194
Minnesota Reading Examinations for College Students	2:1554	59
Minnesota Speed of Reading Test for College Students	2:1555	61
Monroe's Standardized Silent Reading Test	6:798	312
Murphy-Durrell Reading Readiness Analysis	5:679	268
National Achievement Tests: High School Reading Test	5:634	225
National Achievement Tests: Municipal Tests: Reading Test (Comprehension and Speed)	5:648	232
National Achievement Tests: Reading Comprehension Test (Speer & Smith)	5:646	231
National Achievement Tests: Reading Comprehension Test (Crow, Kuhlmann, & Crow)	5:647	231
Neale Analysis of Reading Ability	6:843	370
Nelson-Denny Reading Test: Vocabulary-Comprehension-Rate	6:800	315
Nelson Reading Test	6:802	320
OC Diagnostic Dictionary Test	6:861	382
OC Diagnostic Syllabizing Test	6:827	350

Test	Volume and test number in Mental Measurement Yearbooks	Page in Reading Tests and Reviews
Ohio Diagnostic Reading Test		
Level I		11
Level II		11
Peabody Library Information Test		
Elementary Level	3:538	148
High School Level	3:538	148
College Level	3:538	148
Perceptual Forms Test	6:848	374
Phonics Knowledge Survey	6:828	350
Phonovisual Diagnostic Test	6:829	350
Pictographic Self Rating Scale	5:695	280
Pressey Diagnostic Reading Tests		5
Primary Academic Sentiment Scale		16
Primary Reading Profiles	5:665	252
Primary Reading Test: Acorn Achievement Tests	5:642	230
Public School Achievement Tests: Reading	6:807	324
Purdue Reading Test	5:643	230
Purdue Reading Test for Industrial Supervisors: Purdue Personnel Tests	5:644	230
RBH Reading Comprehension Test	6:817	337
RBH Scientific Reading Test		17

Test	Volume and test number in Mental Measurement Yearbooks	Page in Reading Tests and Reviews
Reader's Inventory		13
Reader Rater with Self-Scoring Profile	6:837	363
Reading: Adult Basic Education Survey, Parts 1 and 2		17
Reading Eye	6:838	363
Reading Skills Diagnostic Test		11
Reading for Understanding Placement Test		
Junior and General Edition		6
Senior Edition		6
Reading Versatility Test		
Paper and Pencil Edition	6:839	365
Basic Reading Eye Edition	6:839	365
Intermediate	6:839	365
Advanced	6:839	365
Robinson-Hall Reading Tests	4:575	197
Roswell-Chall Auditory Blending Test	6:830	352
Roswell-Chall Diagnostic Reading Test of Word Analysis Skills	5:667	255
School Readiness Behavior Tests Used at the Gesell Institute		16
School Readiness Checklist, Research Edition		16
School Readiness Survey		16

Test	Volume and test number in Mental Measurement Yearbooks	Page in Reading Tests and Reviews
Schrammel-Gray High School and College Reading Test	3:500	112
Screening Test of Academic Readiness		16
Screening Test for the Assignment of Remedial Treatments		16
Screening Tests for Identifying Children with Specific Language Disability		13
Slosson Oral Reading Test (SORT)	6:844	373
SRA Achievement Series	6:808	324
SRA Reading Checklist		13
SRA Reading Progress Test		17
SRA Reading Record	4:550	177
SRA Tests of Educational Ability		
Level I		411
Level II		411
Level III		411
SRA Tests of General Ability		411
SRA Youth Inventory		437
Standardized Oral Reading Check Tests	2:1570	71
Standardized Oral Reading Paragraphs	2:1571	72
Stanford Achievement Test: High School Reading Test		7

Test	Volume and test number in Mental Measurement Yearbooks	Page in Reading Tests and Reviews
Stanford Achievement Test:		
Reading Tests		
Primary 1	6:813	331
Primary 2	6:813	331
Intermediate I	6:813	331
Intermediate II	6:813	331
Advanced Paragraph Meaning	6:813	331
Stanford Diagnostic Reading Test		
Level 1		12
Level 2		12
Steinbach Test of Reading Readiness		16
Study Habits Checklist		19
Study Habits Inventory	3:540	150
Study Performance Test		19
Study Skills Counseling Evaluation	6:865	384
Survey of Primary Reading Development	6:814	332
Survey of Study Habits and Attitudes (SSHA)	6:856	378
Survey of Study Habits, Experimental Edition	4:583	207
Survey Tests of Reading		7
Tests of Academic Progress		7
Tests of General Educational Development		
Test 2: Interpretation of Reading	5:683	270

Test	Volume and test number in Mental Measurement Yearbooks	Page in Reading Tests and Reviews
Tests of General Educational Development (cont'd)		
Materials in the Social Studies Test 3: Interpretation of Reading Materials in the Natural Sciences	5:684	270
Test of Individual Needs in Reading		12
Test on the Use of the Dictionary	6:866	386
Tinker Speed of Reading Test	5:687	270
Traxler High School Reading Test	4:559	187
Traxler Silent Reading Test	4:560	187
Tyler-Kimber Study Skills Test	2:1580	80
Understanding Communication (Verbal Comprehension)	6:840	365
Valett Developmental Survey of Basic Learning Abilities		16
Van Wagenen Reading Readiness Scales	3:520	134
Watson-Glaser Critical Thinking Appraisal	6:867	386
Watson Reading Readiness Test	6:851	377
Wide Range Achievement Test (WRAT)		
Level I		391
Level II		391
Williams Primary Reading Test		
Primary I	5:658	246
Primary II	5:658	246
Williams Reading Test for Grades 4-9		8

Index to published research literature in reading

This index provides a reference to research articles which have reported use of the tests described in the *Guide to Tests and Measuring Instruments in Reading*. The document base used to compile the index consists of six basic references published by ERIC/CRIER. The 3,500 articles cited in the basic references were scanned and the tests reported used in the research were noted. These tests are listed alphabetically in the index. The document numbers are grouped because the tests are frequently cited in research articles by name only and not by level. For example, a researcher may report using the California Reading Test, but he may not indicate whether he used the primary level or the intermediate level. Following each entry are the numbers of those documents in the six ERIC/CRIER Basic References which reported use of the test in reading research. The ERIC/CRIER Basic References include the following six bibliographies.

1] **Published Research Literature in Reading, 1950-1963** (ED 012 834, microfiche $1.50; hard copy $19.90 from EDRS/NCR) Includes ERIC/CRIER document numbers 2885-4803.

2] **Published Research Literature in Reading, 1964-1966** (ED 013 969, microfiche $0.75; hard copy $9.10 from EDRS/NCR) Includes ERIC/CRIER document numbers 4804-5345 and 6253-6562.

3] **Recent Doctoral Dissertation Research in Reading,** (ED 012 693, microfiche $2.00; hard copy $11.05 from EDRS/NCR) Includes ERIC/CRIER document numbers 5348-5727.

4] **International Reading Association Conference Proceedings Report on Secondary Reading,** (ED 013 185, microfiche $2.25; hard copy $30.70 from EDRS/NCR) Includes ERIC/CRIER document numbers 5728-5907.

5] **International Reading Association Conference Proceedings Reports on Elementary Reading,** (ED 013 197, microfiche $4.25; hard copy $56.85 from EDRS/NCR) Includes ERIC/CRIER document numbers 5908-6252.

6] **USOE Sponsored Research on Reading,** (ED 016 603, microfiche $0.50; hard copy $5.30 from EDRS/NCR) Includes ERIC/CRIER document numbers 6563-6706.

How to locate a document

A reader can locate a specific document in the ERIC/CRIER six Basic References quite easily. The first step is to identify the document number which appears as a four digit number in the right column of the Index to ERIC/CRIER reading research literature. The second step involves determining in which of the six Basic References the document number is included (this listing of the six basic documents includes the numbers). The documents are listed within each of the Basic References in chronological order with the lowest number appearing in the beginning of the reference and the highest numbers at the end. The reader, once he finds the entry, is supplied with the full citation of the work and an annotation. He can then go to the library and look up the complete article.

Perhaps an example would be useful to demonstrate how to use this reference. The first listing in the Index is for the Botel Reading Inventory. The number to appear in the right hand column is 4986. 4986 appears in *Published Research Literature in Reading, 1964-1966* (since it falls between 4804 and 5345). The full citation given is:

4986 Santostefano, Sebastiano, Rutledge, Louis, and Randall, David. 'Cognitive Styles and Reading Disability,' Psychology in the Schools, 2 (Jan. 1965), 57-62.
 Describes a study in which three tests were devised and used in three separate, but interdependent, experiments.

Purpose was to explore whether the cognitive functioning of children with reading disability could be differentiated in terms of three cognitive styles—1) focusing-scanning, 2) leveling-sharpening, and 3) constructed-flexible. Experimental group was 24 retarded readers with mean age of 10.94 and mean I.Q. of 92.71. Control group was 23 nonretarded readers with mean age of 9.91 and mean I.Q. of 98.39. All subjects were boys and selected from grades three through six.

The user can then locate *Psychology in the Schools* in the library.

How to order ERIC/CRIER Basic References

Each of the *ERIC/CRIER* basic references can be ordered from:

ERIC Document Reproduction Service (EDRS)
The National Cash Register Company
4936 Fairmont Avenue
Bethesda, Maryland 20014

To order any of these documents, the following information must be furnished:

1] The accession number (ED number) of the desired document.

2] The type of reproduction desired—microfiche or hard copy.

3] The number of copies being ordered.

4] The method of payment—cash with order, deposit account, charge.
   a. Add a special handling charge of 50¢ to all orders.
   b. Add applicable state sales taxes or submit tax exemption certificates.
   c. Add a 25% service charge on all orders from outside the United States, its territories and possessions.

d. Payment must accompany orders totaling less than $5.00. Do not send stamps.
e. $20.00 prepaid EDRS coupons are available upon request from EDRS.

EDRS will provide information on charges and deposit accounts upon request.

Test	Citation number in ERIC/CRIER basic references
Botel Reading Inventory	4986
California Reading Test	3179, 3248, 3251, 3258,
Lower Primary	3337, 3345, 3493, 3495,
Upper Primary	3499, 3502, 3516, 3533,
Elementary	3544, 3592, 3631, 3646,
Junior High Level	3665, 3671, 3683, 3693,
Advanced	3738, 3805, 3821, 3851,
	3861, 3862, 3878, 3918,
	3919, 3936, 3956, 3968,
	3979, 3994, 4023, 4024,
	4028, 4073, 4113, 4114,
	4119, 4126, 4156, 4176,
	4211, 4212, 4245, 4247,
	4250, 4272, 4319, 4374,
	4380, 4385, 4389, 4402,
	4433, 4436, 4441, 4478,
	4481, 4498, 4533, 4571,
	4585, 4587, 4605, 4609,
	4632, 4639, 4645, 4668,
	4700, 4706, 4713, 4714,
	4715, 4722, 4751, 4776,
	4777, 4801, 4825, 4826,
	4835, 4836, 4842, 4844,
	4862, 4901, 4904, 4912,
	4919, 4920, 4948, 4949,
	4958, 4966, 4994, 4999,
	5056, 5061, 5085, 5089,
	5097, 5113, 5120, 5127,
	5143, 5161, 5162, 5171,
	5172, 5187, 5193, 5198,
	5214, 5221, 5235, 5236,
	5244, 5303, 5345, 6261,

Test	Citation number in ERIC/CRIER basic references
California Reading Test (cont'd)	6300, 5929, 5936, 6018, 6030, 6038, 6066, 6069, 6141, 6157, 6238, 6242, 5738, 5373, 5377, 5383, 5395, 5415, 5423, 5448, 5457, 5469, 5482, 5490, 5491, 5499, 5506, 5508, 5514, 5515, 5520, 5539, 5545, 5558, 5597, 5608, 5611, 5644, 5647, 5658, 5665, 5670, 5682, 5683, 5693, 5713, 5716, 5720, 5721, 6563, 6566, 6570, 6588, 6589, 6590, 6608, 6622, 6632, 6633, 6674
Commerce Reading Comprehension Test	3952
Cooperative English Tests: Reading Comprehension	2885, 2945, 3027, 3065, 3066, 3067, 3072, 3116, 3117, 3158, 3159, 3172, 3198, 3213, 3232, 3242, 3251, 3292, 3347, 3355, 3366, 3371, 3372, 3377, 3389, 3422, 3426, 3440, 3452, 3483, 3487, 3493, 3502, 3512, 3514, 3540, 3556, 3596, 3628, 3639, 3686, 3695, 3707, 3723, 3763, 3772, 3801, 3812, 3847, 3856, 3864, 3865, 3880, 3928, 3980, 3987,

Test	Citation number in ERIC/CRIER basic references
Cooperative English Tests: Reading Comprehension (cont'd)	4006, 4020, 4032, 4040, 4046, 4150, 4186, 4226, 4285, 4298, 4377, 4450, 4460, 4469, 4476, 4491, 4522, 4527, 4614, 4639, 4653, 4675, 4686, 4694, 4727, 4762, 4800, 4916, 4987, 5002, 5093, 5157, 5404, 5436, 5461, 5478, 5498, 5502, 5588, 5591, 5663, 5762, 5768, 5827
Davis Reading Test Series I Series II	4614, 5164, 5354
Development Reading Tests Primer Reading Lower Primary Reading Upper Primary Reading Intermediate Reading	4725, 4776, 5077, 5142, 6251, 5426, 5472, 5486, 5538, 5628
Developmental Reading Tests: Silent Reading Diagnostic Tests	3974, 4247, 4317, 4776, 5077, 5319, 5426, 5564
Diagnostic Reading Scales	4614, 5467
Diagnostic Reading Test Lower Level Upper Level	3117, 3172, 3182, 3251, 2887, 2960, 2970, 3066, 3088, 3144, 3173, 3283, 3284, 3297, 3308, 3324, 3344, 3345, 3367, 3384, 3385, 3394, 3402, 3416, 3440, 3483, 3498, 3502,

Test	Citation number in ERIC/CRIER basic references
Diagnostic Reading Test (cont'd)	3514, 3522, 3528, 3530, 3539, 3545, 3562, 3584, 3608, 3620, 3634, 3654, 3659, 3676, 3679, 3719, 3758, 3772, 3792, 3797, 3801, 3812, 3849, 3876, 3902, 3913, 3962, 3967, 3987, 3989, 3991, 4021, 4152, 4166, 4174, 4189, 4190, 4191, 4325, 4426, 4467, 4476, 4479, 4522, 4527, 4562, 4586, 4589, 4639, 4641, 4675, 4703, 4728, 4755, 4766, 4777, 4874, 4910, 4968, 4978, 5021, 5088, 5250, 5369, 5414, 5429, 5442, 5465, 5567, 5591, 5659, 5692, 5697, 6576, 6677, 4614
Doren Diagnostic Reading Test of Word Recognition Skills	5479
Durrell Analysis of Reading Difficulty	2892, 2915, 2955, 2959, 3048, 3151, 3226, 3691, 4091, 4156, 4213, 4325, 4433, 4614, 4672, 4674, 4776, 4777, 4842, 5118, 5236, 5292, 5992, 6224, 5496, 5585, 5590, 5613, 5725, 6564
Gates-McKillop Reading Diagnostic Tests	4834, 5495, 6241, 6675
Gilmore Oral Reading Test	3514, 4383, 4468, 4777,

Test	Citation number in ERIC/CRIER basic references
Gilmore Oral Reading Test (cont'd)	4873, 5085, 5121, 5140, 5144, 5255, 5282, 5297, 5339, 6300, 6066, 6127, 6133, 5387, 5393, 5404, 5457, 5469, 5490, 5536, 5604, 5623, 5649, 5678, 5693, 6597, 6599, 6600, 6603, 6608, 6611, 6614, 6616, 6621, 6634, 6635, 6636, 6638, 6639, 6643, 6648, 6679
Gray Oral Reading Test	2892, 2886, 2888, 2902, 2985, 3002, 3024, 3037, 3251, 3315, 3613, 3660, 3815, 3870, 3941, 4261, 4313, 4563, 4639, 4777, 4842, 5076, 5441, 5454, 5466, 5491, 5495, 5542, 5604, 6563, 6649, 6682
Gray-Votaw-Rogers General Achievement Test Level I Level II	3699, 3818, 4776, 4991, 6619
Harrison-Stroud Reading Readiness Profiles	3564, 4776, 4778, 5013, 5021, 5107, 5424, 5427, 5433, 5519, 5525, 5535, 5565, 5611
Iowa Every-Pupil Tests of Basic Skills, Test B Elementary Battery	2904, 2913, 3248, 3322, 3401, 3457, 3488, 3519,

Test	Citation number in ERIC/CRIER basic references
Iowa Every-Pupil Tests of Basic Skills, Test B (cont'd) Advanced Battery	3534, 3732, 3954, 3972, 4078, 4132, 4588, 4776, 4777, 5050, 5051, 5143, 3335, 3387, 3418, 3752, 3848, 3863, 3956, 4076, 4198, 4231, 4251, 4257, 4270, 4419, 4429, 4441, 4452, 4474, 4639, 4740, 4776, 4777, 4920, 5029, 5116, 5196, 5203, 5207, 5289, 6018, 6029, 6038, 5383, 5395, 5397, 5399, 5406, 5431, 5447, 5458, 5489, 5551, 5561, 5621, 5629, 5631, 5676, 5702, 5708, 5727, 6571, 6657, 6667, 6670, 6682, 5803
Iowa Silent Reading Tests Elementary Advanced	2902, 2906, 3031, 3032, 3066, 3080, 3085, 3086, 3136, 3144, 3156, 3178, 3182, 3196, 3199, 3208, 3217, 3245, 3249, 3251, 3257, 3258, 3292, 3346, 3372, 3410, 3440, 3483, 3502, 3528, 3544, 3586, 3608, 3626, 3632, 3640, 3662, 3676, 3679, 3698, 3705, 3737, 3780, 3847, 3910, 3969, 3976, 4011, 4045, 4113, 4186, 4232, 4255, 4285, 4342, 4361, 4424, 4526, 4533, 4614,

Test	Citation number in ERIC/CRIER basic references
Iowa Silent Reading Tests (cont'd)	4639, 4677, 4716, 4777, 5078, 5781, 5358, 5376, 5425, 5474, 5488, 5505, 5528, 5533, 5549, 5556, 5562, 5582, 5650, 5694, 5712
Iowa Tests of Educational Development Test 5: Ability to Interpret Reading Materials in the Social Studies Test 6: Ability to Interpret Reading Materials in the Natural Sciences Test 9: Use of Sources of Information	3175, 3387, 3418, 3752, 3801, 4040, 4051, 4096, 4653, 4762, 4879, 5370, 5461, 6565
Kelley-Greene Reading Comprehension Test	3698, 3712
Lee-Clark Reading Readiness Test	2900, 2918, 3038, 3040, 4124, 4126, 4258, 4451, 4455, 4502, 4605, 4624, 4776, 4778, 4897, 4949, 5113, 5135, 5925, 6103, 6117, 6124, 6224, 5497, 5506, 5519, 5709, 6589, 6599, 6600, 6608
McCullough Word Analysis Tests	4614
Metropolitan Achievement Tests: Reading Upper Primary Reading Test Elementary Reading Test Intermediate Reading Test Advanced Reading Test	2900, 2931, 3033, 3101, 3126, 3226, 3251, 3304, 3335, 3468, 3486, 3506, 3519, 3525, 3531, 3592, 3604, 3642, 3680, 3808, 3815, 4168, 4178, 4355, 4441, 4552, 4584, 4602, 4639, 4697, 4751, 4776, 4778, 4813, 4814, 4849,

Test	Citation number in ERIC/CRIER basic references
Metropolitan Achievement Tests: Reading (cont'd)	4882, 4957, 4982, 5066, 5076, 5124, 5130, 5137, 5166, 5168, 5198, 5206, 6282, 6296, 5911, 5996, 6016, 6124, 5898, 5352, 5361, 5371, 5383, 5393, 5401, 5411, 5424, 5456, 5460, 5481, 5501, 5510, 5521, 5542, 5580, 5609, 5619, 5643, 5658, 5680, 5713, 6564, 6591, 6609, 6639, 6658, 6668, 6676, 6695
Metropolitan Readiness Tests	2900, 3033, 3314, 3437, 3459, 3564, 3633, 3642, 3680, 3699, 3745, 3811, 3819, 4185, 4194, 4253, 4430, 4451, 4624, 4639, 4679, 4697, 4776, 4777, 4778, 4803, 4870, 5066, 5112, 5121, 5135, 5140, 5144, 5149, 5150, 5154, 5172, 5195, 5198, 5199, 5200, 5206, 5208, 5255, 5269, 5282, 5293, 5335, 5343, 6303, 6112, 6127, 6133, 5349, 5352, 5408, 5450, 5459, 5481, 5532, 5548, 5557, 5587, 5595, 5628, 5634, 5647, 5648, 5655, 5680, 5721, 6571, 6595, 6597, 6598, 6599,

Test	Citation number in ERIC/CRIER basic references
Metropolitan Readiness Tests (cont'd)	6600, 6603, 6609, 6610, 6611, 6612, 6614, 6616, 6624, 6634, 6635, 6638, 6641, 6643, 6648, 6651, 6666, 6668, 6679, 6695
Minnesota Reading Examinations for College Students	3698
Minnesota Speed of Reading Test for College Students	3127, 3321, 3600, 3705
Monroe Reading Aptitude Tests	3488, 4483, 4803, 5107, 6116, 5433, 5443, 5557
Monroe's Standardized Silent Reading Test	3338, 5454, 3519, 3613, 4551, 5496
Murphy-Durrell Reading Readiness Analysis	4776, 4778, 5107, 5121, 5144, 5149, 5199, 5208, 5224, 5255, 5282, 5293, 5297, 5343, 5525, 6127, 6133, 6282, 6595, 6597, 6599, 6600, 6603, 6610, 6611, 6612, 6614, 6616, 6624, 6634, 6638, 6643, 6648, 6668, 6679
Neale Analysis of Reading Ability	4607, 4956, 5106, 5994
Nelson-Denny Reading Test: Vocabulary-Comprehension-Rate	2930, 2946, 3087, 3154, 3440, 3483, 3502, 3524, 3677, 3698, 4182, 4368, 4812, 4878, 4895, 4959, 4961, 4970, 4979, 5095, 5184, 5252, 5342, 6253,

Test	Citation number in ERIC/CRIER basic references
Vocabulary-Comprehension Rate (cont'd)	6297, 5752, 5405, 5546, 5617, 5630
Nelson Reading Test	3115, 3251, 3383, 3421, 3667, 3825
Pressey Diagnostic Reading Tests	3848, 4777
Primary Reading Profiles	4151, 4323, 4776
Robinson-Hall Reading Tests	3470
SRA Achievement Series	4414, 4639, 4777, 5138, 5166, 5171, 5427, 5480, 5581, 5696, 6618, 6677
SRA Reading Record	3092, 3251, 3483, 4614, 5090
Stanford Achievement Test: Reading Tests Primary 1 Primary 2 Intermediate I Intermediate II Advanced	2904, 2943, 2953, 2967, 2993, 3013, 3064, 3138, 3181, 3196, 3226, 3351, 3366, 3374, 3462, 3463, 3464, 3514, 3531, 3652, 3660, 3661, 3662, 3705, 3791, 3814, 3850, 3870, 3880, 3927, 3974, 3997, 3999, 4090, 4125, 4143, 4192, 4210, 4220, 4254, 4255, 4280, 4293, 4332, 4355, 4385, 4412, 4430, 4436, 4441, 4493, 4494, 4535, 4572, 4639, 4646, 4670, 4687, 4725, 4726, 4740, 4776, 4777, 4778, 4798, 4799, 4808, 4827, 4844, 4846, 4882, 4897,

Test	Citation number in ERIC/CRIER basic references
Stanford Achievement Test: **Reading Tests (cont'd)**	4931, 4951, 4981, 5021, 5063, 5114, 5121, 5137, 5140, 5144, 5149, 5150, 5158, 5197, 5200, 5202, 5213, 5219, 5224, 5232, 5234, 5255, 5275, 5293, 5297, 5313, 5315, 5328, 6276, 6282, 6300, 5917, 5936, 5968, 6018, 6066, 6073, 6127, 6133, 6178, 5836, 5353, 5365, 5366, 5370, 5375, 5383, 5418, 5432, 5438, 5442, 5463, 5504, 5559, 5580, 5584, 5609, 5632, 5636, 5640, 5667, 5668, 5673, 5711, 5714, 6564, 6571, 6576, 6586, 6587, 6591, 6593, 6595, 6597, 6598, 6599, 6600, 6603, 6608, 6610, 6611, 6613, 6614, 6616, 6624, 6629, 6634, 6635, 6638, 6639, 6643, 6648, 6658, 6668, 6674, 6678, 6679
Tinker Speed of Reading Test	3281, 3282, 3364, 3576, 3908, 3909
Traxler High School Reading Test	3251, 3452, 3483, 4879
Traxler Silent Reading Test	3125, 3251, 3713, 5021
Van Wagenen Reading Readiness Scales	3441, 3488, 4776, 4778

Test	Citation number in ERIC/CRIER basic references
Wide Range Achievement Test (WRAT) Level I Level II	3315, 3338, 3490, 3844, 4008, 4160, 4261, 4435, 4443, 4621, 4639, 4776, 4777, 4873, 5073, 5094, 5111, 5345, 6294, 6115, 6223, 5652, 6620
Williams Primary Reading Test Primary I Primary II	4870

The Nineteen Clearinghouses in the ERIC System

Adult Education
Syracuse University
107 Roney Lane
Syracuse, N.Y. 13210

Counselling and Personnel Services
Services Information Center
611 Church Street
Ann Arbor, Michigan 48104

Disadvantaged
Teachers College
Columbia University
New York, New York 10027

Early Childhood Education
University of Illinois
805 West Pennsylvania Avenue
Urbana, Illinois 61801

Educational Administration
University of Oregon
Eugene, Oregon 97403

Educational Facilities
University of Wisconsin
606 State St.
Madison, Wisconsin 53703

Educational Media & Technology
Institute for Communication Research
Stanford University
Palo Alto, California 94305

Exceptional Children
The Council for Exceptional Children
1499 Jefferson Davis Highway
Arlington, Virginia 22202

Junior Colleges
University of California at Los Angeles
405 Hilgard Avenue
Los Angeles, California 90024

Higher Education
George Washington University
One Dupont Circle, Suite 360
Washington, D. C. 20036

Library and Information Sciences
University of Minnesota
2122 Riverside Avenue
Minneapolis, Minnesota 55404

Linguistics
Center for Applied Linguistics
1717 Massachusetts Ave., N.W.
Washington, D.C. 20036

Reading
Indiana University
200 Pine Hall
Bloomington, Indiana 47401

Rural Education & Small Schools
Box AP, University Park Branch
New Mexico State University
Las Cruces, New Mexico 88001

Science Education
Ohio State University
1460 West Lane Avenue
Columbus, Ohio 43221

Teacher Education
One Dupont Circle, Suite 616
Washington, D. C. 20036

Teaching of English
National Council of Teachers of English
508 South Sixth Street
Champaign, Illinois 61820

Teaching of Foreign Languages
Modern Language Association of America
62 Fifth Avenue
New York, New York 10011

Vocational & Technical Education
Ohio State University
1900 Kenny Road
Columbus, Ohio 43212

Book and cover design by Gerry Roadruck,
Indiana University Office of Publications